Jeni Fong

MAY-LEE CHAI is the author of seven books, including three novels: *My Lucky Face*, *Dragon Chica*, and *Tiger Girl*; and co-author with her father, Winberg Chai, of a family memoir, *The Girl from Purple Mountain*, which was nominated for the National Book Award. She has served as a Chinese-to-English translator for PEN American Center and published a book-length translation of the 1934 autobiography of the twentieth-century Chinese writer Ba Jin. A frequent contributor to the *Jakarta Post Weekender Magazine*, she is the recipient of an NEA grant in prose. She received her M.A. in East Asian studies from Yale University and teaches in the MFA program at the University of North Carolina Wilmington. She has lived and worked in China, where she has been visiting frequently ever since her first trip in 1985.

May-lee Chai can be found on Twitter at @ChinaAtoZ and @mayleechai. She maintains a blog, mayleechai.wordpress.com, and two websites (www.may-leechai.com and www.booksbychai.com).

WINBERG CHAI is the author and editor of more than twenty books on China. Born in Shanghai, Dr. Chai is a political scientist who received his Ph.D. from New York University and who has been teaching about Asia for more than fifty years. He has testified before Congress on China and lectures in China frequently. A professor emeritus of political science at the University of Wyoming, he serves as executive editor of *Asian Affairs: An American Review*.

CHINA A TO Z

Everything You Need to Know to
Understand Chinese Customs and Culture

May-lee Chai
and Winberg Chai

A PLUME BOOK

Contents

CHINA A TO Z

Everything You Need to Know to
Understand Chinese Customs and Culture

May-lee Chai
and Winberg Chai

A PLUME BOOK

PLUME
Published by the Penguin Group
Penguin Group (USA) LLC
375 Hudson Street
New York, New York 10014

USA | Canada | UK | Ireland | Australia
New Zealand | India | South Africa | China
penguin.com
A Penguin Random House Company

First published by Plume, a member of Penguin Group (USA) Inc., 2007.
This edition published 2014.

Copyright © 2007, 2014 by May-lee Chai and Winberg Chai

Illustrations on page 146 by Tiffany Chiang.

P REGISTERED TRADEMARK—MARCA REGISTRADA

LIBRARY OF CONGRESS CATALOGING-IN-PUBLICATION DATA

Chai, May-lee.
    China A to Z : Everything you need to know to understand Chinese customs and culture / May-lee Chai and Winberg Chai.
        p. cm.
    Includes bibliographical references and index.
    ISBN 978-0-14-218084-6
        1. China—Encyclopedias.   I. Chai, Winberg.   II. Title.   III. Title:
Everything you need to know to understand Chinese customs and culture.
DS705.C414 2007
951—dc22   2006102000

Printed in the United States of America
10 9 8 7 6 5 4 3 2 1

Set in Sabon

Contents

Introduction

Since the first edition of *China A to Z*, China's position in the world has grown more important. Economically, socially, culturally, and politically, China's influence cannot be ignored. China now has the world's second largest economy and is projected to overtake the United States for the number one spot by 2017. Once known for producing goods on the cheap, China is no longer the world's sweatshop: the economic boom has helped the country to become the largest consumer market for many goods, ranging from fine art to automobiles, as well as the fastest growing market for luxury goods. As more Chinese tourists travel the world and more students from China choose to study abroad, the opportunities for social and cultural exchange are growing ever greater. At the same time, China and America disagree politically on almost every important issue, including human rights, global warming, investments in Africa and other parts of the developing world, how to handle crises from the Middle East to the South China Sea, and U.S. arms sales to Taiwan, a democracy and longtime U.S. ally that China considers to be a renegade province.

Despite these continuing disagreements and potential for conflict, China's transformation into a powerful, modern nation is a historic feat that deserves the world's attention. The growing economy has allowed hundreds of millions of people to enter the middle class, one of the fastest economic turnarounds in history. It's a remarkable development, especially considering that just over fifty years ago, more than 40 million Chinese starved to death, some under Mao Zedong's disastrous Great Leap Forward policies.

When the United States and China first reestablished diplomatic relations and Deng Xiaoping ushered in the "Open Door Policy" of economic reform in 1979, Chinese were still living under the "iron ricebowl" system. The old Communist system guaranteed everyone a (low-paying) job for life and government-approved housing. The society suffered under these laws: everyone was poor, consumer goods were rarely available and of questionable quality, births were restricted to one child per couple, and political rights were nonexistent. The unleashing of China's economic power under Deng Xiaoping's reforms allowed for some free enterprise and joint ventures with the world's companies. The material quality of life in China improved rapidly, although the political system remained controlled by the Communist Party.

After the Open Door Policy of Deng (who was the paramount leader from 1979 to 1997), China's next generation of leaders initiated and implemented more economic reforms, even permitting capitalists to join the Communist Party. So long as a person had connections—called *guanxi* in Chinese—to high officials, that person's business could thrive. In fact, by 2012 China had the third highest number of billionaires in the world, behind the United States and Russia, and in 2013, China had more billionaires created by the stock market than the United States.

The next challenge for China's leadership has been to transition the export-based economy based on cheap labor into a more mature form that promotes domestic consumption and innovation. Manufacturing has already shifted away from clothes and toys, and now China assembles the world's smart phones, tablets, and personal computers. No longer content to make goods for other countries, China has invested heavily in its universities and research parks, hoping to spark a technological revolution on its own soil. And the effects have been tremendous: Chinese companies are developing green technology, from wind power to solar energy to batteries for electric cars; and entrepreneurs are launching their own social media sites and online shopping sites.

Once repressed under Mao, Chinese artists and writers have gained unprecedented audiences domestically and worldwide now that they, too, are encouraged to create. A Chinese novelist won the Nobel Prize in Literature for the first time in 2012. Investors have paid millions of dollars for traditional artists like Qi Baishi as well as contemporary art pieces. Chinese movie directors, actors, composers, and fashion designers are finding success at home and internationally, creating a period of cultural ferment unlike anything China has experienced since before the revolution of 1949 gave birth to the People's Republic of China.

China's growth has not gone unnoticed by the world. Tourists have made China the third most visited country in the world, record numbers of American students are now studying Mandarin, and many of China's Asian neighbors are expressing concern about the rise of China in their backyard. In turn, China has become embroiled in territorial disputes across Asia from Japan to Vietnam to the Philippines. In 2013, the Pentagon issued a report officially accusing the Chinese government of waging a cyberespionage campaign on U.S. military, government, and business computer systems in order to gain valuable information.

China's unprecedented economic growth has also brought about increased social problems. China remains one of the most inequitable societies on earth—13 percent of the population earns less than $1.25 per day. Migrant workers are demanding more rights, including higher wages, benefits, and the right to live and educate their children in the cities where they work. Women's rights activists have decried traditional values that have skewed the birth rate in favor of boys and that cause unmarried career women over the age of twenty-six to be labeled as "leftovers." Dissidents like artist Ai Weiwei and lawyer-activist Chen Guangcheng have focused worldwide attention on corruption ranging from the lethal bypassing of safety regulations to the flaunting of laws by party officials . . . and have been punished by the government for their actions. Pollution from the rapid industrialization has reached catastrophic levels. The smog over Beijing reached twenty times levels considered safe for humans to breathe and created a diplomatic breach when the U.S. embassy refused to stop broadcasting the particulate levels on its @BeijingAir Twitter feed.

The dismal yellow cloud could be seen from space, a vast miasma covering Northern China like a special effect in a terrifying sci-fi movie. And China's growing car culture has caused China to hold another ignominious title as home to the world's longest traffic jam: a sixty-two-mile standstill that lasted for a miserable twelve days on a stretch of highway outside Beijing.

Napoleon was perhaps the first Westerner to accurately assess China's potential in the world, remarking, "Here lies a sleeping giant. Let him sleep, for when he wakes up, he will shock the world." In the eighteenth century, China seemed dormant, a traditional culture experiencing economic stagnation, unwilling to adapt to a changing world. However, today it is clear that China has awakened. Whether the world will adapt to China's rise peaceably or with increased belligerence remains to be seen.

I have been visiting China since 1985, six years after the United States and China reestablished diplomatic relations. My father, who was born in Shanghai, has been teaching about China for more than fifty years and has been returning nearly every year since the 1980s to witness the changes in the country of his birth. This new edition of *China A to Z* is a culmination of our experiences as China observers and scholars. We hope that these essays will provide readers with a basis for understanding the vast changes occurring in China and help them to benefit the most out of China's rise—whether as tourists, students, businesspeople, or simply armchair travelers.

—May-lee Chai

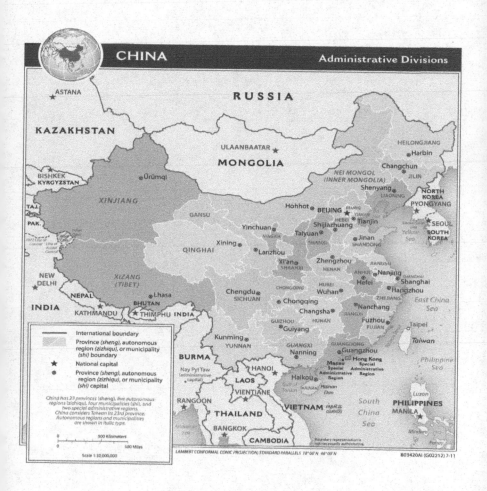

CHINA

Administrative Divisions

ASTANA ★

KAZAKHSTAN

RUSSIA

BISHKEK
KYRGYZSTAN

Ürümqi

ULAANBAATAR ★

MONGOLIA

HEILONGJIANG

Harbin

Changchun

JILIN

NEI MONGOL
(INNER MONGOLIA)

Shenyang

LIAONING

NORTH
KOREA

PYONGYANG

TAJ.

PAK.

XINJIANG

GANSU

Hohhot

BEIJING ★

BEIJING

HEBEI

TIANJIN

Tianjin

Yinchuan

NINGXIA

Shijiazhuang

Jinan

SHANDONG

SEOUL

SOUTH
KOREA

Yellow
Sea

NEW
DELHI

INDIA

Xining

QINGHAI

XIZANG
(TIBET)

Lhasa

NEPAL

KATHMANDU

BHUTAN

THIMPHU INDIA

Lanzhou

Taiyuan

SHANXI

Xi'an

SHAANXI

Zhengzhou

HENAN

ANHUI

Nanjing

SHANGHAI

Shanghai

CHONGQING

HUBEI

Hefei

JIANGSU

Chengdu

SICHUAN

Chongqing

Wuhan

Hangzhou

ZHEJIANG

East China
Sea

Changsha

Nanchang

JIANGXI

Fuzhou

FUJIAN

Taipei

GUIZHOU

HUNAN

Guiyang

Kunming

YUNNAN

BURMA

Nay Pyi Taw
(administrative
capital)

HANOI

LAOS

VIENTIANE

RANGOON ★

THAILAND

GUANGXI

Nanning

GUANGDONG

Guangzhou

Hong Kong
Special
Administrative
Region

Macau
Special
Administrative
Region

Taiwan

Philippine
Sea

Luzon

PHILIPPINES

MANILA ★

Haikou

HAINAN Hainan
Dao

Gulf of
Tonkin

VIETNAM PARACEL
ISLANDS

South
China
Sea

Mindoro

BANGKOK ★

CAMBODIA

Boundary representation is
not necessarily authoritative.

Legend

International boundary

Province (sheng), autonomous region (zizhiqu), or municipality (shi) boundary

★ National capital

⊛ Province (sheng), autonomous region (zizhiqu), or municipality (shi) capital

China has 23 provinces (sheng), five autonomous regions (zizhiqu), four municipalities (shi), and two special administrative regions. China considers Taiwan its 23rd province. Autonomous regions and municipalities are shown in italic type.

0   500 Kilometers
0   500 Miles

Scale 1:30,000,000

LAMBERT CONFORMAL CONIC PROJECTION; STANDARD PARALLELS 18°00'N 46°00'N

803420AI (G02212) 7-11

CHINA A to Z

Animals

Despite Chairman Mao's best efforts to stamp out traditional beliefs during his decades of totalitarian control, many Chinese traditions have persisted, perhaps none more strongly than the Chinese belief in good luck. Numbers, certain alignments of days in a given year, the number of strokes in a written character, homonyms, proper feng shui—all can bring good luck. And since it seems auspicious to begin a book on such a note, we have decided to discuss some of the most visible signs of luck in China today, which are embodied by animals.

Foremost among these are the dragon. Dragons represent the Chinese nation, the emperor, and, at the popular level, grooms. Images adorned with dragons (the male) and phoenixes (the female) are commonly used as gifts for newlyweds as they represent wealth and prestige. Dragons are also believed to rule over the five elements that control one's fate. There are dragons in water, including lakes, rivers, and the ocean. Dragons also live in the earth, and when angered— usually by corrupt officials—they cause earthquakes, a sign that a dynasty or a government is about to lose its Mandate of Heaven and be overthrown. Dragons can control fire, with its ability to both sustain and take human life. Other dragons rule the sky and clouds, proffering or withholding rain from farmers' crops and even bearing augurs for the fate of battles. Finally, celestial (or heavenly) dragons have been thought to impart gifts to mankind, including the earliest form of the written Chinese language, supposedly given to the legendary emperor Fu Xi (c. 3000 BCE). In fact, in some versions of the legend, Fu Xi is half dragon, half man.

Real-Life Dragon Facts

Scientists have speculated that the Chinese concept of the dragon originated with the discovery of dinosaur fossils in northern China. These bones were locally called "dragon bones" and have been ground into powder for use in traditional medicines. "Dragon teeth," which are also used to treat ailments, are believed to be fossilized ivory from prehistoric mastodons and latter-day elephants, which used to roam the land.

Some animals are good luck because their names in Mandarin sound very similar to lucky words. For example, images of bats adorn Chinese traditional art, architecture, embroidery, and porcelain. Far from being seen as the vampiric and frightening creatures of the night as in Western culture, bats are instead harbingers of wealth and prosperity, because their Chinese name, *bian fu*, sounds like the Mandarin words for "to become wealthy" (even though the written characters are completely different).

Similarly, fish are lucky because the pronunciation of their name, *yü*, sounds just like the word for "surplus" or "plenty." Thus, images of fish are used to adorn everything from New Year's cards to scroll paintings, and live fish tanks with bright goldfish in them can be found in the fronts of Chinese restaurants throughout the world, as all Chinese wish for an abundance rather than a scarcity of money.

Monkeys hold a special place in the Chinese imagination. While dragons represent power, monkeys are seen as clever creatures, and in fact, in China's most famous folktale, translated by Arthur Waley quite simply as "Monkey" (also known as "Journey to the West"), the infamous, mischievous Monkey King represents the Chinese nation, and his monkey subjects the Chinese people. Myriad films, television series, puppet plays, operas, and books have been written about the adventures of the Monkey King, who is entrusted by the Jade Emperor in Heaven to aid a devout monk to bring Buddhism to China, aided by the goddess Guan Yin. The Monkey King fights but is never vanquished by many monsters, and he represents a spirit of adventure, mischief, cleverness, loyalty, martial arts prowess, and ultimately kindness—all qualities that the Chinese people value in themselves.

Finally, the twelve animal signs representing the years according to the ancient lunar calendar are traditionally believed to bestow upon babies born under their signs certain lucky qualities. According to legend, the Lord Buddha invited all the animals of the world to a banquet. The first twelve to arrive were rewarded when he named a year after each, in the order in which they appeared in his heavenly palace. The first in the twelve-year cycle is the rat. The rat's lucky qualities include a survivor's instincts and a way with money. Next comes the ox, whose steadfast nature allows ox children to plow through adversity and attain their goals. Tigers, known as King of the Forest because the markings on their foreheads resemble the Chinese character for "king," are strong-willed and powerful, enabling them to succeed in life. Rabbits are refined, elegant creatures who will enjoy the comforts of life because their charm will allow them to get their way. Dragons of course are the embodiment of power and leadership potential. Snakes, unlike in Western culture, are seen as wise creatures whose intellect makes them formidable in all their endeavors. Horses are swift, strong, spirited animals, hard to tame, with wild hearts that will allow them to pursue exciting lives. It used to be considered bad luck for girls to be born in the Year of the Horse, but this is no longer the case. Sheep (also known as rams or goats, as the Chinese character represents all three animals) are artistic, charming, mercurial, stubborn creatures who pursue their path in life with refinement. Monkeys, as described above, are clever, mischievous, and much beloved by Chinese parents. Roosters are detail-oriented, verbal, perhaps a bit bossy, but they know they want to rule the roost and will do their best to succeed. Dogs are loyal, strong, and patient. And babies born in the Year of the Pig are sometimes considered the luckiest of all, as pigs represent wealth, an easygoing nature, and a life of abundance.

Architecture

Perhaps nothing is as startling to both Chinese and foreign visitors alike as the rapid changes to the skyline of China's cities.

In its efforts to modernize its cities, the Chinese government has embarked on a redesign campaign that is unprecedented in world history. City planners estimated that 95 percent of Shanghai's pre-1949 architecture was completely replaced by the time the Summer Olympics arrived in Beijing in 2008. Only the historic Bund on the Huangpu River (known as the Waitan in Chinese) and part of the French concession's historic architecture were completely preserved. In Beijing, twenty-five thousand workers labored around the clock for years to build the new sports stadiums and Olympic village on the city's northern border, while within the city, the historic *hutong*s—the winding alleyways lined with courtyard homes—were razed to make way for new highways, high-rises, and shopping centers.

As a result of the building boom, China consumed 55 percent of the world's concrete and 36 percent of all steel produced in 2004. And there was more construction taking place in Beijing in 2005 alone than in the whole of Europe for the previous three years, according to the BBC.

A large number of the contracts for China's new architecture are going to foreign firms, both a source of pride and a scandal within the country. Chinese architects are embittered that their own designs are considered inferior or at least less prestigious than the work of non-Chinese firms. For these foreign architects, "China is a land of dreams," according to a *New York Times Magazine* report. The Swiss firm Herzog and de Meuron, hired to design the new Olympic Stadium (dubbed "the Bird's Nest" by Beijing locals for its unusual scraggle of exposed beams), exults that China is a land without inhibitions when it comes to new building projects. The more radical, the more likely the government will approve the design in an effort to seem not only modern but cutting-edge, even avant-garde.

The new Shanghai Heritage Museum (designed by Xing Tonghe), shaped like an ancient bronze fifth-century BCE *ding* cooking pot, stands next to the neon-lighted Grand Theater, with its curved roof that evokes nothing so much as a skateboarding park (built by French firm Arte Charpentier and Associates). At first glance, the juxtapositions of style are rather dissonant. But when Shanghai natives are asked how they feel, they most commonly reply, "The two buildings show we are both traditional and modern, Chinese and international."

Other projects are less enthusiastically received. While locals loved the "Bird's Nest" stadium during the Olympics, its post-Olympics career has been less than illustrious, as attempts to turn it into a "snow park" with man-made ski slopes and a Segway racetrack have failed to make money. Locals are even less kind when referring to the National Grand Theater (designed by Paul Andreu) built in the late 1990s, dismissing it as "the egg" for its ovoid shape. Meanwhile the sinewy Beijing airport (designed by Lord Norman Foster) is thought to resemble a dragon's body and thus is viewed positively.

Sometimes foreign firms' efforts to evoke China's past backfire. The China National Offshore Oil Corporation's headquarters in Beijing was intended to resemble a Shang dynasty (3500 BCE) vessel, but alas, to locals it looked like a giant Western-style toilet bowl. A skyscraper in Shanghai designed by a Western firm (Kohn Pedersen Fox) was likewise panned when the architects decided to put a giant circle at the summit to relieve wind pressure. Local authorities nixed the design, which was for the Japanese-owned Mori Building Company, because they felt the circle evoked the Japanese flag. (The project went ahead after the architects changed the circle to a less-politically incorrect trapezoid.)

International critics tend to favor Western architectural designs over older Chinese ones, which often feature traditional tiled roofs with upswept eaves placed at the top of a modern skyscraper's rectangular column. These critics dismiss such buildings as "big roof" or "big hat" designs. Cultural critics expressed alarm when Beijing's city planners hired Albert Speer's eponymous grandson to oversee the redesign of the city. Where the Chinese saw clear central lines and avenues that evoked Beijing's imperial past, many in the West were reminded of Hitler's penchant for the grandiose.

One of most surreal trends in architecture is the penchant for the nouveaux riches to imitate famous buildings and monuments from around the world and set them in their hometowns. Throughout China, there are multiple replicas of architecture both mundane and sublime, from Dutch hamlets and windmills to Orange County, Southern California, suburban tract houses to grandiose versions of Versailles and Monticello. Context matters little to the patrons: for example, the White House has been reincarnated as everything from a seafood restaurant to a local government office to a single family home, and the Eiffel Tower's doppelganger can be found straddling a highway in Hebei Province.

Perhaps the changes to China's cities can best be summed up by the thoughts of their residents.

In Chongqing, amid a sparkling new suburb of generic white rectangular skyscrapers built to house the growing population, a local guide who worked for the city government offered his opinions on all the changes to his city. To many foreign tourists' eyes, the stilt houses built along Chongqing's mountainous terrain and the ancient city wall (both of which were being demolished) were far more charming than the generic cinder-block-style housing projects now being erected. He disagreed heartily. "Chongqing is like that statue," he said, pointing to a courtyard statue of a large-boned naked woman astride a lion. "A traditional face but riding the lion of modernity."

On the other hand, a scholar from Nanjing University had a very different opinion when asked how he felt about China's foray into the architectural wonderland. "We have a saying: 'For ten years the government destroyed the countryside,'" he said, referring to Mao's disastrous deforestation projects, communes, and neglect of public works like dams. "'For the next ten years, the government is going to destroy the cities.'"

Art

Since the age of the Roman Empire, Europeans have been fascinated by Chinese art—and have been willing to spend large sums of money to acquire it. From silks to porcelains to sculptures, art was a large part of China's trade surplus throughout history. In the nineteenth century, when the Qing dynasty was particularly weak, foreigners made off with all manner of Chinese artwork, from scroll paintings to larger-than-life-size Buddhist statuary to entire walls painted with religious imagery, many of which became fixtures in museum collections around the world. Recently, though, China's wealthy elite have been setting records in auction houses to "repatriate" lost treasures and return them to the Motherland. Wealthy Chinese investors looking for a relatively safe place for their money have been bidding on traditional and contemporary pieces, creating one of the hottest—and most robust—art markets in the world. In 2011, Chinese buyers spent $18.1 billion on art, surpassing the U.S. art market.

Chinese art encompasses a great diversity of forms, from traditional works painted on scrolls or fans, carved jade, lacquer and porcelain, to sculptures in stone, bronze, and wood to calligraphy and murals. A magnificent famille rose turquoise vase with an imperial seal on the base dating from the Qing dynasty sold for $14,332,650 in 2012 through Bonhams auction house. The most talked about sale of 2013 was a white Song dynasty porcelain bowl that the owners bought at a garage sale for $3 in New York, then sold for more than $2 million at auction.

The rise of China's art market stands in stark contrast to other Asian countries' rise, such as Japan. When Japanese businessmen and conglomerates began bidding on art with their newly acquired wealth in the 1980s, they made headlines for the record prices they were willing to pay for Western art, including the $39.9 million bid that made Van Gogh's *Sunflowers* the world's most expensive painting in 1987. Today's Chinese art lovers are proving to spend even more. China's elite thus far have preferred to bid on Chinese artworks rather than European masters, such as the record $67.1 million paid for twentieth-century master Qi Baishi's watercolor *Eagle Standing on Pine Tree*, purchased in 2011 by a Hunan TV and broadcast executive, or the record $10 million paid for a Chinese contemporary work, Zhang Xiaogang's *Forever Lasting Love*, a dystopian triptych depicting naked and emaciated figures.

The change in fate for Chinese arts might seen ironic considering that Red Guards set about destroying traditional art during the ten years of the Cultural Revolution (1966–76), burning any paintings they could get their hands on and combing the countryside in groups to destroy traditional Buddhist artworks on mountainsides and in temples. However, the arts have always played an important cultural role in China, and the Maoist bias against traditional artwork has proven to be more a historical blip than a lasting cultural trend. As art scholar Dr. Ch'u Chai wrote in his bestselling book, *The Changing Society of China*, "Of all the expressions of Chinese civilization, it is Chinese art that has made the lasting contribution to the culture of the world."

Watercolor or Ink Paintings

Known in Chinese as *shan shui* (literally "mountain and water" paintings), these works emphasize the brush skills of the artist rather than the ability to capture three-dimensional space on a sheet of paper or focus on religious symbolism as is prominent in much of Western art history. Landscape paintings have traditionally been more valued in

Chinese history than figurative works or cityscapes. *Shan shui* are mounted either on a vertical scroll for hanging, or a horizontal scroll that is meant to be opened and viewed one arm-length at a time, emphasizing the intimate relationship between owner and painting.

Calligraphy

Contrary to many myths, the calligraphy that appears on Chinese paintings is not necessarily describing the scene depicted. The graceful brushstrokes are considered an art form irrespective of the meaning of the text, and can showcase a classical poem, the calligrapher's remarks, a sign of ownership of a famous painting, or an official edict. Calligraphy is not meant to be easy to read; in fact, some styles are illegible even to people literate in the traditional characters and classical grammar of the text. Connoisseurs appreciate the gradations in the ink, which reveal the great control of the calligrapher, the historic style of the calligraphy (there are innumerable scripts), and the delicate shape of the characters.

Contemporary Art

Since the reform period began after 1979, China's contemporary artists have become some of the most daring in the world. For example, Zhang Huan covered himself in honey and allowed flies to converge upon his body in a show in Beijing, and in another performance piece, he lay naked on a block of ice as an exploration of the body and spiritual self. Other contemporary artists like to create a dialogue with the socialist realism themes of Mao-era art, such as Zhang Xiaogang's famous paintings of dry-eyed families dressed in Mao suits and soberly staring straight at the viewer of the painting. Photographer Liu Bolin uses his art to critique the social problems associated with China's rapid urbanization, and his method is unique. Liu covers himself in body paint so that he blends nearly perfectly into his backgrounds—from brick walls to buildings slated for demolition—then has assistants photograph him in place.

Perhaps the most famous of the contemporary artists is Ai Weiwei, whose conceptual work has explored themes of destruction and culture. In the 1990s, he took priceless Chinese urns and repainted them with logos for contemporary brands like Coca-Cola, and in one instance photographed himself simply dropping one urn and smashing it to smithereens. One of his most famous recent works is made of several million hand-painted sunflower seeds that museum visitors may walk through or lie in. He is also credited with co-designing the "Bird's Nest" stadium for the 2008 Beijing Olympics. After the 2008 earthquake in Sichuan, Ai made an exhibit of plastic backpacks in honor of the more than five thousand schoolchildren killed when their schools collapsed. His continuing efforts to uncover the causes of their deaths (activists believe the schools were built with substandard materials and were not built to code) as well as other dissident activities have caused Ai to run into problems with the government. In 2011, he was beaten by the police in Chengdu, Sichuan Province, and later, he was detained for eighty-one days by the government. After being forbidden from leaving China, Ai set up cameras throughout his house, providing a "live feed" on his website and to his hundreds of thousands of followers online.

While most Chinese art, ancient or contemporary, has commanded good prices, largely due to the demand of Chinese buyers themselves, it is still possible for people to buy quality, original works. Most Chinese buyers are not necessarily art lovers per se, but are investors, so they focus on purchasing famous works as advised by auctioneers or financial planners. Visitors may still buy wonderful works of art by local artists who may not be famous or popular but are certainly talented and creative. While hotels often offer high-priced mass-produced works, visitors can find original, hidden treasures by visiting any of China's schools for the arts, where students are often willing to sell their works to pay for their bills. Remember that Ai Weiwei was once such a starving artist when he lived in New York City in the 1980s. Who knows where the next Ai will come from?

Banquets

Banquets are the single most important way that Chinese greet friends, business colleagues, diplomats, and even enemies. If it's a truism that all the "real business" is done outside the boardroom, for example, in pubs in England, on golf courses and squash courts in America, or during after-work drinking binges in Japan, where potential partners and rivals can interact informally and size each other up, then in China this type of relationship-building is done with banquets.

As a result, whether you go to China as a student, a tourist, a businessperson, or a returning family member from overseas, you will experience a banquet.

They differ from Western banquets in that the tables are round, not rectangular, so there is no visible head or foot. That does not mean that seating is egalitarian. Traditionally, guests of honor were seated with their backs to the wall, the hosts (or most junior members of the host's party) with their backs exposed to the door. The legend behind this is that once in Chinese history a devious king invited his rival to a banquet, supposedly in a bid for peace. While they were eating, an assassin stepped inside the room—unseen by the guest, who had his back to the door—and stabbed the unsuspecting guest to death. From that time onward, to show true friendship, the host must have his back to the door. (Naturally, among young people, families, and close friends, such formalities need not be observed.)

Banquets are often served in private rooms within larger restaurants. One, this affords privacy. Two, this helps the host save face in case a rival banquet at a nearby table should have fancier food. In fact, many junior executives prefer to pay extra for the private banquet rooms simply to avoid any possibility of getting into an expensive ordering rivalry with a neighboring table.

Banquets in the West generally follow a set pattern of dishes, with hors d'oeuvres first, followed by a salad, perhaps a soup, main courses, then a dessert. Chinese banquets will have different kinds of foods depending upon the region and the occasion. Expect that there will be many, many courses. Traditional hospitality requires that the guests be offered far more than they could possibly finish eating. Therefore, it is wise to eat a little of each course rather than heartily indulge or you might not make it to course twenty-seven.

Banquets also are generally served "family style," in which platters are placed on a lazy Susan that rotates in the center of the round table rather than an individual plate of food being given to each diner.

Typical menus include a set of cold dishes to begin. These might be cold boiled and salted peanuts, crunchy jellyfish noodles, sliced vegetables like lotus root or greens, one-thousand-year-old eggs (which are not really that old but are hard-boiled and prepared in sauces so they become dark and translucent), flavored seeds, sliced cold meat, and local delicacies. The next courses will most likely involve hot foods. Nowadays the Chinese like to mix Western specialties with traditional dishes, so it's not unusual to be served escargot sautéed in clarified butter as one course, then Chinese-style sea slug or giant prawns or lobster sashimi, then a series of beefsteaks. Raw salads have also come into vogue although once Chinese balked at eating anything uncooked. Most banquets include at least one soup, which is unlikely to be served at the beginning of the meal because soups are used to change the palate or else to finish a banquet so that one's stomach is completely full. Little sweet cakes might also be served to change the palate in between courses. Their arrival does not signal the end of the meal by any means. Various kinds of tea also are used as palate cleansers. A whole fresh fish is considered essential for most banquets unless various other seafoods have already been served, such as whole crabs, whole prawns, eels, and so on. Fresh cold fruit generally signals the end of a banquet.

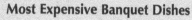

Most Expensive Banquet Dishes

Shark fin soup
Swallow's nest pudding
Shark stomach
Abalone dishes
Peking duck
Exotic animals

Banquet Etiquette

Even if you really don't feel like eating something, take a sample for your plate or rice bowl. As the guest, you will be expected to be served first or serve yourself first. If you don't take a sample, your hosts will feel awkward and will not be able to take a sample either. Servers will come and replace dirty plates with clean ones so you can let the server simply take away something if you really don't want to eat it.

Often your hosts will make a series of toasts. Hold your glass with both hands, one flat on the bottom, the other around the base of the cup. It's not necessary to clink glasses as one does in the West. Simply raise it with a smile toward the person making the toast then to other senior officials then to the more junior members and take a sip. If you must make a toast, simply say something friendly, such as a thank-you to your hosts for their hospitality and the lovely meal or the beautiful city you are visiting or a generic remark about your appreciation for the friendliness of the Chinese people. No need to make a business pitch, such as "Here's hoping you choose our company and we all become very prosperous." Generic works best in these situations.

If you really don't like alcohol or you have an ulcer, let your hosts know and you can make your toasts with bottled water or soda pop. Women are not expected to drink as much as men. You can touch the glass of alcohol to your lips without even drinking, in fact. If you are a man, try not to drink a lot with each toast as there may be many, many toasts, and getting drunk is a distinct possibility. Also, if you down your alcohol, this will put pressure on your hosts to do the same, and it might put them in an awkward situation. They might have a full day and night of work to attend to after the meal or a long commute or they may have to write up notes about the meal for their company. Don't inadvertently turn a banquet into a drinking contest.

Sometimes your hosts will actually put food onto your plate or rice bowl. They are giving you the choicest bits and you should thank them. Make a pretense of eating, even if you don't really want to. It's a polite gesture. If you notice that someone's plate is empty or he or she seems to like a particular dish, spin the lazy Susan slowly in that direction and urge the person to have some more. Your encouragement for others to eat more is considered polite.

Banquets will end rather abruptly. Don't expect any serious business to have been discussed. The banquet is a formality, a requirement of being a gracious host. It's not the place where decisions are made. However, your behavior will be observed, and your trustworthiness as a human being also judged.

Banquet Nightmares

Most Chinese do not yet have any understanding of the Western concept of "being on a diet." After one hundred fifty years of war and political struggles, the Chinese associate being too thin with being unhealthy. Most Chinese are proud to put on a little girth. (Unfortunately, China now has the second highest obesity rate in the world, behind the United States, so attitudes at some point will have to change as unhealthy eating patterns brought upon by new prosperity will lead to health problems. However, that day has not yet come for most Chinese.)

But if you are on a diet and you are at a banquet, there are some things you can do to keep from blowing your diet at every meal. First, let your hosts know you have certain food "allergies" or food "restrictions." Blame your doctor. Your Chinese hosts don't want to kill you even though they might be serving you an extremely high-cholesterol meal and you have heart disease. A very effective means of saving their face and your diet is to take what is offered, eat (or pretend to eat) a tiny bit, and then say, "Oh, this is so delicious, but I mustn't eat more. My doctor absolutely forbids it. But I just wanted a little taste." Your hosts will feel that they have given you a secret pleasure but they won't insist you eat more of something dangerous to your health.

How to Avoid Eating Unbearable Things

Another situation might arise where you are served something you just frankly cannot bear to eat. It might be those fried eels with their little faces staring up at you from your rice bowl. Or fresh young quails on a stick that appear to have been fried in oil while still alive, judging by the death grimaces on their faces. Or maybe snake just isn't your thing. Here being a foreigner comes in handy. You can feign chopstick incompetence. If they put something on your plate and you can't bear it, move those chopsticks like crazy but just drop that stuff before it ever reaches your mouth. Your hosts will be so embarrassed for you, you will become truly invisible. If perchance your hosts should send a server from the restaurant your way to assist you, simply whisper to the server to please take your plate away. The server won't lose face—he or she didn't order this food, after all. Thus, it's a culturally safe way to get rid of something you just don't want to put into your mouth.

A banquet is not a good time to lecture your hosts about what you consider appropriate to eat. For example, you may find shark fin soup personally offensive. But until you know your hosts extremely well and you can all talk about personal matters with ease, denouncing the Chinese practice of eating shark fin soup midbanquet is not going to help anyone. It's too late to save the shark, it will embarrass your hosts, and your behavior will most likely be read as immature as opposed to rational and convincing.

If you are in a more informal situation, such as on a tour, let your guide know about food preferences early on, such as vegetarianism or allergies. If something unpleasant comes up later on the tour, which you didn't anticipate, you can always bring up that you have a "restricted diet." One family friend of ours was served Peking duck at every single lunch and dinner banquet he attended on a three-week tour of China. As a result, he never wants to eat it again as long as he lives. If you find a similar pattern happening to you, tell your guide that you need to vary your diet and your doctor will be upset if you eat Peking duck at every meal because it is very rich. Ask for some blander food—such as fresh greens or a fish—and say something like "Peking duck is a wonderful luxury but my doctor warned me I must stay away from duck. I'll enjoy watching everyone else eat it, but I'm afraid I must make this special request. Sorry to trouble you." This way you save your guide's face—you're not blaming him or her for ordering the same damn food at every meal, or accusing the guide of trying to ratchet up the price or, who knows, help out a restaurant owner/secret partner by bringing a tour group to the restaurant then consistently ordering the most expensive thing on the menu. All of these are possibilities, but no point in bringing them up. Politeness and an appeal to your own health issues will most likely get you the food you want.

True Health Concerns

Finally, if you have severe allergies, naturally you should tell your hosts first and foremost before any meal. They will gladly accommodate you and tell the chef to prepare special dishes just for you. The Chinese want a banquet to leave a good impression. Even friends of ours with life-threatening peanut allergies, diabetes, shellfish allergies, MSG reactions, and such have gone to China and had many enjoyable banquets. Just let your hosts know any special dietary requirements in advance.

Bargaining

Bargaining is an art form much beloved by the Chinese. However, there is a common misconception in the West that bargaining is simply about getting a cheaper price. No. Bargaining to the Chinese is like seduction to the French. The process is as important as the actual end result.

First and foremost, bargaining is about establishing a relationship between yourself and the merchant. The merchant is not your adversary and should not be treated as such. The merchant is the object of your seduction. Try to find a common ground. If you are Asian, emphasize common roots. "Can you give a special deal to a fellow Chinese (or a traveling Korean, a Japanese who loves China, etc.)?" If you are not, emphasize the distance you have traveled. "I've come all this way to see China. Such a wonderful country! Is there any way you can give me a special price?" Flatter the merchant. Suggest options, such as, "Can you call your supervisor?" Not all salespeople are allowed to make price reductions themselves so do not say this in an insulting way but try to emphasize that you understand this salesperson would of course like nothing better than to give you a deal, as he or she is such a nice person, but of course you understand a salesperson must consult with a boss.

Watch how other people bargain. Make more than one trip if you can to the stall, stand, or store that you are visiting to show your interest, but like a good flirt, you play hard to get and act as though you cannot make up your mind about the item you wish to purchase. See if the merchant will make a first move and offer you a discount.

Then there's the more proletarian but ever effective, "If I buy more than one, can I get a discount?" Again, you are showing your love for the merchant's product and respect for his or her business instincts.

In big department stores, bargaining is generally not permitted. However, you can ask salesclerks if there are any sales and they will be glad to point out that merchandise to you. In fact, many Chinese department stores have myriad promotions going on at any given time—including free gifts with purchases (such as a freshwater pearl), scratch-type lotto tickets, discounts on other merchandise if you buy a certain amount of goods in the store, and even free digital photos of yourself (or rather, your head transposed onto a model's body).

In large cities, some groups of Chinese bargain hunters have now taken to using the Internet to plot how to mob certain showrooms at a certain time to demand a group discount. This is not bargaining per se but bullying and not recommended for non-Chinese to participate in.

Beijing

Beijing, formerly known as Peking, is the capital of China and perhaps China's most famous city. Because of the 2008 Summer Olympics games, the city experienced a massive influx of government cash so that it became China's showcase to the world. As soon as the International Olympic Committee announced Beijing as its choice in 2001 for the 2008 games, the government announced a new goal: that each resident of the city would learn one hundred English phrases. Construction of the massive and impressively modern Olympic facilities began soon after. As a result, such architectural wonders as those dubbed "the Bird's Nest" (the National Stadium) and "the Water Cube" (the National Aquatics Center) have been keenly debated in popular and architectural journals around the world for their avant-garde designs. Today the Water Cube is the family friendly "Happy Magic Water Cube" water park, featuring such standards as a wave pool, "lazy river," and thirteen water slides, whereas the "Bird's Nest" stadium struggles to find a purpose at all. Perhaps this seems an unexciting fate for the once-vaunted projects, which cost an estimated $51 million and $480 million respectively to build, but such is the nature of contemporary Beijing, where the sublime and the mundane routinely rub shoulders.

Beijing is a fascinating city that has been at the center of some of history's most important events. The most visible ancient architectural wonders date from the last dynasty, the Qing (1644–1911), when the

Manchus who ruled China left their distinctive cultural aesthetics on the city. In addition to the Forbidden City, where the various emperors traditionally lived, the imperial family's pleasure palaces remain as well, including the Summer Palace, with its multicolored, exquisitely painted buildings, lush grounds, and perhaps most impressive of all, Marble Boat, which the Empress Dowager Cixi famously built using the funds supposedly earmarked to build a real navy for China in the late nineteenth century. Prince Gong's Mansion, the garden palace of one of the princes from the reign of Emperor Xianfeng (1851–62) is every bit as opulent as Versailles, with its lakes, swans, halls, and private opera house (with daily performances for visitors), as well as mysterious life-prolonging feng shui symbols like the bat-shaped pond, the Longevity Pavilion, and calligraphy carved into stone. Domestic tourists from as far away as the Burma border flock to this exotic palace, so it is also a fabulous place to people watch, as Han Chinese and ethnic minority tourists far outnumber Westerners.

For even older historical sites, one can visit the Ming dynasty (1388–1643) Drum Tower or the many altars of the Temple of Heaven, which also has the famed Echo Wall, where a word whispered at one end of the curved wall can be heard at the other end.

Even older yet, the Mongol-built Beihai Park, which is believed to have been the original location of Kublai Khan's palace, now holds many historical treasures including the White Dagoba—built for a seventeenth-century visit by the then Dalai Lama—and the famed Nine Dragons Screen, a symbol of imperial power.

Because Beijing was the capital of China under Mongol, Han, and Manchu rule (three different ethnicities), the city's diversity is present in its architectural history. It is likewise very obviously diverse in the present. There are mosques, Daoist temples, Buddhist temples, Christian churches, and of course the most famous landmarks of Communist Party power.

The Great Hall of the People, located on the western side of Tiananmen Square, is where the National People's Congress meets. Also off Tiananmen, Mao's portrait still hangs on the Gate of Heavenly Peace, where Mao first proclaimed the birth of the People's Republic of China on October 1, 1949. And Chairman Mao himself is still available for viewing, as his mausoleum is located on the southern end of Tiananmen.

For those interested in contemporary politics, the vast Tiananmen Square, where pro-democracy demonstrators lived, danced, and were driven away at gunpoint in 1989, is fully open to the public. Today, however, families are more apt to be flying kites, riding bicycles, or taking pictures in front of Mao's portrait than staging political protests and the square is well guarded by soldiers and plainclothes policemen.

Of course, Beijing is also a very modern city replete with dance clubs, jazz clubs, bars, world-class restaurants, art museums, galleries, shopping malls, glittering five-star hotels, Western and Beijing opera houses, and all the other hallmarks of contemporary urban society. However, it would be a shame to visit Beijing without investigating some of the city's remaining *hutongs*—mazelike alleys with courtyard homes that represent the nonimperial, pre–Communist Party Beijing, the true essence of Beijing's residents. Most of the *hutongs* have been razed to make way for businesses and high-rise apartment buildings, but near the Forbidden City, a historical zone has been created to preserve some of Beijing's most famous indigenous architecture.

Bo Xilai Scandal

The scandal that brought down one of the Chinese Communist Party's fastest-rising stars sounds like a plot straight out of a James Bond movie: a British businessman gets too close to one of China's most elite power couples and ends up dead, his body cremated within twenty-four hours, while his family in England is told that he'd died of a heart attack after a night of heavy drinking. Friends are surprised as the man was a teetotaler. Then, the police chief of Chongqing, a metropolitan area of 30 million, seeks refuge at the U.S. consulate in Chengdu and provides shocking information—that the Brit was murdered by the jealous wife of the party secretary (chief) of Chongqing, a leader who was on the fast track to becoming one of the inner circle of the Communist Party. This 2012 case exposed the vast network of connections underlying the so-called Red Princelings, the grown children of Communist Party elites.

The players in question revolved around Bo Xilai (pronounced "Boh She-Lye"), who at the time was considered a "progressive" political leader in China, one of the twenty-five members of the all-powerful Politburo of the Central Committee of the Chinese Communist Party. Bo came from a distinguished, well-known family whose father had been Deng Xiaoping's right-hand man with the title of vice premier of China. As party secretary of the megacity of Chongqing, Bo was known as a reformer, fighting for the common people, constructing subsidized housing for the tens of thousands of low-income workers in the city. He also led a campaign to crack down on organized crime, a rarely discussed but pervasive problem in China. He ordered his police chief, Wang Lijun, to investigate and arrest hundreds of corrupt party officials and businessmen. Many ended up being tried and executed. Rumors spread that he wasn't just hunting criminals, but using his authority to crack down on anyone who threatened his authority. Still, he had widespread support among the people of Chongqing.

Bo encouraged a new spirit of civic-mindedness to counter the pervasive materialism in China and led massive public sing-alongs of Mao-era songs, reviving nationalistic sentiments. He claimed he wanted to rebuild a new China after Mao's model—that is, a more equitable, socialist model—and was widely expected to succeed Hu Jintao as China's next leader in 2013.

Suddenly, scandal broke out publicly in February 2012 when his chief of police, Wang Lijun, fled to the U.S. consulate in Chengdu and told American diplomats that Bo wanted to have him killed. He said he'd refused to cover up for a crime committed by Bo's wife. The crime? Wang said she'd poisoned her longtime business associate, a British man named Neil Heywood, in his hotel room in Chongqing.

What happened next was unclear. The United States apparently refused to grant Wang asylum because of rumors that he had tortured political enemies. At any rate, he was released from the consulate into the authority of the central government in Beijing, where Bo would not be able to silence him.

Soon thereafter, the world media exploded with the Bo Xilai scandal. The *Wall Street Journal* ran a long article about the once-glamorous Mrs. Bo, comparing her to Jacqueline Kennedy Onassis, and later reported that Heywood had supplied information about the Bo family to MI6, the British intelligence agency. The *New York Times*, *Washington Post*, *New Yorker*, *Guardian*, and other Western media provided constant updates on the unfolding investigation. *Time* magazine put the story on the cover of its May 14, 2012, issue entitled, "The People's Republic of Scandal: Murder. Lies. Corruption. Can China Face the Truth?" Entire books dissecting the scandal appeared in the overseas Chinese presses from Hong Kong to Taiwan.

Each article revealed deeper layers of the corruption present in

China. While official salaries are low, reports revealed that most government officials lead wealthy lifestyles, amassing millions or even billions from kickbacks for business deals and investment schemes. The Bos were the perfect example of this type of incredible wealth. Their son attended a pricey British prep school, arranged for by Heywood, and later went on to graduate school at Harvard. (He also had a preference for being chauffeured around Beijing in an Audi—once with then U.S. ambassador Jon Huntsman's daughter). Mrs. Bo's investment firm was reported to have been worth hundreds of millions of dollars. And Bo was reportedly bugging central government officials' phones and offices.

The official Chinese government statement was published by the *Beijing Review* on August 23, 2012, in an article named "A Gripping Murder Case." It stated simply that Bo's wife and her personal aide, Zhang Xiaojun, had poisoned Heywood in his hotel room. Then with the help of Bo Xilai's deputy, Police Chief Wang Lijun, she had ordered the body to be cremated the next day. Eventually all three were tried in Chinese courts: Mrs. Bo was given a suspended death penalty, her aide and the police chief sentenced to nine and fifteen years in prison respectively. The only rationale given for the crime was a statement attributed to Mrs. Bo, saying that she feared Heywood wanted to harm her son after a business deal had fallen through.

Meanwhile, the disgraced Bo lost all his official positions and was placed under arrest in 2012. The following year he was sentenced to life in prison after being found guilty of bribery, embezzlement, and abuse of power.

While many articles speculated about the web of tangled relationships and paranoia that led to the murder of Neil Heywood—a business deal gone awry? a love affair gone sour? a hit job on a foreign spy?—the truth behind the case may never be known. What the scandal did reveal was the dark secrets of China's new elites: their rivalries, their power struggles, their privileged lifestyles, and their access to wealth and power based on family ties.

Body Language

Chinese tend to stand closer to other people than Americans do, even when they are not in crowds. It is also common in Europe to come up right next to the person you're talking to, but we Americans tend to like a large circle of space around us. We lounge. We stride. We take up space. Perhaps five thousand years of living in a densely populated country is the reason Chinese stand close, but it is also a sign of politeness. To stand at a distance from a colleague or friend and shout would seem unfriendly. However, some Americans can find it disconcerting at first when a Chinese friend or colleague moves into one's spatial comfort zone.

Chinese also tend to be more "hands-on" than Americans, but this generally extends only to people of the same sex unless the man and woman are a couple. Even then, open displays of affection are uncommon even for married couples of a certain age while they are increasingly common for young Chinese in their twenties and below. For example, if two women are good friends, it is not uncommon for them to walk arm in arm down the street to shop. Similarly, young men can put their arms across each other's shoulders and stand very close with no sexual connotation whatsoever.

Some physical contact relates to age. Younger people are expected to take the arms of much older people to help them up or down stairs, through narrow passageways, or to step over curbs or anything that might cause the older person to trip.

Chinese tend not to make as many hand and arm gestures as Americans. Americans should try to refrain from pointing directly at someone when making a point or gesticulating into what they assume is empty space around them; otherwise they might just strike a colleague who is hovering nearby.

Sexual Harassment

If you are a woman and a Chinese man is touching you a lot, do not write this off as normal behavior of a different culture. To accept this behavior would be to give the impression that you are open to his sexual advances. Instead make your displeasure known quickly and firmly and try to get away from the man. If you are in a crowded area, shout "*Bu!*" very loudly (pronounced "Boo!") and look angry so that others might assist you or you might embarrass the man into going away. (*Bu* means "no" in Chinese and, if said forcefully, it will be pronounced in the correct tone. It is the easiest word to pronounce under duress if you don't speak Chinese and that's why we recommend it here.) Unfortunately, a persistent stereotype exists in China that American women are "easy" because of images from Western movies, where women are sometimes depicted to be very easy indeed.

To avoid giving the impression that you are sexually coming on to a Chinese person, the most important thing to remember is that touching members of the opposite sex can easily be misinterpreted. And if a misunderstanding should occur, smile to show that your intentions are friendly while apologizing if the Chinese person seems offended.

Cross-Cultural Changes

China does not have as many strict prohibitions regarding body language as other Asian countries, such as Japan, where even blowing your nose in public discreetly into a tissue can be considered an affront; Thailand, where you must never point your foot or shoe at someone; or Cambodia, where touching someone, even a child, on the head is considered very disrespectful. And the Chinese are working hard to understand what Americans consider normal and friendly. For example, when then President Hu and President Bush met at the G-8 summit in 2006, Hu greeted Bush with open arms to embrace him in a hearty hug. This is not typical Chinese behavior, as no Chinese leaders are ever seen hugging each other in greeting, but an obvious sign that Hu had been studying American body language. In this regard, the Chinese tend to be more forgiving of American movements that might have caused stares a mere decade ago.

Buddhism

Buddhism was founded by an Indian prince, Siddhartha Gautama (ca. 566–486 BCE), after he became enlightened—that is, discovered the "truth" that human existence is based on suffering because of our desires. To free ourselves of suffering, and the cycles of birth and rebirth that humans must endure, we must follow the eightfold path: right view, right resolve, right speech, right livelihood, right effort, right mindfulness, right concentration, and right action. In other words, be kind to all in word, action, and thought.

Achieving this state of enlightenment means one has achieved Nirvana and will no longer have to be reborn as a human to suffer through the cycles of karma (essentially, good and bad things that happen to you because of good and bad things you did in past lifetimes).

Buddhism was introduced into China from India during the Han dynasty in the first century CE, when Indian Buddhism spread along the Silk Road first to China's westernmost province of Xinjiang, where it moved from the ancient capital of Changan (present-day Xi'an) inward to Luoyang in Henan Province. During the Sui dynasty (581–618 CE), Buddhism became the state religion of China.

At various times throughout Chinese history, Buddhism blended with folk religious practices as well as Confucianism and Daoism. At other times, Buddhism found itself in opposition to these other religious and philosophical traditions.

"Zen" Buddhism (as it is called in the West after the Japanese term) is known as Chan Buddhism in China. It emphasizes attaining enlightenment through meditation. Zen has influenced many poets and works of art, which are striking for their simplicity of line and strong graphic qualities as well as use of negative (blank) space.

Today many sects of Buddhism are practiced in China. Although the Communist Party officially espouses atheism, and members must be atheists, Chinese citizens have the right to practice religion, so long as their sect is approved by the government and obeys Chinese laws. As a result, Buddhist monasteries and nunneries are once again flourishing across the country after being severely persecuted during the Cultural Revolution under Mao's leadership.

The Shaolin Temple located in Henan Province is unquestionably the most famous monastery in China. Tens of thousands of domestic and foreign tourists travel to this mountain temple every year to see contemporary Shaolin monks practice the unique form of martial arts that has immortalized them in film and fiction.

However, there are other less famous but equally active monasteries, temples, and sites for Buddhist pilgrims throughout the entirety of China, many of which are being renovated by the Chinese government in acknowledgment of their huge appeal to tourists, both the faithful and the merely curious. Giant Buddhist statues carved into mountainsides can be seen in Emei Shan outside Chengdu in Sichuan Province as well as Luoyang in Henan Province. Many pilgrims still take to heart the adage that before dying they should show their devotion to the Buddha by climbing Huang Shan and Tai Shan (Yellow Mountain in Anhui Province and Mount Tai in Shandong Province), believed to be sacred sites because of their great beauty and proximity to the heavens. Meanwhile, in the Xishuang Banna Autonomous Region next to Burma (Myanmar), many sons of the ethnic minorities who live in this southern part of Yunnan Province are expected to serve as apprentice monks for at least one year in their lives to gain merit for their parents as well as to learn about their own culture separate from the Han Chinese curriculum that they are taught in public schools. The Buddhism practiced among these groups is very similar to that of Thailand and Cambodia. However, in provinces that border Tibet, many ethnic Tibetans as well as Han Chinese practice the Tibetan tantric form of Buddhism (although they are not allowed to follow the teachings of the Dalai Lama, who lives in exile in India).

Tourists irrespective of religious faith are generally welcome to visit Buddhist temples although visitors may not be allowed to enter inner sanctuaries. It is best not to dress in scanty clothing; men should always wear shirts and women should not bare a lot of cleavage or wear short-shorts or miniskirts out of respect for the monks. Some temples allow you to take pictures, others do not. Signs are generally posted if they do not allow photographs. When in doubt, ask.

Canton
(Guangzhou)

Guangzhou (pronounced "gwahng joe") was formerly known in the West as Canton and is the capital of Guangdong Province in southern China. "Canton" became famous in the West as most of the overseas Chinese diaspora originally came from Guangdong Province, leading to the construction of Chinatowns throughout the world where Cantonese, the language of Guangdong Province, was the most commonly spoken dialect, not Mandarin.

The port city of Guangzhou has always had an international bent as it was one of the earliest points of entry for foreigners coming to China. The Romans arrived here around the second century CE. Much later, in the sixteenth century, Portuguese traders arrived, looking to expand their trade in Chinese ceramics, teas, silks, and spices. Within a few decades, Jesuits arrived, looking to convert Chinese souls to Catholicism. The British first arrived at Guangzhou in the seventeenth century, with ships from the East India Company looking to trade with China. The Qing dynasty, alarmed by the increasing foreign presence at the port, confined all foreigners to the nearby island of Shamian and authorized a single merchant group, known as the *cohong*, to oversee China's trade with the outside world. The British decided to tip the trade imbalance in their favor by dumping cheap opium onto the Guangzhou market, creating addicts who would later be willing to pay much inflated prices. The Qing government tried to stop the British opium trade, leading to the Opium War, which the British with their superior arms were able to win. As a result, the Chinese government was forced to cede nearby Hong Kong Island to Great Britain.

Guangzhou has also been the birthplace of many Chinese revolutionaries. The leader of the Taiping Rebellion (1848–64), Hong Xiuquan, who nearly toppled the corrupt Qing dynasty, was born just west of Guangzhou. It is widely believed that Hong first came into contact with Western missionaries in Guangzhou, which is how he came upon the idea that he, like Jesus before him, was the son of God and it was his duty to try to bring God's kingdom onto earth; thus his revolution began. Dr. Sun Yat-sen (1866–1925), founder of modern China and the first president of the Republic of China, was born in a village near Guangzhou as well. His movement to overthrow the imperial system was effective and ended the Qing dynasty—China's last—in 1911. Later, after warlords took over northern China, and the Republic of China that he had so dreamed of establishing faltered, Sun set up base in Guangzhou, where he organized the Nationalist Party to wage campaigns against the other warlords. Guangzhou was also the center for early Chinese Communist Party activities in 1925–26, during which time Mao Zedong was based in the city (having fled Shanghai, where Chiang Kai-shek was based).

Guangzhou today is known for its exquisite cuisine, such as dim sum, and also its adventurous residents' willingness to eat just about anything—from dogs to cats, rats, live shrimp, endangered species, and unusual species not found in other provinces. These eating habits have given Chinese in general the reputation for culinary revolution, but in fact most Chinese from outside Guangdong marvel at the daring of the Cantonese palate. Unfortunately, these adventures in dining occasionally have dire consequences—as the 2003 SARS epidemic is now believed to have originated in Guangzhou after people began eating civet cats (a wild animal quite unlike the domesticated pets), which then caused the virus to be transmitted from animal to human.

Perhaps because Guangzhou has always been marked by an adventurous spirit—as shown by the number of sojourners, revolutionaries, and gourmands it has spawned—

the city also was one of the first to embrace market reforms and capitalism. Even in the late 1980s when other Chinese cities were still marked by squat concrete, Soviet-style buildings, a few so-called free markets (where budding entrepreneurs could sell their wares) and many government-run enterprises, Guangzhou was building skyscrapers, attracting investors from abroad (especially among the large overseas Chinese community with roots in the province), and fast becoming China's first modern city. Its proximity to Hong Kong—and shared Cantonese dialect with Hong Kong residents—also helped Guangzhou to bridge the divide between a government-planned economy and a free market economy.

Today Guangzhou, with more than 12 million residents, remains one of China's most sophisticated, prosperous, and expensive cities. In a bold move with implications for the rest of China, the municipal government in 2012 announced the strictest measures in the country to reduce by half the number of new cars on its streets, including license plate auctions and lotteries. The central government in Beijing has generally frowned upon such measures for fear of damaging the growing auto industry. Although Guangzhou is also a major auto manufacturing hub, city officials felt it was more important to take steps to improve air quality and reduce gridlock in response to growing public outcry. The city's growing middle class no longer accepted the decades-old model of putting short-term economic growth over quality-of-life issues, a change in attitude that could very well be the next new trend that originated in Guangzhou.

How did Guangzhou come to be called Canton?

Many scholars believe "Canton" derives from a French misunderstanding.

When the French Jesuits came to the port of Guangzhou, they mistook the name of the province for the name of the city. Hence the word "Canton" derives from the French version of the local pronunciation of Guangdong, "kahn-tohn."

The vowels were shortened by later English arrivals to Canton.

Cars

Once a nation associated with its millions of bicycles, China is now the second-fastest-growing market for cars in the world. Millions of Chinese have already purchased cars and millions more are expected to make purchases in the coming decade as homegrown automotive companies are able to provide more affordable models for the domestic market.

Already new car sales have reached 18 million annually in China (compared to 14.5 million in the United States) but the room for growth is enormous: whereas there are roughly six hundred cars per one thousand people in the United States, there are only forty-four per one thousand in China as of 2013. Owning a car has become part of the Chinese dream; as one female contestant explained on a popular television dating show, "I'd rather cry in the back of a BMW than smile on the back of a bicycle."

Despite heavy tariffs, sales of luxury cars have been growing steadily over the last decade and are predicted to surpass the United States by 2016. In fact, when Rolls-Royce launched a special $1.2 million "Year of the Dragon" version of its Phantom model, all eight were sold in less than two months.

Meanwhile, China is seeking to make a splash in the foreign automobile market, building car factories in Wuhu, Anhui Province, for example, and supplying automotive parts of high quality that are cheaper than those produced in the United States, Germany, or Japan.

And in 2012 a Chinese company took over the storied British Black Cab company, a longtime symbol of modern London that was prominently displayed in the opening ceremony for the 2012 Summer Olympics in London.

Car brands have their own associations in China. Audis are seen as the car of choice of government officials, Buicks are a family model, and Ferrari and Porsches are the favorite of the "Red Princelings"—the children of wealthy and connected government officials. China's own Chery QQ hatchback may have been designed with the domestic market in mind, but as one Chinese businessman told the *Guardian* newspaper, if he drove such a low-end car to meet a client, the business deal would be "doomed" before he ever reached the door.

Cars can also take on political significance. During anti-Japanese street demonstrations following a political standoff over the contested sovereignty of the Diaoyu Islands (the Japanese also claim them, calling them the Senkaku), a mob pulled a Chinese man out of his Toyota Corolla and beat him so severely, he was paralyzed.

The Chinese love affair with the car has had negative consequences for the environment. Congestion now reigns in China's cities. In one contest sponsored by the media group Bloomberg, a bicyclist was better able to navigate Beijing, beating a Porsche by nearly a half hour. And China holds the ignominious record of worst traffic jam for a twelve-day, sixty-two-mile standstill on a national highway outside Beijing in 2012. Worst of all is the quality of air in the capital city. Smog levels literally blew the charts in 2013, measuring 755 on a scale of 0 to 500, where 500 was already supposed to be too toxic for humans to breathe.

Road deaths resulting from traffic accidents are high, although how high remains a matter of debate. The Chinese government issued official figures in 2011 showing a decrease in deaths at 62,387 people, although researchers claim the real toll is likely much higher, saying police records show 81,649 deaths in 2007, and death registrations for the year show that 221,135 died because of car crashes.

What this means for the ever-pragmatic tourist is that it's a very good idea to use the restroom before embarking on a car trip.

The other essential piece of knowledge you will need to know about cars is that you should *never* assume a car will stop for a pedestrian in its path. One American student of ours commented poignantly about watching a Chinese pedestrian get struck by a car while attempting to cross the street at a designated crosswalk. "He might have survived, if not for the fact that every other car turning onto the street ran over him, too."

In the early to mid-1980s, such accidents were not uncommon either, but back then drivers had an excuse: during the Cultural Revolution red lights meant go (red being the color of revolution and Marxism) and green lights meant stop. When Deng Xiaoping ushered in the reform era in 1979, traffic light meanings were changed to conform with the rest of the world. Older drivers may not have gotten the message. Also, in an attempt to save their headlight bulbs, which in China's nascent market-based economy were not that easily attainable, cars and trucks tended to drive at night with their headlights off.

Today, however, it seems drivers are merely impatient, cross, and distracted (there are no enforceable laws banning cell phone use or even preventing drivers from watching satellite TV in their cars—handy during long traffic jams but deadly at other times). Drivers are also fairly self-confident that when it comes to a showdown between a car and a pedestrian, the pedestrian will not emerge victorious. Therefore, it is a very good idea to cross the street with a group of people. Running over an individual may be hazardous if a cop happens to be nearby, but running over a massive group of people will definitely dent the driver's car, and people are really fond of their cars. As China's city streets tend to be quite crowded, it is not difficult to find a group to cross with, even when jaywalking.

But remember, never assume a car will slow down for you alone just because you happen to be in its path!

Chiang Kai-shek

hiang Kai-shek (1886–1975) remains one of the more colorful and notorious figures of twentieth-century history and
the role he has played in modern Chinese history will remain
controversial for a long time.

Chiang (in Mandarin: Jiang Jieshi) rose to power in the 1920s,
largely through his influence with the notorious Green Gang of
Shanghai, which controlled much of the city's political and financial
underworld. He became the leader of the famed Northern Expedition, a military expedition against China's warlords to try to unite
China under the control of the Nationalist Party (also known in English as the KMT, after its spelling at that time in history, the Kuomintang). At the same time, he organized a campaign to break ties
with the Chinese Communist Party, his erstwhile allies, and staged a
massacre of their cells in Shanghai in 1927.

By 1928, Chiang had succeeded in convincing the warlords to fly
the flag of the new Chinese Republic and swear allegiance to him. He
soon established the new capital in Nanjing. He also married the
powerful and ambitious Soong Mei-ling, the American-educated
daughter of wealthy Bible salesman Charlie Soong. (He abandoned,
or at least conveniently forgot about, his first wife in order to do so.)

Generalissimo Chiang, as he now called himself, allowed the Japanese to invade and take over most of Manchuria, but when the Japanese staged a fight in July 1937 at the Marco Polo Bridge outside

Beijing, Chiang ordered his troops to fight back, eventually attacking Japanese ships in Shanghai. Chiang hoped that by bringing the war to the West's favorite port city, he would gain sympathy. Instead, the better-equipped Japanese Imperial Army marched inland to his capital and by December 1937, its soldiers had sacked the city in what would become known as the infamous Rape of Nanjing.

After the Japanese strike at Pearl Harbor, America allied itself with China. Unfortunately, Chiang did not get along with U.S. general "Vinegar Joe" Stilwell, who spoke fluent Mandarin and loved the Chinese people, but couldn't stand Chiang's corrupt government. Chiang, Stilwell claimed, was more intent upon using his military resources to fight the Communists than the Japanese, and his wife's family were reportedly lining their own bank accounts with American aid dollars. Stilwell took to calling Chiang "the Peanut," after the shape of the Generalissimo's famously bald head, and Chiang finally prevailed upon President Roosevelt to remove Stilwell from his command overseeing the China-Burma-India theater in 1944.

After being kidnapped by General Zhang Xueliang and released only after vowing to stop his counterproductive civil war, Chiang did form another alliance, the so-called United Front, with the Communists (1937–45) to fight together against the advancing Japanese military.

After World War II ended, from 1945 to 1949 Chiang waged an open civil war with Mao Zedong's People's Liberation Army. By 1949, President Truman was no longer willing to aid the Generalissimo, and it was clear Chiang had no chance of winning the civil war. He then fled with his troops to the island of Taiwan.

From the 1950s to the 1970s, Chiang ruled over Taiwan under a state of martial law and vowed to "take back the mainland" from Mao. He died on April 5, 1975, without attaining his goal.

Today Chiang's hometown of Fenghua in Zhejiang Province has been renovated as a tourist attraction. Before that, his cultural visibility in the mainland, besides vilification in textbooks, was limited to a sly visual reference in director Zhang Yimou's 1995 mobster classic, *Shanghai Triad*, in which the gangland boss played by veteran actor Li Baotian was rumored to have been modeled, at least physically, on the Generalissimo.

Children

Chinese people generally love children, which makes the One Child Policy restricting families to a single child all the more ironic. One of the traditional symbols of good luck for the New Year are pictures of chubby, round-faced children surrounded by the accouterments of prosperity—colorful kites, giant fruit, musical instruments, and the like.

Still, it can be startling to see a poster on a Chinese school's wall exhorting its students to allow "foreign friends" to take their pictures. The posters typically show a large and very blond couple with cameras smiling and pointing at a pair of Chinese children, who obligingly smile back and pose for the foreigners' photographs. In effect, Chinese are training their children from a very young age that it is their patriotic duty to act as cultural ambassadors in order to create a favorable impression of China.

Foreign children are similarly adored in China and it is not unusual for Chinese to want to come up to the kids, take their picture, or even pinch a cheek. However, American children are not trained to be cultural ambassadors but rather are versed since kindergarten in the concept of "Stranger Danger." As such, American kids are taught to avoid strangers who greet them, smiling, and call to them to come over.

Thus, if your children find themselves surrounded or swamped by smiling Chinese strangers, who may only want to take a picture or be friendly, your kids might just freak out. If this is the case, a little parental intervention can resolve an otherwise traumatic experience for all parties.

In this situation, smile broadly and say, "I'm sorry, my child is very shy." You can also claim your child is very tired. Then while firmly grasping your child, free him or her from the surrounding crowd and move on to a new area, away from the curious child watchers.

Even if the Chinese in this situation don't understand English, your smile will signal that no ill will is intended. However, it's important to get your child away from a crowd quickly, because an even larger crowd is likely to form just to see what the first crowd is up to. It's also important not to show anger, as this attitude is only likely to draw an ever bigger crowd.

In major cities where foreigners are common, such scenes are less likely to occur. However, many Chinese from the provinces are now flocking to the cities to look for work or as domestic tourists, and sometimes staring at cute foreign kids is part of the new urban experience for them.

If you find that this type of situation is happening frequently, talk to your tour guide or someone at your place of employment or to a Chinese person you know and let them know what's happening. A good tour guide will shoo away such crowds. A good friend will let you know what areas are more internationalized and perhaps more comfortable for your children. There's no need to suffer in silence.

Chinese Communist Party

Currently, China is under the total and absolute control of the Chinese Communist Party, whose authority supersedes even that of the Constitution. The Chinese Communist Party began as a number of separate groups formed by Chinese intellectuals in Beijing and Shanghai to study Marxism after the fall of the Qing dynasty in 1911. At that time, China was nominally a republic but in fact had disintegrated into a number of warring provinces led by warlords and their armies.

In 1921, Moscow's Comintern sent an agent to China to link China's budding communists with its own party apparatus. He attended the first organized Chinese Communist Party Congress in the French concession of Shanghai on July 1. There were only twelve delegates, including a young library worker named Mao Zedong, representing a total of fifty-seven members nationwide. From these inauspicious beginnings would grow the world's largest Communist Party.

The Second Party Congress was held in June and July 1922 in Hangzhou, although official party records curiously list Shanghai as the meeting place. At this meeting, the party adopted a constitution and a manifesto. The Second Party Congress also made a formal decision to join with Moscow's Comintern and establish a political bureau within the party. Finally, the party pledged to cooperate with the Nationalist Party's leader, Sun Yat-sen, to work to overthrow the warlords and unify China.

However, after Sun died in 1925 of cancer, his successor, Chiang Kai-shek, decided to outlaw the Chinese Communist Party and ordered the killing of its members in Shanghai in April 1927. An estimated five thousand party members and union representatives were executed. By November 1930, Chiang began the first of six military campaigns to exterminate the Chinese Communist Party and its army. Mao led his followers on the famous Long March of six thousand miles to escape the Nationalists and established a new base in a rural part of northwest Shaanxi Province known as Yan'an.

As the threat of Japanese invasion became more obvious toward the end of 1936, Manchurian warlord Zhang Xueliang (pronounced "jahng shweh lee-ong") kidnapped Chiang in December and refused to release him until Chiang promised to unite with the Communists to fight Japanese aggression in what became known as the United Front.

When the United States, Great Britain, and other Western powers entered the war in the Pacific at the end of 1941, they too encouraged Chiang to cooperate with the Communists as they feared a civil war would only work to Japan's advantage.

However, the Nationalists under Chiang never truly stopped fighting the Communists, as Chiang considered them an even greater threat to his hold on power than the Japanese, whom he felt the West would be able to defeat. Indeed, his paranoia proved correct, although it is hard to gauge if Chiang's insistence on pursuing civil war while being attacked by the Japanese was, in fact, a main reason why so many generals defected to Mao's side after Japan surrendered in August 1945. By this time, party membership had increased from forty thousand in 1937 to 1.2 million.

Mao's People's Liberation Army ultimately won the civil war and established the People's Republic of China on October 1, 1949, with Mao Zedong as its chairman. Thus the Chinese Communist Party became the single most important power in China.

By 2013, the Communist Party had 3.5 million organizations throughout China, with some 80 million members controlling the country's political, social, and military affairs. As for economic affairs, the party began cooperating with private sector entrepreneurs and companies, including joint ventures with foreign-owned firms, under the guidelines of the "Open Door Policy" enacted by Deng

Xiaoping in 1979 to revitalize the Chinese economy after it had been devastated by Mao's endless political campaigns. China was admitted to the World Trade Organization in 2001.

As for international affairs, the party is obligated to adhere to all international treaties and protocols to which it has become a signatory, and it must abide by international laws as well as the charter and decisions of the United Nations and its numerous agencies.

After the death of Deng Xiaoping in 1997, the Chinese Communist Party had three different leaders: Jiang Zemin (1989–2002); Hu Jintao (2002–2012); and Xi Jinping (2012–present).

How were these leaders selected? Jiang and Hu were personally designated by Deng before his death as the so-called leaders of the third and fourth generation. Deng considered himself as the leader of the second generation of the Chinese Communist Party as Mao was the leader of the first generation of Chinese under the rule of the party. Xi is considered the leader of the fifth generation of Chinese under the CCP. He was officially selected at the party's Eighteenth National Congress in 2012, which is held every five years. The delegates of the Congress were selected (the Chinese use the term "elected") by local party congresses, which are established throughout local and provincial regions in China.

The selection process is secretive and not at all transparent to the Chinese people. There is a long process that proceeds the final selection, during which national and provincial leaders nominate potential leaders. They attend secret meetings where these leaders negotiate and bargain for their proposed candidates. Retired high officials also play a critical role in the selection process for new leaders. Jiang Zemin is believed to have played a central role in the selection of Xi as the new party leader.

Currently, China is under the so-called collective rule of the twenty-five members of the Politburo of the party's Central Committee. Within this Politburo there is a Standing Committee of seven men who together rule China on a day-to-day basis, making the final decisions on all policies governing China to be ratified by the twenty-five-member Politburo. How much individual power Xi as party chief now wields is hard to estimate. His power is most likely dependent on winning allies in the seven-member Standing Committee.

There are several rules that party members must follow when nominating potential leaders. These rules are made by the Central Committee's Organization Department. These rules include the following: (1) candidates must have a college education; (2) candidates must have a variety of leadership experiences, such as having worked in different areas of China and at different departments; (3) candidates must be firmly embedded in the party's current ideology and must have graduated from a recognized party school for cadres; (4) the candidates must have passed satisfactory evaluation by the party's Disciplinary Committee, a separate and independent branch within the party; (5) the candidates must belong to one of the major factions within the party, such as the Party Youth League or the military, for example; and (6) the candidates must be under sixty-five years of age. Finally, while the party is an authoritarian organization, it does have rules that prevent uneducated members from becoming leaders, no matter how personally popular.

Chongqing

hongqing, formerly known as Chungking, was the wartime capital of China during the Japanese invasion of World War II. Located at the confluence of two rivers, the Jialing and the Yangtze, it is also a city built upon a mountain. Both these factors proved essential to Chongqing's survival during World War II, when the Japanese flew more than 9,500 sorties over the city and dropped nearly 22,000 bombs from 1938 to 1945 in an attempt to destroy the Nationalist government. Because of the rivers and humid climate, Chongqing is a very foggy city, and Japanese bombers in those days did not have radar; thus the fog protected many vital targets. In addition, the population of Chongqing built thousands upon thousands of air-raid shelters, digging directly into the mountain base of the city. Some of these shelters were only large enough for one or two people to squat inside. Others could hold battalions of soldiers and even supply trucks.

Today Chongqing (pronounced "chohng cheeng") is a mix of new and old, with remnants of former bomb shelters converted into shops and dance clubs while modern skyscrapers break the horizon line where once only the city's ancient wall stood. The city center is adorned with giant video screens projecting endless streaming advertisements and videos, evoking comparisons to the movie *Blade Runner*. (Fortunately, Chongqing's air quality is better.) The city was named a Special Economic Zone in 1998, accelerating its development, and the entire metropolitan area now comprises some 30 million people.

Tourists may visit many World War II historical sites, which include Zhou Enlai's bunker and the Stilwell Museum, which is filled with videos, artifacts, and photographs from the era when General Joseph Stilwell served as President Roosevelt's adviser to Generalissimo Chiang Kai-shek. Unfortunately, the airfield where the famous Flying Tigers were stationed is now under water due to the building of the Three Gorges Dam, but visitors may see photographs of the air force jointly run by Americans and Chinese in various historical displays in the city. Chongqing is unique in Chinese history in that the Nationalists, the Communists, and the Americans all had representatives working together here during various periods in World War II in a united effort to defeat the invading Japanese army and air force.

Chongqing is renowned for its fiery hot cuisine, especially the hot pot. Similar in concept to the Western dish fondue except without the cheese, hot pots are tureens with a fire beneath and filled with a spicy, oily broth. Many courses are served, of everything from noodles to lettuce to meats and fish, which are then dipped into the hot pot to cook and steep in the spices. Sichuan peppercorns provide an unusual sensation different from Thai or Indian "hot" spices in that after a first rush of heat the mouth begins to feel numb. If, however, the heat does not subside, a spoonful of white sugar or something sweet can help greatly to cleanse the palate. Most restaurants will provide a mid-meal sweet, such as a tiny petit four for this purpose. If you feel the need to reduce the heat in your mouth sooner, don't hesitate to ask your waiter or waitress for something sweet. Water alone will not do the trick.

Outside Chongqing the modern world slips away rapidly and visitors can see giant Buddhist statues carved into the mountainside in the nearby town of Dazu or visit the famed natural hot springs, now a resort known in Mandarin as *shan dong*. Farmers can be seen working in terraced fields that climb the steep mountains in seemingly endless spirals, water buffalo walk beside the new superhighways, and traditional stilt houses built off the sides of the mountains are still visible, although plans to raze all these old buildings and house the people in high-rises instead are under way.

Chongqing is also one of China's "three furnaces" (the other two are Wuhan and Nanjing), so named because of the extreme heat and humidity of the summers. So, be forewarned if you are planning a summer trip to the city.

Visitors should definitely partake in the city's penchant for public dancing, called "baba" dancing after the local dialect's term for parks. In 2012 alone, nearly a million people participated in Chongqing's myriad dance contests. Before his fall from power, former party secretary Bo Xilai made use of his city's proclivity for public dancing with mass musical sing-offs and dance events using Mao-era standards to boost civic spirit (and his own political fortune). Public dancing in Chongqing's many public parks and city squares remains a vibrant part of the megacity's culture, where current musical tastes favor international pop standards from K-Pop rapper PSY to Beyoncé and Lady Gaga.

Colors

In October 2005, when China's two *taikonauts* landed back on Earth after becoming the first Chinese to orbit the planet successfully, the two men were greeted with giant pink bouquets of flowers. Later, bedecked in flower garlands, they continued to hold their pink bouquets as they sat in a convertible and waved to the ecstatic crowds who had come to witness the historic landing.

From an American point of view, this scene might have seemed unusual because pink flower bouquets are generally not given to men, unless you are in Hawaii, where flower leis are routinely given to both sexes. However, in China pink is not a gendered color the way it is in America. Pink is seen as a shade of red, and red is the color of celebration, good luck, and happiness.

Traditionally in pre-1949 China, brides wore red clothing and red veils for their marriage ceremonies. Red envelopes filled with

money were given as presents during the ceremony, as well as to children for the New Year. Red is the color on firecracker wrappers, many imperial seals, and on the background of the Chinese flag. Red is easily the most important color in China. Today when you want to say that some actor or actress is very popular, you say they are *feichang hong!*—that is, they are very red! For these reasons, both Communism and Coca-Cola benefited from the traditional Chinese affection for the color red.

White has traditionally been associated with death, corpses, and ghosts. An unbleached cotton, a sort of off-white color, was the traditional color to wear to a funeral. "Ghost money" (pinyin: *gui zhi*, pronounced "gway juhr"), which is burned at funerals and on festivals such as Qing Ming to remember the dead, was printed on undyed off-white paper.

However, nowadays because of Western influences, brides can be seen wearing Western-style white wedding dresses—although it is not uncommon for them to change into red traditional-style *qipao* dresses during the reception.

Chinese in general tend to view colorful things more positively than monochromatic ones. For example, all colors are acceptable for children's clothing so long as they are bright and cheerful, so young babies and boys and girls can be seen in clothes with pink and blue on them—as well as yellows, greens, purples—regardless of gender.

Adults can wear all colors, but the New York City obsession with black as the ultimate chic uniform has never been fully accepted in China. In Beijing and Shanghai, Hong Kong and Guangzhou, you will see young people in their twenties occasionally sporting an all-black look, but in general brighter colors are preferred. If you are inclined to wear black a lot, don't be surprised if your Chinese hosts or guide comes up to you to say, "You look so sad and depressed. What's wrong?"

Chinese cultural connotations associated with color have also influenced the language, sometimes in contradictory ways. For example, when the word "yellow" (in pinyin: *huangse de*) is used as an adjective for a book, magazine, or movie, it means that thing is pornographic. Yet, the term "Yellow Emperor" refers to the mythic founder of the Chinese people and thus the common ancestor to all Chinese in the diaspora. The phrase "land of the Yellow Springs" refers to a traditional Buddhist concept of the afterlife or paradise.

Green is generally a neutral color, yet the expression "to wear a green hat" (pinyin: *dai lü maozi*) when referring to a man means that he's been cuckolded. Therefore, men should not wear green-colored hats, knit or otherwise, when visiting China lest they elicit giggles.

The term "black society" (pinyin: *hei shehui*) refers to the world of organized criminal gangs. It does not have anything to do with skin color.

And whereas the color red itself has positive connotations, the expression "to have red eyes" means that someone is very jealous or envious of another person.

Nevertheless, in practical terms, if you're giving a gift to someone, red or pink wrapping paper is always appropriate and does not conjure up images of envy but simply signifies a celebration and a wish for good luck. When choosing a bouquet, unless it's for a funeral, bright colors are preferable to white flowers unless the recipient is very familiar with Western tastes or into the avant-garde art scene.

And if you're a guy, and someone gives you flowers as a welcoming gift or a thank-you for a performance (singing at assemblies is a popular activity at many schools), think like the Hawaiians and enjoy their beauty.

Confucianism

Confucianism is a system of ethics based upon the teachings of Kong Qiu, also known as Kong Fuzi (thus in English he became known as Confucius), who lived roughly between the years 551 and 479 BCE. He believed that mankind would be in harmony with the universe if all behaved with righteousness and restraint and adhered to specific social roles. He emphasized the study of classic works of literature, the worship of ancestors, and submission to authority. The five principal relationships upon which all society should be based, according to Confucius, are as follows: filial piety between father and son (meaning the son must obey and respect his father, in both life and death), loyalty between ruler and subject, harmony between husband and wife, precedence of the elder over the younger in family relations, and trust between friends. Trust between friends is the only horizontal relationship; the rest are hierarchical.

However, these guidelines also insist upon reciprocity. For example, the filial piety of the son should be reciprocated by the love of the father, and the obedience of the subject should be reciprocated by the fairness of the ruler.

It should be remembered that Confucius lived during a very chaotic period of time in Chinese history known as the Warring States period, during which time China was not a unified nation but in fact a series of little fiefdoms that fought with each other constantly, causing much human suffering. He emphasized allegiance, loyalty, and obedience as a way to end this constant warfare.

After he died, his teachings (written down by his disciples in a book called the *Analects*) were adopted by the Chinese imperial states throughout the centuries, although modifications and different interpretations of his teachings continued to be made. One of the most important factors of Confucianism in its many interpretations is an emphasis on education. This aspect of Confucianism is still very much in practice in China as well as the other Asian countries deeply influenced by Confucianism, including South Korea, Japan, Taiwan, and Singapore.

Many temples were built to honor Confucius over the centuries and even today in rural areas some Chinese pray to Confucius as a kind of wise saint for his help in their daily life—even though Confucius himself never talked about religion, famously saying, "If you are not able to serve men, how can you worship the gods?" and "If you do not know life, how can you know about death?" (*Analects*, XI, II). He considered himself a statesman and philosopher rather than the founder of a religion, but over time Confucianism took on religious aspects.

In 1911, when the last emperor of China was overthrown, Confucianism was officially out of favor in China. Leading intellectuals blamed Confucianism's emphasis on studying the past, obeying authority, and respecting elders at the expense of the ideas of the young as a force that had kept China "backwards" in terms of technology and political culture compared to the West. Indeed, the Confucian emphasis on a benevolent, paternalistic form of government and obedient citizens contradicts aspects of Western liberal democracy, which is based on the principles of individual rights and social contracts between the government and its citizens.

During the Cultural Revolution, Chairman Mao launched a movement known as the "Campaign against Lin Biao and Confucius" in 1973–74. Lin Biao had been named as the official successor as future chairman of the Communist Party but had died in a mysterious plane crash in 1971. Linking Lin and Confucius was a seemingly bizarre and random act of dogma, especially considering that both men were already dead, but Mao ensured that it spread across the country. (Some political theorists say the campaign was a veiled attack on another of Mao's contemporaries, Zhou Enlai, who was still alive.) At any rate, the various Kong clans in China, as the living descendants of Confucius, went through living hell while this campaign lasted. In fact, one branch was not able to rebuild its Confucian temple until 1992.

Today, there is a resurgent interest in Confucianism, perhaps as a way to counter Western criticism of China's political system, but also as a source of pride in China's ancient culture and the brilliance of its philosophers. Confucius's hometown of Qufu in Shandong Province is a major tourist attraction. More recently, former President Hu Jintao in 2006 called upon government officials to return to Confucian moral ethics as a way to counter corruption and growing inequality within Chinese society, and he approved funding for more than three hundred "Confucius Institutes" to be established around the world to offer classes and resources about Chinese language and culture.

Corruption

Corruption permeates every level of Chinese society and is one of the greatest problems facing China today. This assessment does not come simply from foreign critics, but from China's current president Xi Jinping and former president Hu Jintao, both of whom publicly declared when they took power that cracking down on corruption was a major goal of their presidencies. Hu obviously failed, while Xi's efforts remain to be seen.

Scandals in China run the gamut from merely distasteful to completely lethal.

Numerous officials have been caught in sex scandals. In one notorious case, a Chinese Communist Party member kept two twin-sister mistresses in apartments paid for with government money; in another, provincial officials naively posted photos online of themselves embarking on an orgy. Real estate scandals are also widespread—including the cases of so-called Sister House, in which a bank vice president used fake IDs to purchase forty-one homes in Beijing. Scandals involving cars are also not unfamiliar, as illustrated by the case of the son of a high-government official who crashed his Ferrari in Beijing in 2012, killing himself and one passenger (the daughter of a Tibetan government official) and injuring another female passenger. The driver was not identified in the official press, and all mention of the crash was soon deleted by government censors from the web. However, private netizens kept the story alive online, and foreign journalists were able to track down the sole survivor as well as college friends of the driver to confirm details of the accident, which is widely believed to have derailed the official's expected promotion to the highest levels of government.

When safety regulations are flaunted, corruption actually can sicken or even kill. For example, bribing food inspectors has led to recycled cooking oil being used from one restaurant to the next (a practice known as using "gutter oil"), massive food poisoning incidents, ordinary meat mislabeled as organic being sold in major chain stores, and the overuse of antibiotics in some chickens that found their way into the KFC franchise's supply chain. Furthermore, use of substandard building materials is blamed in deaths across the country, where buildings and structures have collapsed, from bridges to highway overpasses to schools. In the case of the 2008 Sichuan earthquake, elementary schools for migrant workers' children were not built up to code to withstand an earthquake and came tumbling down, resulting in more than five thousand children's deaths.

It's hard to say if Chinese society is becoming more corrupt than ever before, or if the Chinese people are simply more aware of the corruption because of social media and cell phone cameras that have allowed ordinary citizens to report bad behavior. The government often tries to hush up coverage of corruption in the media, preferring to handle its own opaque investigations. Ordinary citizen bloggers, sometimes using pseudonyms, have taken to posting examples of official misdeeds—from sex scandals to construction problems to land grabs to cover-ups over crimes ranging from rape to murder. While censors often take the posts down within hours, many of these bloggers have gained hundreds of thousands of followers online and a celebrity status that, for the time being, protects them from official harassment.

Perhaps the people most hurt by corruption are China's rural residents and unemployed, older workers. Both groups have largely been unable to benefit from the economic reforms that have fueled growth and wealth in China's coastal cities. Laid-off workers are often promised pensions or some form of compensation but then after a few payments, they are given nothing. As a result, many unemployed workers, especially those cut from the rolls of the cumbersome state-run enterprises that are being phased out of the new, faster-paced Chinese economy, are banding together to protest their disenfranchisement. It is not uncommon in some of the poorer inland cities to see workers bearing placards with their grievances spelled out in large Chinese characters.

Farmers face a different problem. Often they find that their land is being confiscated by corrupt local officials who cut deals with factories or other profit-making ventures to build upon the cheap real estate—cheap because the farmers aren't adequately paid for their land. As a result, rural poverty continues to grow. Furthermore, the farther one lives from the central government in Beijing, the easier it is for corrupt local officials and businesspeople to exploit farmers, as they have no way to make their grievances heard. Heroic Chinese reporters and lawyers, often self-trained, have tried to bring the plight of farmers to the public's attention and force the government to help. However, local corruption is such that lawyers are often arrested and beaten by police, who are paid off by the officials or companies, and reporters can be censured or fired for covering stories that are not first approved by the Communist Party, which still controls the media. However, Chinese journalists have grown increasingly bold in challenging what they see as a blight on their society and in demanding more freedoms for the media.

Most foreign tourists will not have to deal with large-scale corruption. Because the tourism industry is seen as essential to China's growing economy and as its "face" in the international arena, it is highly competitive and watched over by the central government. The smaller-level corruption one typically encounters may involve detours on your tour bus to businesses, restaurants, and trinket stands where suddenly your guide announces, "It's time to take a rest." The idea is that everyone is forced off the bus and will make purchases and/or eat. The tour companies or guides then get a cut from the business owners.

When planning a tour, be wary of smaller, lesser-known companies. If anyone is offering incredibly low prices, special access to ancient treasures, an itinerary that covers vast amounts of territory in very little time, or the like, be skeptical. Ask for references from satisfied tourists. Check the Internet and travel magazines for complaints. If something sounds too good to be true, it probably is.

Businesspeople will have to be vigilant at every step of the process of building their company base and brand in China, from quality control to ever-shifting contracts. Even government support does not guarantee escape from corruption. Businesspeople from countries where bribery is illegal face a particular disadvantage, as the practice is rampant in China, and many nations have no problem with how their businesspeople operate. However, it's almost impossible (not to mention illegal) for Americans to compete in the bribery arena. For example, Taiwanese are well-known for offering special "gifts" to local officials to help their businesses along. Such gifts can include diamond-encrusted watches, expensive luxury goods, and even out-and-out cash payments.

Alas, everyone suffers. The best you can hope to do is know who's in charge of your venture, tour, study abroad program, English-teaching program, or whatever you're involved with. When something goes awry or you feel you are being squeezed, try to reach the most senior official or person in charge of your program. That person will be most able to stop lower-level people from harassing you or your company. It's also good to make as many Chinese friends as possible, as they have had to deal with corruption their whole lives and have many coping strategies and networks of friends you can tap into.

Cultural Revolution

Officially known as the Great Proletarian Cultural Revolution, the period from 1966 to 1976 was Mao Zedong's ultimate political campaign to change China according to his personal interpretation (some might say fantasy) of communism. Proclaiming the people "a blank sheet of paper" upon which he felt a new culture could be inscribed, Mao set about remaking society from its very foundations. Uprooting millennia of Confucian values, Mao turned students against their teachers, the young against the old, even children against their own parents. While Mao proclaimed this upheaval was necessary to root out "counterrevolutionary" elements that he claimed to have discovered hidden within Chinese society, allegedly attempting to overthrow his Communist revolution, in fact much of the Cultural Revolution was anchored in a far more prosaic motivation. Mao was in the midst of a power struggle within the Communist Party and he did not want to give up the reins of power to the so-called pragmatist revisionists who had slowly begun to make economic reforms in the early 1960s.

After the horrors of Mao's failed policies of the 1950s led to the deaths of more than 30 million Chinese, largely from famine and related illnesses, many in the party secretly called for Mao to step down. In fact, he did turn over power to reformist Liu Shaoqi, who was named president in 1959. Slowly, Liu began to introduce new political and economic programs—for example, allowing peasants to sell produce on the open market in cities rather than to work exclusively in communes. He also reintroduced the manufacture of light consumer goods. Perhaps Mao thought Liu was betraying the revolution with his baby steps toward capitalism. Perhaps Mao was merely jealous that Liu's policies seemed to be working better than Mao's had in raising the people's standard of living. It's hard to say now what motivated Mao's furious return to power in 1965. Only the devastation that followed is clear.

In 1966, Mao Zedong, aided by expert propagandists who portrayed him as a near godlike father figure, savior, and plain-living man of the people, called upon the youth of China to form gangs known as Red Guards to protect China from the "capitalist roaders," "counterrevolutionary spies," and "running dogs of the West" that he claimed were trying to wrest control of China. In August, Mao used his influence to change the composition of the Chinese Communist Party's Central Committee and purged the party of pragmatists, including Liu Shaoqi and Deng Xiaoping. Liu was imprisoned in a dank concrete cell, where he later died of cancer. Deng was sent down to the countryside to perform hard labor and be "reeducated" by the peasants.

The party changed its leadership secretariat, which had been helmed by Deng, into a new "Cultural Revolution Group" chaired by Lin Biao, a military man, and Mao's wife, Jiang Qing. By April 1969, a new party constitution was approved, with "Mao Zedong Thought" enshrined as the official ideology of the Communist Party of China. All Chinese were required to read, and even memorize, Mao's so-called Little Red Book of quotations. Other forms of literature were banned, and "counterrevolutionaries" caught with contraband books could be beaten, tortured, sent down to the countryside, or at worst killed.

In 1968, all schools were officially closed and no more entrance examinations for college were given. The children of "class enemies"—that is, intellectuals, former capitalists, or petit bourgeois from prerevolutionary days (pre-1949 China), as well as former members of the Nationalist Party who had decided to remain in China after Chiang Kai-shek fled to Taiwan in 1949—were outright denied an education and sent away from the corrupting influence of their parents to live in the countryside, where they were told to "learn from the peasants." (The peasants, shocked to find their villages inundated with city kids who knew nothing about planting, farming, herding, or rural life, were not necessarily pleased to have so many new mouths to feed, nor did they understand how exactly they were supposed to educate these young people. In some rural areas, out of traditional respect for educated people, they treated the newcomers with deference and kindness. In other areas, out of bitterness, spite, and revolutionary fervor, they abused the city youth without mercy.)

Meanwhile, in the cities, the children from the "correct" social background—that is, the Red Guards—found their power increasingly growing out of control. They were told to destroy anything and everything "old" and therefore "feudal," in the vocabulary of the day. As a result, they set about destroying temples, ancient statues, imperial tombs, historic gardens, libraries, universities, shops, homes, and museums. Similarly, anything with a connection to the West was seen as subversive and destroyed, including books, musical instruments, even medical equipment. Parents and teachers were denounced for their "feudal" ways and made to wear tall dunce caps and humiliating placards listing their alleged sins around their necks. They were forced to stand in the sun for hours, kneel on broken glass, or endure being paraded through the streets as onlookers jeered, spat, and threw rocks or rotten food at them. Many people were beaten to death publicly.

However, rival bands of Red Guards soon formed and they began to fight among themselves. Sensing that the revolution Mao had fomented was growing beyond his control, Mao proclaimed new policies to encourage the Red Guards to disband and also to go into the countryside to learn from the peasants and become real revolutionaries. Many idealists eagerly set off for the countryside, while often the more cynical (and more violent) stayed behind in the cities. When the schools reopened in 1969, it was these former Red Guards who often benefited the most. However, children from peasant families were also given a chance to attend city universities, in a kind of massive affirmative action program to make up for the generations of lost opportunities their families had had to endure as poor peasants, and thus many formerly rural youths benefited from the new topsy-turvy social order.

As a result of the near total chaos China found itself mired in due to Mao's radical policies, a split formed within the Communist Party again, this time between Mao and his former ally, Lin Biao. In September 1971, Lin allegedly attempted to have Mao assassinated. When the plot failed, Lin tried to escape to the Soviet Union but his plane crashed under mysterious circumstances in Mongolia, killing Lin and all aboard.

To fill the power vacuum, Mao's wife, Jiang Qing, organized a so-called Gang of Four to serve as the new leaders of the Cultural Revolution and ensure that Mao's policies would not be challenged.

In September 1976, Mao died. Two new groups within the Communist Party emerged, trying to counter the power of the notorious Gang of Four. One group was led by a senior party and military leader, Ye Jianying, who held the title of defense minister, along with Vice Premier and Public Security Minister Hua Guofeng. The second group was headed by erstwhile economic reformer Deng Xiaoping.

The groups temporarily joined forces. Upon Mao's death, Hua became the new premier with Deng as vice premier. Together with their combined allies they were able to have the Gang of Four arrested and put on trial publicly. Officially, the excesses of the Cultural Revolution were then blamed on the Gang of Four rather than Mao, who still retained a cultlike following. Then the two groups fought for power. Hua could not maintain his hold on leadership and soon real power went to Deng, with the help of Marshal Ye, who deserted Hua.

In 1979, Deng traveled to the United States to negotiate normalization of relations between the two countries and initiated an Open Door Policy for China, meaning that China was no longer to be isolated from the world but would allow foreigners in to study, work, and invest while small numbers of Chinese would be allowed to study and work abroad.

By June 1981, Hua Guofeng officially resigned his position as premier and Deng nominated his protégé, Zhao Ziyang, a provincial official, to succeed Hua. However, all real power remained in the hands of Deng, whose ties to the military and party elite, dating from the early years of the Communist Party's formation and tribulations during the Sino-Japanese War and Chinese Civil War, gave him credibility that the younger party members could not compete with.

Thus, it could be said, the policies of the Cultural Revolution finally came to an end.

Today it is still not known exactly how many people died in the decade-long Cultural Revolution. Low estimates run in the millions. And while the Communist Party officially condemned the policies of the Cultural Revolution in 1981, very little about the Cultural Revolution is actually taught in Chinese schools, and researchers both within China and from abroad are often arrested if they try to delve too deeply into records from that era. Movies depicting this era are almost immediately banned. Perhaps too many government bureaucrats who are still in power at the provincial level—or higher—owe their positions to their activities during the Cultural Revolution. Perhaps the government believes that digging up past sins will only lead to renewed bitterness and undermine the party's legitimacy once again. At any rate, the result of this official silence is that a generation of young people knows almost nothing about this period of time in Chinese history.

Some older Chinese complain that even their own children don't believe their stories when they try to tell them what the Cultural Revolution was like. However, chic Cultural Revolution–themed cafés, decorated with fake big-character posters touting Maoist slogans, are popular in the more affluent cities. Some middle-aged Chinese even express nostalgia for the idealism of the era compared to the cutthroat competitive, winner-take-all style of capitalism that characterizes much of China today. And many Chinese farmers, utterly impoverished by the new Chinese economy, have set up shrines to Chairman Mao in the countryside, where they pray to him as a kind of ancestor to all peasants for help, so great are their feelings of hopelessness in the contemporary world, where basic medical care, education for their children, and on occasion even clean drinking water may be beyond their reach. After all, today no one is urging anyone to "learn from the peasants."

Dalai Lama

The current Dalai Lama is the paramount spiritual leader of Tibetan Buddhism. He was born Tenzin Gyatso in 1935 in eastern Tibet. When he was two years old, other Tibetan lamas gave the child a series of tests that proved to them he was the new, fourteenth reincarnation of the Dalai Lama.

In 1950, China invaded Tibet as part of Chairman Mao's policy of consolidating Chinese territory under Communist rule. The American CIA briefly supported a Tibetan independence movement but then abandoned the project as other regions in Asia took precedence. After China tried to enforce Communist, atheist values in Tibet, the Dalai Lama recognized he was in danger and fled to northern India, where many Tibetan refugees had established a community in Dharamsala. Since that time, the Dalai Lama has been considered the leader of the Tibetan community in exile.

The Dalai Lama has traveled around the world preaching the values of compassion, as embodied by the ideals of dissolution of one's individual ego and replacing that with selflessness and wisdom. He does not formally espouse Tibetan independence, unlike many other Tibetans in exile, but prefers to use the term "autonomy" to describe his hopes for Tibetan self-government as a part of China. He has said that he does not believe China would grant Tibet full independence, and that seeking such a state could lead to outright war. Thus far, the Chinese government has refused to negotiate with the Dalai Lama on the future of Tibet.

The Dalai Lama received the Nobel Peace Prize in 1989.

In general, most Chinese do not understand the Western fascination with the Dalai Lama, although recent trends in literature show a growing interest in Tibetan Buddhism. Images of the Dalai Lama used to be officially banned and anyone caught with one could be arrested. However, as China becomes more secure in its relations with the West and less fearful that an outside power will try to use Tibet as a means to overthrow the Communist Party, images of the Dalai Lama have resurfaced, generally in outer provinces where ethnic Tibetans live and where Tibetan Buddhism is practiced. For example, the *New York Times* has reported that Inner Mongolian motorcyclists like to dangle pictures of the Dalai Lama from their bikes, a practice which has not resulted in prosecution.

Daoism

Daoism (originally spelled "Taoism" in English) is one of the four major native religions of China—the other three being ancestor worship, Confucianism, and Buddhism after it merged with native Chinese rituals. It is also intimately connected with the development of Chinese herbal medicine as well as rituals associated with traditional weddings and funerals.

Daoism rose out of the writings of Laozi (also spelled "Lao-tsu"), who was believed to have lived in the sixth century BCE, making him a contemporary of Confucius. Unlike Confucius, who traveled from state to state to campaign for political reform, Laozi lived apart from mainstream society, seeking longevity through experimentation with Chinese herbal remedies. His writings were originally collected into two books, but they were combined under orders of the Emperor Jing (156–141 BCE) during the Han dynasty into one book known as the *Dao De Jing* (often translated into English as *The Way of the Dao*, which is redundant, as *Dao* means "way" or "path"). In one passage, Laozi explains the Dao in the following fashion:

> *Man conforms to Earth;*
> *Earth conforms to Heaven;*
> *Heaven conforms to Dao;*
> *and Dao conforms to the way of nature.*

Laozi's work, written in the terse language of classical Chinese, contains only five thousand characters, making it open to varied interpretations over the centuries. Thanks to the influence of another Daoist philosopher, Zhuangzi (369–286 BCE), the *Dao De Jing* became enshrined as one of the pillars of classical Chinese literature. Zhuangzi elaborated on the concept of Dao, describing it as the life force within all things:

> Dao has reality and evidence but no action and form. It may be transmitted, yet not possessed. It existed before Heaven and Earth and lasts forever. It caused spirits and gods to be divine and Heaven and Earth to be produced. It is above zenith, yet not high; it is below the nadir, yet not low. It is prior to Heaven and Earth, yet has no duration.

Daoism teaches that liberation of the human spirit or soul is achieved when a person lives in harmony with the empty, spontaneous, and natural essence of the Dao—that is, the "way" or "path" of the universe. (Is it any wonder Daoism became extremely popular with the counterculture movement in America in the late 1960s and '70s?) Longevity can be achieved by following the path of "nonaction" (in Chinese, *wu wei*)—in other words, trying to live in harmony with nature.

Today, Daoist priests often perform complex rites involving the healing of the sick, salvation of the souls of the dead, and exorcisms, and they have even been known to advocate certain sexual practices to promote immortality. Although Laozi had no intention of forming a religion, Daoist rituals have become intertwined with traditional and ancient folk religions in the countryside, and thus Daoist temples have existed in China for nearly two thousand years and have even developed a strict regimen of required studies for its priests.

Daoist art, including surreal—one could say trippy—images of Daoist sages riding through the heavens atop fish and other assorted creatures, can be found in museums and temples throughout China.

Deng Xiaoping

W hen Deng Xiaoping died in 1997, *Time* magazine issued a special report with Deng on its cover, calling him "The Last Emperor." The term was especially apt because, like an emperor, Deng ruled with absolute power in his last decades and his word alone was sufficient to determine policy in the People's Republic of China. For the last twenty years of his life, he in fact held no official title, such as president (a post occupied by Yang Shangkun) or premier (the position held by Li Peng).

Born in 1904 in Sichuan Province, Deng was a veteran of the famed Long March, during which the original founders of the Chinese Communist Party, in order to escape persecution from Generalissimo Chiang Kai-shek and his Nationalist government (1911–49) literally walked some six thousand miles from Nationalist-controlled territory to Shaanxi Province in remote northwestern China. As a result, Deng had impeccable credentials as a Communist and rose quickly through the party ranks after the founding of the PRC in 1949.

During the Cultural Revolution (1966–76), Deng fell out of favor with Chairman Mao Zedong, China's paramount leader at that time. In 1963, Deng was one of the party members who had urged economic liberalization in China under the new chairman, Liu Shaoqi, while Mao went into temporary retirement. With more free enterprise allowed and less state control of the economy, China's people soon began to enjoy a higher standard of living. However, Mao was furious, as he felt these capitalistic policies contradicted the essence of communism. Mao also wanted to return to power, no matter the consequences, and launched the Cultural Revolution to do so. Chairman Liu and his wife were both imprisoned. Deng was sent into "internal exile," which generally meant some kind of work camp in the countryside. Deng's son was paralyzed for life after jumping from a second-story window in an attempt to escape a band of Red Guards—teenagers and other youths loyal only to Mao—whom he feared would beat him to death.

Deng could not advocate his economic policies again until after Mao's death in 1976. By 1979, Deng had consolidated his base within the Communist Party and become vice premier. He traveled to the United States (previously considered an enemy of China) and reestablished diplomatic ties with then president Jimmy Carter. And perhaps most memorably of all, he initiated a series of economic reforms known as the Open Door Policy, which he justified in China as "building socialism with Chinese characteristics." Under this policy, the authoritarian Communist Party maintained political control while the country's economy was allowed to operate under a dual system: a planned economy in some sectors and a capitalistic, market-driven private economy in others.

As a result, China began its emergence on the world economic scene with a complex mix of state-owned enterprises, shareholding, public ownership, foreign direct investment, joint ventures with foreign companies and countries, and collective ownership. Stocks and bond markets have sprung up throughout major Chinese cities and more than a million private enterprises have been incorporated. It was Deng who coined the phrase "To get rich is glorious." And it was also Deng, responding to critics within the party who worried that foreign influences would corrupt Chinese society, who replied, "When you open a window, some flies are bound to come inside." In other words, China needed fresh air and a few flies could be dealt with.

Unfortunately for the party, some of those "flies" turned out to be a yearning for greater political freedom and democracy. In April 1989, students began to assemble at Beijing's Tiananmen Square calling for more transparency in government, an end to corruption, and more rights for Chinese citizens. By June, more than 1 million Chinese citizens were believed to be camped out on Tiananmen Square demanding political reform. On June 4, the People's Liberation Army was called in to clear the demonstrators and to restore order to the capital. Although Premier Li Peng gave the order for the army to use force, it is widely believed in both China and abroad that Deng Xiaoping gave his approval for this action or Li would never have been able to do it. The resulting tragedy was dubbed the Tiananmen Square Massacre by the Western media and is known in China as the June Fourth Incident, or simply Six Four (pinyin: *liu si*). Unknown hundreds, even thousands, of Chinese civilians—as well as many soldiers—died in the ensuing chaos.

Because of the bloodshed on June 4, 1989, and Deng's steadfast refusal to open up political reform in China, his legacy remains mixed. Without his foresight, brilliance, and political savvy, China might never have opened up to the world and would certainly not be enjoying its current prosperity. His first two political successors, Jiang Zemin and Hu Jintao, were considered to be his handpicked protégés. However, Deng's decision to approve the use of force to stop the political demonstrations at Tiananmen Square and the subsequent bloodshed remain a stain on his record that will not soon be erased.

Dialects

Although Mandarin Chinese is the official language of China, there are in fact myriad dialects of Chinese in addition to separate languages (such as Tibetan, Mongolian, Manchu, Tai, and Korean spoken by minority peoples). However, in the seventeenth century the Qing dynasty began to establish "correct pronunciation institutes" to try to make the Beijing pronunciation of Mandarin the "standard" pronunciation of the elite, who could afford schooling and thus would train to become part of China's vast civil service bureaucracy. In 1913 the Republic of China's Ministry of Education created the Commission on the Unification of Pronunciation to again try to establish a standard national language. In those days, and currently in Taiwan, that language was called *guo yu*—that is, the "national language" or the language of the governing elite (hence it became known as "Mandarin" in English). However, after 1949, the Communist government decided to call so-called standard Chinese *pu tong hua*, or the "common language" so as to downplay the elitist angle. Despite all these efforts, the reality is that thousands of mutually incomprehensible local dialects of Chinese still exist and in fact flourish in China today.

Officially, there are between seven and twelve main dialect groups, but there are innumerable subdialects within each official regional dialect. For example, Mandarin itself can be broken into two or three main subgroups spread throughout northern, central, and western

China. There are five main dialects of Cantonese (all mutually incomprehensible) spoken throughout Hong Kong, Guangdong Province, the Guangxi Zhuang Autonomous Region, Macao, and parts of Hainan Island. Hakka (Kejia) dialects are spoken in the provinces of Guangdong, southwestern Fujian, Hunan, Yunnan, Guangxi, Guizhou, Sichuan, Hainan Island, Taiwan, and many parts of the Chinese diaspora in Asia including Singapore, Malaysia, and Indonesia. Many Hunanese speak their own dialect, known officially among linguists as the Xiang dialect. The so-called Min dialects are spoken throughout Fujian Province, eastern Guangdong Province, Hainan Island, large sections of Taiwan, and other Chinese communities in Southeast Asia. Gan dialects are spoken in Jiangxi, eastern Hunan, and the southeastern corner of Hubei. Wu dialects are common in Zhejiang, southern Jiangsu, and Anhui.

So, how different are Chinese dialects from Mandarin and from each other? Very. Not only are the tones different—for example, Mandarin has four tones while Cantonese has nine—but the grammar can be completely different as well. Linguists have found that French and German share more in common than Mandarin and Shanghaiese (often grouped as part of the Wu dialects). As one longtime Shanghai resident and expert in Shanghai dialect told us, Shanghaiese is actually a combination of five different languages, including words adopted from the Chinese pronunciation of French and English. The dialect reflects the fact that Shanghai was always a city of immigrants from other parts of China, the man said proudly. These immigrants combined their separate dialects and learned to communicate with the guards of the French- and English-speaking foreign concessions in the city (pre-1949), creating a unique and decidedly multicultural language.

Hong Kong and Guangzhou (formerly Canton) residents speak a similar form of Cantonese, while inland residents of Guangdong are more apt to speak Taishanese (also called Toisan dialect) or several other less common dialects. Because the Cantonese people made up the largest group of Chinese going overseas for business and immigration before the 1980s, Cantonese in its various forms is the most widely spoken form of Chinese in America. It is also widely spoken among the business elite in Cambodia, Vietnam, the Philippines, Singapore, and other Asian countries.

Differences Between
Mandarin and Cantonese

Good-bye
Mandarin: *Zai jian*
Cantonese: *Joi gin*

Please give me that book.
Mandarin: *Qing gei wo nei ben shu.*
(Literally: Please give me that volume book.)
Cantonese: *Mmh goi, bei go ben sui bei ngoh la.*
(Literally: Please give that volume book to me polite-request-modifier.)

More formal Cantonese request: *Cheng bei go ben siu ngoh la.*
(Literally: Please give/to that volume book me polite-request-modifier.)

A final word of warning on dialects. There are many homonyms in Chinese; the difference of one tone or one consonant can change a phrase from innocuous to obscene and vice versa. For example, the very common phrase meaning "to not have" is pronounced *mei you* ("may yoh") in Mandarin, but in Nanjing dialect the same phrase sounds, to American ears at least, a lot like a very common Mandarin slur against one's mother. Thus, if you are speaking in Mandarin and someone responds with a phrase you cannot place but that sounds vaguely obscene, never assume that's the case. When in doubt, remain calm and try to find someone who can translate for you.

Dissidents

The nature of political protest has changed completely since the days of the pro-democracy student demonstrations at Tiananmen Square in 1989. Today many protests occur in cyberspace, where bloggers, activists, and concerned citizens post information that would otherwise be suppressed. From posting news about car accidents involving the children of prominent government officials to spreading photos of officials stepping out with mistresses or sporting bling too expensive for their salaries, private netizens have kept ahead of the official news media on reporting many scandals.

Many prominent social protests have occurred via the blogosphere. Dissident Hu Jia blogs extensively about human rights abuses and social justice topics, including the harassment of AIDS activists. The 2010 Nobel Peace laureate Liu Xiaobo famously posted his call for political reform online: his petition, Charter 08, called for democracy, republicanism, Constitutionalism, and respect for human rights. Although his petition received nearly ten thousand signatures, Liu was arrested and sentenced to eleven years in prison "for inciting subversion of state power," and his wife, the poet Liu Xia, was placed under house arrest. She has been under government surveillance ever since. Other activists like artist Ai Weiwei make extensive use of cyberspace to communicate with the world. Despite being arrested and detained for eighty-one days before he was finally accused of tax evasion, Ai continues to be active on China's microblogs as well as

Twitter, where he comments on Chinese and world events. Although the government censors the Internet, with more than 500 million Internet users in China, there are simply too many bloggers and too many ways to express opinions for the censors to stop them all.

Dissidents vary in what they want and how they go about their protests. Most Chinese are deeply patriotic, even when they are demonstrating against something the government has done, and are not seeking an overthrow of the government and the Chinese Communist Party, as was commonly reported in the Western press during the protests at Tiananmen in 1989. Instead most protesters are trying to alert the Chinese central government in Beijing to local corruption that is hurting their livelihood. For example, many farmers' land is appropriated to build a new factory, parking lot, highway, or some other kind of economic infrastructure. When they are not compensated as promised, their only recourse is a villagewide protest in the hopes of attracting the central government's attention. Similar protests are waged when they discover toxic waste is being dumped into nearby streams, lakes, or underground aquifers.

These kinds of protests demonstrate two important facets of contemporary Chinese culture. One is that the common people have faith that the central government will help them if they can only get the word to the right official. (In many ways, this sentiment reflects historical patterns in which peasants sent petitions to the emperor in Beijing to report local corruption.) Second, these protests show the level to which corruption pervades Chinese society. These protests also reveal the extent to which the market economy is pressuring rural areas desperate for new sources of income. Local officials, businesspeople, and sometimes even the police may be in cahoots not because they are evil, but rather because they are trying to bring revenue to their impoverished villages and small cities. The price they pay for these ventures is often pollution, dislocation of farmers, and slow returns on investments, which delays compensation.

Chinese lawyers who have defended farmers, workers, the poor, the sick, and other disenfranchised groups have recently come under attack. Sometimes they are beaten by local thugs and even the police. Chen Guangcheng, a self-taught, blind lawyer who was named in *Time* magazine's 2006 cover story "Time 100: The Lives and Ideas of the World's Most Influential People," was arrested by the local government in Yinan County, Shandong Province, after he defended peasants who had been forced to undergo abortions or sterilization operations. His trial was postponed when hundreds of supporters gathered outside the courthouse, and he was jailed again for an indeterminate time period. Because the Chinese legal system is not transparent, some people who are arrested may not discover the charges against them until the day of their actual trial. Eventually, Chen was sentenced in 2006 to four years and three months in jail for allegedly fomenting a riot.

In 2012, he made headlines again with a daring nighttime escape from the compound in Northern China where he was under house arrest after being released from prison. Without disclosing the network of people who aided him, Chen made it to the U.S. embassy in Beijing, in time for Secretary of State Clinton's visit to the capital. Ultimately Chen was released to a hospital in Beijing, where he was then allowed to leave for "study" in the United States.

Other sources of dissent are religious in nature, rather than political or economic. For example, ten thousand adherents of the Falun Gong movement staged a sit-in at Tiananmen Square in 1999 to protest what they considered unequal treatment of their religion. The central government was so alarmed by their sudden show of strength, discipline, and singlemindedness that it banned the sect as a cult and began arresting its members. Other, more quiet protests can be found in the ever-growing number of underground Protestant churches. Officially, Christianity is not banned but adherents must go to government-regulated churches. Many poor, unemployed urban workers have found solace in Christianity but prefer their own church groups, which meet informally in people's homes, outside the watchful eye of the government. Other religious protesters include Muslims from Xinjiang Province and Tibetans loyal to the Dalai Lama—both of these groups have members who believe their provinces should be autonomous from China.

A very visible form of dissent is public, urban street demonstrations. While such events may be de rigueur in France and common in the United States, they erupt in China only when an issue is extremely emotional. For example, after the United States accidentally bombed the Chinese embassy in Yugoslavia in May 1999, killing three people, tens of thousands of students in cities across China held major demonstrations. Similarly, in 2003, violent protests occurred after four hundred male Japanese tourists hired prostitutes for what was described in the Western press as a "public orgy" on the anniversary of Japan's invasion of Manchuria in 1931. On both occasions protesters threw rocks at the U.S. and Japanese embassies and sometimes roughed up foreigners they thought were American or Japanese.

During anti-Japanese protests in 2011, a Chinese man was paralyzed after a mob pulled him from his Toyota Corolla and beat him in the street.

Protests can seem to descend upon a city out of thin air and an incident can escalate from a street protest to a full-scale demonstration within twenty-four hours.

To survive such street demonstrations, remember to keep your cool. Don't take pictures in public. Innocent bystanders have sometimes had their cameras ripped from their hands while they tried to photograph protests and found themselves bodily lifted up and delivered over the heads of the mob in a kind of mosh-pit reversal. Chinese demonstrators don't want to be identified by the police in your photographs so they obviously do not appreciate being photographed.

Finally, if you find yourself in a demonstration that is turning violent or raucous in any way, get the hell off the street as fast as you can. If you are caught up in a mob, lie if you have to, and if it's an anti-U.S. demonstration, don't hesitate to claim Canadian citizenship. Similarly, Japanese tourists or people who look Japanese should claim Korean heritage or Asian-Canadian heritage, for example, if an anti-Japanese protest breaks out. And so long as the prime minister of Japan continues to visit the Yasukuni Shrine, where Japanese war criminals from World War II are buried, there will continue to be protests against the Japanese government.

As for the old-fashioned pro-democracy dissidents from the Tiananmen Square era, most are based overseas now, and within China the memory of Tiananmen and its bloody end has faded considerably. Many young people have never even heard of the protests.

As for visitors to China, talking about such issues should be restricted to private conversations with friends. Most Chinese are far more savvy about what dissidents are saying than they will let on in public. Friends and colleagues will have no problem expressing their opinions in private once you have gotten to know each other well. But this is not a subject for strangers to discuss.

Dynasties

ynasties in China refer to the period of political reign headed by a king or emperor and his descendants. There have been more than thirty dynasties throughout Chinese history, from the legendary first Xia dynasty (c. 2205–1766 BCE) to the last dynasty, the Qing (1644–1911), which ended in revolution when the Republic of China was founded in 1912.

The first emperor who unified China's territory took "Qin" (pronounced "chin") as his reign name. His dynasty lasted a relatively short time, from 221 to 207 BCE, during which he ruled with an iron fist, conscripting tens of thousands of poor Chinese farmers to leave their land and build the Great Wall along China's northern border. In an act of extreme cruelty, these slaves were not allowed to return home even upon death and their bones were interred in the wall. This act violated traditional religious beliefs of the period, which insisted that a person's bones should be buried in his ancestral village or the soul of the deceased would become lost and wander the earth endlessly (for without the offerings of food and prayer and spirit money at the ancestral temple, the soul could not bribe the Judge of Hell and ensure future generations' prosperity). In a particularly poignant folktale, a farmer's widow (sometimes it is his mother instead) comes to the Great Wall looking for the bones of her dead husband. She cannot find him and kneels on the stones, weeping. The Jade Emperor in Heaven takes pity on her and a lightning bolt bursts from the sky, splitting open a section of the wall, thus revealing her husband's bones. She is able to carry them home to his village where he can be properly interred.

Emperor Qin is most famous now for the army of terra-cotta warriors that he had buried in his tomb to protect him in the afterlife. A portion of the tomb has been excavated outside present-day Xi'an, and visitors are allowed to see the warriors in their original underground tomb as well as in local museums.

One unusual feature of Chinese dynasties, which set them apart from European royalty, is the Mandate of Heaven. This concept meant that no emperor was allowed to rule simply because of his bloodline. Instead he was responsible for setting a moral example for his officials and for his people. If he grew corrupt and the people suffered, rebellion was a legitimate political and ethical recourse. Hence any peasant who could gather an army could overthrow an emperor and found a new dynasty. If the new emperor could bring prosperity to China, then he was considered to have successfully gained the Mandate of Heaven. His sons—or nephews—were expected to succeed him politically, but again they could be overthrown if judged unfit to rule. There was no belief that only certain bloodlines, members of the nobility, or descendants of an erstwhile king should be the emperor. In this sense, Chinese dynastic rule was curiously democratic.

On the other hand, there was no legal limitation on the power of the emperor—no separate nobility (after the Tang dynasty, 618–907 CE) or separate religious clergy to challenge his power—and hence the concept of the separation of powers did not take root in traditional China as it eventually did in the West.

Women in Power

Empress Wu, who ruled from 9 to 23 CE, between the Western and Eastern Han dynasties, was the only female empress in Chinese history.

However, recent archaeological finds have shown that there were females who wielded great power.

Lady Fu Hao, who died around 1200 BCE, was a general who led an army of seventy-five thousand men in battle. Her tomb, discovered in the late 1970s, showed that she was buried with four bronze ax blades that had been used in beheadings.

The Empress Dowager Cixi ruled as regent in the last decades of the Qing dynasty, as the male heirs mysteriously died before they could become of age. Pu Yi, the last emperor, came to power only after her death.

Dynasties

Chronology

Xia   2205–1766 BCE

Shang   1766–1122 BCE

Zhou   1122–221 BCE

Qin   221–207 BCE

Han   206 BCE–220 CE

Three Kingdoms 220–280 CE

Jin   265–420 CE

Southern and Northern Dynasties 420–581 CE

Sui   581–618 CE

Tang　　618–907 CE

Five Dynasties　　　907–960 CE

Northern Song　　　960–1126 CE

Southern Song 1127–1279 CE

Yuan　　1279–1368 CE

Ming　　1368–1644 CE

Qing　　1644–1911 CE

Economy

The Chinese economy has undergone some of the most dramatic changes in the world, and possibly human history, over the past one hundred years. In 1911 China was still a poor country, struggling under an ineffectual emperor as foreign powers carved its territory into "spheres of influence," in which foreign countries were allowed to take all the resources out of the country and pay nothing back in return. After the 1949 Communist revolution, China struggled under Mao Zedong's revolutionary policies and could barely feed itself; in fact, more than 40 million Chinese starved to death from 1959 to 1962. However, by 2012, China had a GDP of $11.4 trillion, making it the second largest economy in the world behind the United States.

What has made this difference? First, a series of reforms since Mao's death have allowed China's economy to open up to the world. Under Mao, China followed the Soviet model of a planned economy. After the death of Mao in 1976, Deng Xiaoping came into power and introduced his own idea of "socialism with Chinese characteristics," which allowed for some experiments in capitalism. For example, Deng established several Special Economic Zones (SEZ) on the Eastern Seaboard, where total capitalism could be practiced within these zones.

The next major change occurred under Deng's successor, Jiang Zemin, who introduced the concept of the "Three Represents" to the

Communist Constitution. This allowed capitalists to join the Chinese Communist Party. Jiang almost completely changed China's economic system in function, if not in name, by adopting measures of nineteenth-century "state capitalism," with members of the Chinese Communist Party as stakeholders and owners of new enterprises with huge rewards. As China's economy prospered, members of the Chinese Communist Party became millionaires (and sometimes billionaires), increasing the incentives of the ruling class to keep the capitalist reforms in place.

Additionally, China's economic miracle has been aided by the rest of the world's policies toward China. Since the 1970s, many Western nations, particularly the United States, have allowed tens of thousands of young Chinese men and women to enroll in Western universities, to study and learn the newest technology and inventions as well as economic theories and investment strategies. Many of them returned to China and contributed to the growth of society.

Furthermore, Western companies invested billions of dollars in setting up joint ventures and manufacturing and research and development centers in China. In exchange for developing the Chinese economy, these companies were able to make use of China's large and cheap labor force which the government guaranteed would be stable and well behaved by banning any outside unions.

Finally, China has developed many sound governmental policies, despite being a Communist totalitarian system. It has invested heavily in improving the country's infrastructure—from roads to railways to bridges and airports—and it has spent hundreds of millions on trying to create a world-class educational system. China was careful not to get drawn into any expensive wars, despite its sometimes bellicose rhetoric, and the country did not launch any wasteful political campaigns as it had under Mao.

What remains to be seen is if China can continue its economic growth and adapt its policies for its new social realities. Economic inequity is high in China, second only to that of South Africa, according to some indices. Most growth has been driven by government investment. Experts say in its next phase of development, China must bring together government funds with more private capital to create sustainable growth. Moreover, no country in human history has survived only on the basis of economic growth. There must also be a fundamental reform of the political structure and of China's social policies. China's rapid urbanization will demand the ruling Communist Party meet the needs and demands of a large middle-class society, with hundreds of millions of young, educated citizens. Nor can China ignore the needs of its rural residents, who have not benefited from China's urbanization and who still lack a basic social safety net. Finally, China must tackle the problem of corruption, which exists at every level of society. Only then will the world know if China's economic miracle is here to stay.

Education

China has one of the most competitive education systems in the world, where children must take an exam after elementary school to determine which middle school they will attend. This test, usually taken at the tender age of ten, can determine one's fate for life. Middle schools vary highly in quality and getting into the best schools with the best facilities is almost essential in order to eventually go to college—unless one's family is extremely wealthy.

The Official System

The education system is divided into sections. First, children often attend the neighborhood *you'er yuan*, roughly equivalent to American preschool and kindergarten. As in many of America's more expensive enclaves, competition to get your child into the best preschool is often keen and bribes are not unheard of. Connections, or *guanxi*, help as well. From there children spend five years in elementary school. Next comes the onerous entrance exam for middle school, or rather, the first three years, known as *chu zhong* (literally: early middle school), roughly equivalent to junior high in America. During their third year in junior high, students must again take an exam to determine whether they will be permitted to continue on to senior high, known as *gao zhong*, which lasts for another three years. In the final year of senior high, students must again prepare for and take the truly painful national college entrance examination. Students are allowed to list a number of colleges that they would like to attend should their scores be high enough. Traditionally, students are not allowed to choose their majors but are assigned majors based on their test scores.

In July, test scores are released and many students' hopes are utterly crushed when they discover they did not score high enough to attend any university.

The Back-Door System

In Chinese there is an expression for solving a problem by bypassing the normal bureaucratic route. It's called *zou hou men*, or "going in the back door." Naturally, the education system has its own series of back doors.

The exam system was created out of a sense of fairness, so that the best and brightest could be chosen objectively to go to school in a time of limited resources for the country. There have been various exam systems in China since the Han dynasty, with the Imperial Exam System, which tested males on their knowledge of memorized classic texts and rewarded them with official government posts, lasting roughly from the Tang dynasty to 1911, when the last emperor was overthrown and the Republic of China established.

However, cheating has been documented throughout Chinese history and continues in the present in various forms.

For example, many middle schools now have a private side and a public side. Students without money but who pass the exams may attend the public side, which is mostly free (although some schools are charging tuition and fees for expenses). Students whose parents are willing to pay private tuition rates can get their child placed in the private side of the school regardless of test scores.

Alternative Schools

For those parents and students who lack the financial resources to pay their way into a top school or to devote a year of their life just to study for an entrance exam, more and more alternative sources of education have sprung up in China. Naturally, they all charge a fee but they feed a hunger in China for education and skills needed to compete in China's fast-paced economy. There are private night schools where one can attend classes to supplement one's schooling or to continue learning while working at one job in the hopes of getting a better one or a promotion, private colleges where one simply pays tuition to be admitted, and even distance-learning programs that originate in foreign countries. There are also schools called TV universities in which students watch videos of professors' lectures and then take the exams.

All these institutions vary in quality but they attest to the desire of Chinese people to better their job prospects through education.

Educational Expansion

The Chinese government has been steadily building more universities to accommodate the endless demand. In 2006, the National Development and Reform Commission reported that 4.1 million students would be graduating from universities in 2006, an increase of 750,000 students from the previous year.

However, as more students graduate, they discover the jobs they had hoped to find after their decades of hard work are not necessarily appearing. By 2011, reports showed 16.4 percent of the college-educated urban population nationwide between the ages of twenty-one and twenty-five was unemployed. Perhaps even more painful were statistics that showed new college graduates were four times as likely to be unemployed as young people who had only an elementary school education, due to the greater number of factory jobs available. While many grads continued to be supported by their parents while looking for an ideal white-collar position, many factory jobs went unfilled.

Rural Education

Despite urban students' complaints, their situation is nearly ideal compared to that of rural children, whose parents often cannot pay the fees necessary for their children to attend school at all. Girls are especially hard hit by rural poverty and are more likely than their brothers to have only an elementary school education. Even then, what they are taught may not be up to par with the curriculum in city schools. This social problem was documented in director Zhang Yimou's 1999 film *Not One Less*.

World-Class Universities

Despite these disparities, China is intent upon building up one hundred of its top universities into world-class institutions. The government is providing major funding for these universities, similar to America's Ivy League, in an initiative called the "21st Century Number One Project" ("21/1" for short). For example, the world-famous Beijing University (also known as Peking University) and Qinghua University (formerly spelled "Ts'ing Hwa" and known as China's MIT) were each given 1.8 billion RMB ($225 million) from the government for improvements; and Fudan University in Shanghai, Zhejiang University, and Nanjing University were each given 1.2 billion RMB ($150 million). Needless to say, graduates from these schools do not have the same difficulty finding jobs but rather field multiple offers from foreign graduate schools as well as multinational corporations and information technology (IT) companies.

Study Abroad

Hundreds of thousands of Chinese students are opting out of the misery of the exam system by studying abroad. Others are looking for a leg up in the competitive job market by gaining international experience. Many families pool resources, taking loans from extended family and friends, so that one child can go to a university in another country. More than 1.3 million Chinese students went abroad to study in 2011, a 23 percent increase from the previous year. China was the largest source of international students in the United States, where 734,000 Chinese chose to study in the 2010–12 school year. And so long as an overseas degree confers more prestige than one from a local university, Chinese students will continue to look for options abroad.

Ethnic Minorities

If you visit Xishuang Banna, an "autonomous region" in southern Yunnan province bordering on Burma (Myanmar), you might find that Chinese friends will warn you to take care. You might even hear comments from urban, Han Chinese about the ethnic minorities there, such as, "They are like wild people!"

One reason many strange tales abound about China's minority populations is that unlike America's diverse population, they are not for the most part integrated into Chinese mainstream society but are "allowed" to practice their own cultures and religions as they have been passed down through the centuries. As a result, China's minorities often dress and look quite different from Han, who make up the majority of the population of China and who for the most part wear contemporary Western fashions. For example, the women of the Dai minority still wear the long colorful skirts of their ancestors, silver belts, and side-buttoned blouses. The Hani women favor black, pleated kiltlike skirts with elaborately embroidered leggings, black woven tops, black headdresses, and thick silver ornaments in their earlobes. Their teeth are often dyed red from chewing betel nut. Many men in Yunnan sport elaborate tattoos on their legs and arms. And true to one story that we assumed was legend, some tribesmen do wear leopard pelts tied to their belts, supposedly captured without the aid of weapons other than their fists. Young men dressed in the orange robes of monks ride on bicycles and motor scooters en route from village to temples, where they can study the religion, language, and history of their people outside the Han-dominated curriculum of China's public schools.

In fact, China officially recognizes 56 distinct ethnic groups, although the true ethnographic divisions could easily run far more than one hundred. (In fact, the 1964 census listed 183 different ethnic groups. It's not clear why the government chose to change the classifications.) In China's imperial past, the government often used ruthless force to try to Sinicize other ethnic groups and turn their territory into vassal states. During the Cultural Revolution, Red Guards again wreaked havoc on minority temples, art, and the people themselves as they brutally tried to impose Mao's form of communism, combined with their own sadistic violence, onto these cultures.

Today Chinese anthropologists travel the country and try to record the nation's varied ethnic groups' beliefs and customs. There is a feeling that time is running out to make these studies as the modern economy is making vast changes to minority regions. No longer able to survive in the twenty-first century on herding, ancient agricultural techniques, and barter-type markets, many minority groups in outlying regions far from China's booming coastal cities find themselves struggling to adapt. In Inner Mongolia motorcycles are becoming the travel mode of choice among the nomadic Mongols, when just a decade earlier horses and yaks provided most transportation. In southern Yunnan, hunting is no longer as valuable a skill for a young man as is trafficking in heroin, which has resurfaced in China's cities on a scale not seen since before the 1949 Communist revolution. AIDS, too, has come to minority areas, sometimes through traffickers who return to their villages after testing the wares, sharing needles, and becoming ill, not realizing that when they take a wife, they are passing on the deadly infection. AIDS has also devastated some communities in the so-called Golden Triangle, where poppy production is lucrative and easy to accomplish in the warm climate, as needles were reused to vaccinate everyone in villages for simple things like flu shots or vitamin injections. While the government has tried to make HIV drugs more accessible and affordable to the rural poor, stigma, ignorance of what causes the disease, and lack of access to any modern health care at all continue to stymie these efforts.

Some classifications of minority groups are completely outdated. For example, the government still groups the matrilineal Moso society, known among Han as the Country of Women for its preference for daughters over sons, together with the Naxi, who are decidedly not matriarchal. In Moso culture, women own the property and pass it along to their daughters, they do not marry their male lovers, and there is no traditional word for "father"; whereas in the Naxi culture a bride on her "honeymoon night" must escape from her husband's village and run all the way back to her mother's village—which could be many miles and days away—sometimes with bare feet, while a search party of Naxi men comes to collect her. If she does not make it to her mother's home, thus proving her virtue in some kind of unusual chastity ritual, when the men of her husband's village catch up to her, she will be treated as a slave and greatly disrespected. Very different cultures indeed! Yet they are still classified as the same according to the Chinese census.

Minorities in China are accorded different rights from the Han majority. For example, minorities are not obligated to practice the One Child Policy lest that lead to genocide. They are granted a certain degree of autonomy in how they express their culture and are not forced to participate in Han festivals or religious beliefs. However, autonomy is limited in many respects. Children are still taught in Mandarin (or the local Han dialect) in school rather than in their culture's own language. Some groups—such as Tibetans and Muslim Uighurs—are considered separatist threats to the Chinese state and are policed very strictly. Han migration to minority regions is also seen as a threat by many minorities, as a means to dilute their cultures.

Yet China's minorities do manage to keep quite a bit of their traditional cultures intact, even as they adapt to the rapidly changing world. Tourism provides one major source of revenue for China's minority groups and as a result they tend to be very welcoming to visitors.

From highest population rank to lowest, the following is the list of China's official fifty-six ethnic groups (please note that multiple spellings are occasionally used in China and in history books): Han, Zhuang, Manchu, Hui, Hmong (called Miao in China), Uighur, Yi, Tulia, Mongolian, Tibetan, Bouyei, Dong, Yao, Korean, Bai, Hani, Li, Karakh, Dai, She, Lisu, Gelao, Lahu, Dongxiang, Wa, Shui, Naxi, Qiang, Du, Xibe, Mulam, Kirgiz, Daur, Jingpo, Salar, Bulang, Maonan, Tajik, Pumi, Achang, Nu, Ewenki, Jing, Jino, De'ang, Uzbek, Russian, Yugur, Bonan, Menba, Oroqin, Drung, Tatar, Hezhen, Gaoshan, and Lhoba.

Face

Face is perhaps the most important concept to understand about Chinese culture and also perhaps the most difficult as it reflects values that are so very different from those in contemporary America. Truly, the Chinese concept of face is the yin to America's yang. Face is your public persona, your social standing, your pride, your dignity, your scruples. "Saving face" is the act of preserving that appearance of dignity, and it is something that Chinese will go to great lengths to preserve. "Losing face" is the ultimate disgrace.

Whereas in America, thanks in part to the popularity of talk shows like Oprah Winfrey's and the embrace of psychotherapy, we no longer feel the need to keep our "dirty laundry" a secret. We Americans reveal relatively intimate details about our lives in public all the time. Turn on the television and you will see celebrities openly talking about overcoming drug addictions, spousal abuse, sexual abuse, alcoholism, diseases, and so on. And we as a culture generally applaud people who come clean about their past and describe their struggles. For example, when President George W. Bush first ran for president, he spoke openly about overcoming his addiction to alcohol when he was a younger man. No Chinese official would ever do such a thing. It would be considered a devastating loss of face and almost impossible to overcome.

A Chinese proverb warns, "A family's ugliness [misfortunes] should never be publicly aired." (Pinyin: *Jia chou bu ke wai yang*.)

A traditional insult is to say that someone "has no face" (pinyin:

bu yao lian), which means that person has no principles. By the same token, one of the worst things that can happen to a person is to "lose face" (pinyin: *diu lian*). That is why one proverb warns, "A person needs face as a tree needs bark." (Pinyin: *Ren yao lian, shu yao pi.*) Without the protection of your good social standing, a person cannot survive.

With that proverb in mind, the April 2006 visit by then Chinese president Hu Jintao to the White House illustrates how differences in Chinese and American cultural conceptions of social standing can lead to enormous difficulties from the point of view of maintaining face. President Hu had insisted he be given a "state visit" just as his predecessor, President Jiang Zemin, was given in 1997. However, President Bush insisted the visit was an "official visit," a more neutral term. To overcome this difference, the Chinese media translated "official visit" as "state visit" and Hu's face was initially saved. Similarly, President Hu insisted he be given a twenty-one-gun salute just as Jiang had received instead of the nineteen-gun salute that President Bush's advisers had planned. In the end, Hu received the twenty-one-gun salute. Again, his face was saved. However, President Hu also wanted a state dinner and President Bush only provided a state lunch. Therefore, many Chinese news outlets did not mention the meal at all. Finally, disaster struck during the actual greeting ceremony on the White House lawn when a voice over the loudspeakers introduced Hu as president of "the Republic of China." Alas, that is the official government name of the island of Taiwan, which the *People's Republic of China* considers a renegade province and not an independent nation. Then while President Hu gave his official speech, a protester from the banned Falun Gong religious group loudly heckled him from the press stands. It took three minutes for the Secret Service to escort the woman away. In the last act of humiliation, as President Hu tried to leave the raised platform upon which he and President Bush were standing, he started to walk away in the wrong direction. President Bush hastily reached out and grabbed Hu's suit jacket and pulled him back to the stand. While from an American point of view, this action might seem a tad casual for a president, it was not out of the ordinary for President Bush, who has taken great pains to cultivate an image as a casual, down-to-earth Texan. However, from the

Chinese point of view, this pulling on Hu's jacket was seen as deeply insulting, as though President Bush were treating Hu like a child, to be tugged here and there. As a result, the White House visit was downplayed in the Chinese state media and instead Hu's visits to Microsoft chairman Bill Gates's home and Boeing's massive Washington state facilities were emphasized.

While this incident might seem minor or even humorous from an American point of view—just another public relations snafu but certainly not signs of a vast conspiracy to denigrate China—the Chinese had the opposite reaction. Conspiracy theories dominated Chinese chat rooms as Internet users revealed the embarrassing details that the official Chinese press had omitted, with the vast majority of Chinese expressing the opinion that President Bush had deliberately tried to make President Hu look bad and that this was a sign that the American government looked down on China.

Again, one should never underestimate the importance that Chinese put on maintaining face.

From a practical point of view, visitors to China should always keep in mind that when something goes wrong—at work, at school, on a tour—they should never openly, publicly, and loudly blame their guide or colleague, even if it is entirely that person's fault. If there's a problem, always speak to the person involved in private. Be careful not to assign blame to the person. Use the passive voice, such as "A problem has occurred," rather than "You made a mistake. We were supposed to do such-and-such, but you did this-and-that instead." Flatter the person you are speaking to: "I know this is not your fault, of course, but I know you will be able to think of a way to help solve this problem." Or "I need your help. I know you are very clever and understand these things so perhaps you'll be able to think of a solution."

Open confrontation will usually result in the person denying responsibility or feigning complete ignorance.

Family

The Chinese word for "nation" is made up of two characters: the first, *guo*, means "state" or "kingdom" while the second, *jia* means "family." Thus the importance of family as a central component of the nation is clear.

History

However, the nature of the Chinese family has changed radically over the course of the last one hundred years, so that the makeup of today's families would be nearly unimaginable to Chinese living a mere three generations earlier. Traditionally, a family was patriarchal, with the oldest living male having the most power and authority. This was usually the grandfather, whose sons would be expected to live either within the family compound or nearby in the same village and work in the family business or tend the family fields. Wives came from outside the family and were considered outsiders their entire lives. Their duties were to provide heirs and to serve their in-laws, mostly their mothers-in-law. Girls were considered less valuable than boys, as girls would marry and move away whereas boys would stay nearby and take care of their parents in old age. A woman gained power only through her sons.

After the humiliating Treaty of Versailles in 1919, in which

Western powers awarded Chinese territory to Japan, Chinese intellectuals came to realize how weak China as a nation had grown and began demonstrating for reform. The anarchist writer Ba Jin wrote his most famous novel, *Family*, to this effect, offering a scathing attack on the stultifying hierarchy and generally loveless misery the traditional family system engendered. His book inspired many young people to seek "love matches" as opposed to arranged marriages. The state also realized the need to educate its women, and in 1920 China began allowing a few women to attend its public universities. Communist cells further attacked the traditional family structure and vowed to uphold the principle of gender equality to modernize China.

The war years brought many of these reforms to a halt as people simply struggled to stay alive. However, with the Communist victory in 1949, the Chinese family once again became the subject of intense scrutiny. Chairman Mao's policies rearranged village life around communes, shared property, and mass dining halls. Fearing change was coming too slowly, during the Cultural Revolution Mao tried to remake Chinese society from top to bottom by encouraging young people to denounce their own parents and to attack teachers and other elders who normally had been held in respect. The resulting chaos changed Chinese society all right, but not for the better.

Contemporary Families

The most dramatic and, thus far, lasting changes to the Chinese family came about in 1979 when the One Child Policy was inscribed in the constitution, allowing Chinese families to have only one child. For the first time in Chinese history, almost an entire generation of Chinese would be born without siblings, and parents would be forced to treat their girls as well as they would a son, as they had no chance of getting a son. In urban areas, the results were most noticeable as daughters became the object of the same parental pressure to succeed and to excel in school. Parents' expenditures on their one child became the single most important factor in their lives as this was their one and only chance for the family to survive in China's increasingly competitive market-driven economy.

Now in urban areas, many couples resemble their counterparts in the West. Young men and women live together without marrying. Some never want to have children (to their parents' dismay). Both men and women with good educations are career-oriented and confident. Social critics contend that the "only-child syndrome" has created a generation of little emperors and empresses, used to getting their way, never having to share their parents' and grandparents' attention or affection, and thus thinking of satisfying their personal desires first and foremost. Other critics say the system has created a stressed-out generation, forced to excel and carry the expectations of four grandparents and two parents to succeed on their shoulders without any siblings to share the burden. These only children will be forced to care for six elderly people for the rest of their lives and if they marry, one couple will have to take care of twelve elderly people and one child of their own in an increasingly expensive society.

Divorce

Divorce was once an almost unknown phenomenon in China. When in the 1930s a Chinese sociologist documented a few hundred cases of divorce in Shanghai, it was the cause of much lamenting: Chinese society was obviously disintegrating, many prominent political figures and intellectuals concluded. In 1995, there were more than a million divorces in China, a new milestone. And today divorce is easier to obtain than ever (although divorce rates are low by Western standards at about 2.8 million per year). Where once under the Communist system a couple had to have their work units' (i.e., employers') permission to divorce, amendments to the legal system now make it an entirely personal matter. Cities lead the nation in divorces, with Beijing's divorce rate at 39 percent, Shanghai a close 38 percent, and Shenzhen 26 percent, with infidelity cited as the number one cause of divorce in 2012. In 2006, for the first time, a website was devoted to helping divorced individuals cope with their newfound loneliness. Tens of thousands of Chinese have since flocked to the site, seeking advice and solace. Meanwhile, in Shanghai the first class of trained marriage counselors (all 140 of them) graduated in 2006 as well.

Rural Families

On the flip side, family life in the countryside has taken a tremendous hit because of both the One Child Policy and the new economic reforms. Because rural Chinese still prefer sons to daughters for a number of cultural and economic reasons, there is a grave imbalance between the number of boys born relative to the number of girls. (Abortions, female infanticide, and depositing baby girls with "orphanages" have been the major causes of this imbalance.) Officials estimate that rural areas are missing 40 million girls—that is, 40 million girls who should have been born and reared there but were not. One awful consequence is an increase in kidnapping—young women are snatched from elsewhere in the country and sold in the countryside as brides. Also, females in the countryside are growing up in greater isolation. Whereas traditionally they might have been part of a community of women—the daughters, wives, mother-in-laws, and grandmothers in villages—they are now more isolated than ever, and they are forced to do more work. The pressure to bear a son is greater than ever, and unfortunately many women are beaten if they do not, as ignorance about the male's role in producing a son endures. As a result, depression is great.

According to the World Health Organization, every four minutes a woman in China kills herself, and China is the only country in the world where more women than men commit suicide. Every year roughly 1.5 million women try to kill themselves and some 150,000 succeed. In rural areas, female suicide rates are three times higher than in cities.

Chinese organizations, both grassroots and governmental, are trying to address the problem with support groups and training programs for rural women. However, all agree that in the short term, pressure on women in rural families is only going to increase.

Curiously, while sonograms used to determine the sex of a fetus are permitted, even in rural areas, educational programs to explain to men that only they can provide the Y-chromosome needed to produce a son, as well as IVF treatments specifically used to produce male heirs, are not available in the countryside. Of course, these programs would most likely make the imbalance in the male-to-female sex ratio of babies being born in rural areas greater; however, they could possibly decrease violence against wives and mothers. Another option would be to provide an FDR-esque New Deal for China's farmers so that they have a social net and are not entirely dependent upon sons to take care of them in their old age. However, the Chinese state, with encouragement from the West, has been dismantling its social net since the 1980s and has shown no inclination to return to its more socialist policies of the past.

Obviously something drastic needs to be done to alleviate the burdens facing rural women. What exactly that something is has not been determined.

Farmers

Why are China's 656 million farmers, slightly less than half of the population, so often referred to as "peasants" in English when this seems like a pejorative term? In fact, it has to do with the feudal economic system. Peasants differ from farmers in that they do not own the land upon which they are born and which they till, and yet they are bound to their land. China's farmers in this sense are most often economically truly "peasants." They have the right to grow crops on their land but they do not own their land. Private landownership was banned shortly after the Communist Party took over the country in 1949, and today most peasants are too poor to buy their land under the new reformed economy. Commercial enterprises in the new market-based economy may purchase the land upon which the skyscrapers, factories, shopping centers, and so on are built or they negotiate a long-term lease from the Chinese government.

China's farmers up until 2006 could not technically legally leave the land upon which they were born and upon which their residence permits (called *hukou* in Chinese) were based. As such they truly were peasants in the medieval economic sense of the word. Today the *hukou* system has been modified because the government officially recognized a trend that had been occurring for decades: that is, millions of farmers were leaving their land and moving to the cities to find work. Without this labor force, China's cities could not have developed as rapidly as they have; there would be a vast shortage of construction workers and factory workers; and the cost of labor would skyrocket.

Still, Chinese farmers in the city (dubbed "the floating population") face endless legal discrimination. Because of the *hukou* system, they are like so-called illegal immigrants in their own country.

They cannot legally send their children to public school nor can they use the hospitals or medical facilities in the city without paying extra money up front. They also do not have access to welfare benefits. This saves the city governments tremendous money from having to provide these services (which are not funded by the central government); however, it places tremendous burdens on the farmers. They are faced with a difficult choice: either stay in their villages and earn very little money, or move temporarily to the cities to work while leaving their children behind, often to be raised by grandparents. Young men who move to the city often find they cannot save enough money to attract a spouse, and young women face numerous kinds of discrimination and gender-based harassment. For example, if a young woman from the countryside should become pregnant by a man in the city, her child is not guaranteed a city registration that would allow the child to attend a city school. Instead the baby is assigned the mother's *hukou*.

So why do farmers want to leave their villages in the first place? Perhaps the most important reason is that it has become almost impossible for them to make a living simply by farming. A farmer can make the equivalent of $180 per year raising crops or animals. That's not enough to pay for medical expenses or schooling for their children. So when young people (and sometimes even children) are able, they leave their parents' farms to work in city factories or construction work or other hard-labor jobs that many city people do not want, all in the hopes of making more money and sending it home to help their parents or saving it up to start their own businesses so that they can afford a family of their own.

The second reason farmers leave is that their farmland is increasingly being confiscated by developers. One way cities have found to raise revenue to pay for all the services for their official residents is to expand their boundaries. That means confiscating farmland on the outskirts of the city and allowing developers to bid on it. In order to make a profit, city officials give the farmers much less in compensation than they receive from the developers. As a result, farmers are left with no way to make a living.

This outrageous dilemma has led to myriad protests—some estimate more than two hundred daily—across China as desperate farmers fight off the developers and officials who have colluded to take their land. These fights can involve tens of thousands of farmers who band together from different villages and try to protect their land or demand more compensation. Local police are called in and in recent years many of these protests have ended in violence, with both police and farmers seriously injured. While the police have guns, the farmers have their farm implements and greater numbers. Still, it is the farmers who can be carted off to prison.

Whether protests and pledges from the central government's highest leadership, namely President Xi Jinping and Premier Li Keqiang, to improve living conditions for China's farmers will actually greatly benefit this generation of farmers remains to be seen. Much prejudice remains against China's peasants among urban dwellers who see them as a reminder of China's rural and—in their eyes—backward past. As a result, one of the worst insults a city person can use is to call someone else "a peasant."

Fashion

When bilingual Chinese-American designer Alexander Wang was appointed as the head of Balenciaga in 2012, fashion insiders felt it signaled a sea change in the way the industry views China. No longer just a cheap workforce sewing clothes for the world, China is now considered the fastest-growing market for luxury and fashion goods. Wang himself had developed three stores for his own namesake line in China before being tagged for the Balenciaga top spot. While executives at the European fashion house insisted Wang's success in China and language skills were "not criteria" for his recruitment, they did say his heritage was "an extra value."

Chinese spending on fashion and luxury goods is expected to surpass that of the current top markets of the United States and Japan by 2020, according to the *Harvard Business Review*. Designers and luxury brands have courted Chinese consumers at home and abroad, with everyone from Prada to Chanel to Diane von Furstenberg setting up boutiques in China and making sure their flagship stores in the West have Mandarin-speaking clerks for the waves of mainland tourists who flock there. Some brands, like Estée Lauder, have created new lines just for the Chinese market. And others like Adidas have learned to tweak their products to capture Chinese fashionistas' imagination. For example, Adidas offered a $3,100 fur-trimmed leather trench coat as well as high-heeled tennis shoes in addition to its more typical sneakers and sweatshirts to capture more than 11 percent of China's $23.8 billion sportswear market (behind industry leader Nike, which held just over 12 percent of the market in 2012).

China's fashion tastes run from foreign luxury brands to downright quirky. While Chinese supermodels are the newest faces on the world's runways, China's unlikely top model was a seventy-two-year-old grandfather. The five-foot-eight-inch-tall, 110-pound former rice farmer from central Hunan Province became an Internet sensation in 2012 after he modeled some of the women's fashions for his granddaughter's online clothing store. Liu Qianping donned wigs, sunglasses, miniskirts, and colored tights for his gig as a fashion plate, which resonated with China's netizens. Mr. Liu found himself fielding offers from newspapers and even television talent shows in China as a symbol of the country's new prosperity and opportunities for personal happiness. "There's no comparison with the way things are now," Mr. Liu told reporters when asked to reflect upon the changes he'd witnessed over the course of his life. "Life now is so rich."

Feng Shui

eng shui (pronounced "fung shway") literally means "wind and water." However, in practice feng shui refers to the harmony inherent in the universe that people should try to harness in order to find balance in their lives. It is this balance that will allow for the greatest success. Traditionally, the Chinese believed that following the principles of feng shui could lead to improving one's health, wealth, family life, and relationships. Throughout the Chinese diaspora, feng shui masters help to determine the optimum place for building homes and offices, arranging furniture, how each room in the house should be used, and even the color scheme based on the owner's personal feng shui chart.

The origins of feng shui came from the teachings of Daoism, which was founded by the philosopher Laozi (formerly spelled "Lao-tzu") in the sixth century BCE. Daoists believe the universe is created by a force called qi (pronounced "chee"), and that this force is composed of two elements: yin, the negative force, and yang, the positive force. There are also five important elements within this universe: water, earth, metal, fire, and wood. All of these elements must be in harmony for a family or individual or even a city or nation to succeed.

For example, in Hong Kong, I. M. Pei's stunning modern design for the Bank of China skyscraper in 1982 set off alarms as local residents thought its sharp angles sent bad qi in the direction of their homes. Furthermore, the two white finials at the top of the tower looked like incense sticks placed before shrines of the dead—and evoking the dead on a large scale is a definite feng shui no-no.

In perhaps the biggest scandal, the designs for the new Hong Kong International Airport on Lantau Island originally stirred many protests among local residents. The airport was built on reclaimed land from the ocean near Lantau and a smaller island was leveled in order to create enough space for what would become the world's largest airport. Old-timers argued that its position would deflect positive qi from Hong Kong. When it opened in 1998, amid the growing East Asian economic crisis that had begun in 1997, feng shui experts blamed the new airport for ruining Hong Kong's economy. In fact, some Hong Kongese felt the whole project was a mainland Chinese scheme to destroy Hong Kong so that Shanghai could replace it as the financial capital of China—even though the airport was designed by a British architect and had been in the planning stages well before the 1997 handover to mainland China. However, such incidents show the continued influence of feng shui in Chinese political and cultural life.

Although the Communist government has tried to stamp out such beliefs as "superstitious," feng shui has in fact resurged as an industry on the mainland, and consultants are paid large sums of money by both Chinese and Western firms looking to build corporate headquarters, factories, and even private villas in the most auspicious locations.

Feng shui has become so popular among China's business elite that the Peking University School of Economics offers a class on the subject as part of its Executive Master of Business Administration program.

Festivals

There are practically as many different kinds of festivals in China as there are different kinds of people. Chinese citizens in Xinjiang celebrate the Muslim festival of Ramadan; other minorities such as the Dai in the southwestern province of Yunnan celebrate Po Shui Jie, or Water Throwing Festival, much as it's practiced in Southeast Asian countries, and young Han yuppies in the coastal cities celebrate Christmas (although generally without the religious aspect). To elaborate on all of China's festivals would take an encyclopedia set. Thus, we will instead focus on the main Han festivals, and visitors who happen to encounter other festivals can enjoy their good luck.

Chinese Han festivals generally do not fall on a fixed date but rather on dates that change from year to year, as they originated using the lunar calendar. Traditionally, they can be divided into two groups: festivals honoring the living and festivals honoring the dead.

Festivals Honoring the Living

Lantern Festival

Chinese New Year, or Spring Festival, is the first and most important festival of the new year. (See page 241 for "Spring Festival.") It ends fifteen days after the start of the lunar new year with the Lantern Festival. By now the waist-high mounds of red firecracker papers have been swept from the streets and sidewalks, the dragon dances and lion dances have been completed, and family feasts have been eaten. Thus, the Lantern Festival is a more subdued event than other Spring Festival activities. One of the most charming aspects of the holiday are the lantern parades, featuring children carrying exquisite and complex paper lanterns lit with real candles inside. Even pre-schoolers take part in this event. Whereas in America, children are generally not given real fire to hold, especially encased in large paper objects, Chinese children do indeed get to carry real lanterns and real flames. Once, in Nanjing, a four-year-old's paper goldfish did, in fact, catch on fire. The little girl calmly placed it on the ground beside her as the inferno blazed away and stood very still, hands folded, quite assured that some adult would come and save her. And indeed a group of teachers rushed over, grabbed the flaming lantern, and stomped it out. The child never shed a single tear. Chinese children, being for the most part only children and much beloved by parents and two sets of grandparents, are calm in such situations in ways almost unimaginable to those of us raised in America, where a similar event might invoke utter panic in a child so young. (Take note: if your children are invited to participate in a lantern festival, be sure to watch them in case of similar lantern flare-ups.)

The Dragon Boat Festival

This festival takes place on the fifth day of the fifth lunar month, which means it can occur sometime between May and June. (In America, it seems Dragon Boat Festivals may take place at almost any time of the year. For example, Denver celebrates with Dragon Boat races in the summer whereas San Francisco's Dragon Boat races take place at the same time as the Mid-Autumn Festival.)

The highlight of the Dragon Boat Festival is of course the races. The long, canoe-shaped boats can range from forty to one hundred feet in length, with as many as eighty rowers. The competition can be fierce, especially in southern China, where the warmer climate and many lakes and rivers make practice for the Dragon Boat racing teams possible.

There are multiple origins for the festival, including honoring the spirit of water dragons, considered to be the most powerful of the dragons and essential for providing water for crops. However, the races also have a historical element in that they honor a poet and scholar, Qu Yuan, who lived in the third century BCE. Disgusted by the corruption of a king who would not heed his counsel and who went to war needlessly, Qu Yuan drowned himself in the Milo River in Hunan Province. Local villagers raced in their boats to find his body before he drowned but could not save him in time. So instead they threw rice into the water to prevent the fish from eating his body.

In honor of Qu Yuan, one of the most important festival foods is a glutinous rice dish called *zongzi*, which are bamboo leaves stuffed with sticky rice and other fillings that may be sweet, salty, or may contain meat to flavor the rice. (When eating a *zongzi*, unwrap the bamboo leaf as you would the corn husk around a tamale but do not eat it. Only eat the rice within.)

Festival of the Cowherd and Weaving Maiden

This festival, based upon constellations in the sky, is growing in popularity and has in fact been dubbed China's Valentine's Day in the Chinese press. The original legend centers on the story of thwarted young love. The daughter of the Jade Emperor of Heaven, the so-called Weaving Maiden, falls in love with a common cowherd. They marry and live on Earth together for several years, during which time in their bliss she forgets to weave her celestial cloth and the cowherd forgets to tend his water buffalo. The Queen Mother of the West—a goddess—becomes alarmed as Heaven and Earth grow chaotic without cloth and with water buffalo running about here and there. Thus as punishment, she banishes the Weaving Maiden back into the heavens. The cowherd attempts to follow (how is unclear), but the Queen Mother won't allow him to do so anyway and instead creates the Great River (known in the West as the Milky Way) in the sky to keep them separate. (According to Western astronomy, the cowherd is the Western-named star Altair in the constellation Aquila and the Weaving Maiden is the star Vega in the constellation Lyra.)

While in ancient times, this holiday was celebrated largely by women and girls, who made offerings for fertility, happiness in marriage, and the like, today it is a popular dating holiday where gifts are exchanged and lovers make dates at fancy restaurants.

The Mid-Autumn Festival

This festival is similar to the American holiday of Thanksgiving, as it has traditional agricultural roots celebrating a good harvest. According to the lunar calendar it falls on the fifteenth day of the eighth month, meaning it can occur sometime between September and October. Today the Mid-Autumn festival in urban areas is a time of street fairs, performances, parties among friends, and of course feasting upon the traditional moon cake.

Moon cakes have fallen out of favor lately in China—although everyone is expected to give them as gifts. Boxed sets of the pastries—stuffed with various fillings, such as lotus seed paste, red bean paste, melon seeds with duck eggs, pumpkin, mixed dried fruits, coconut, and more—can be very pricey indeed. However, many young Chinese say they despise the things. Scandals in the late 1990s revealing that some moon cake factories were using rotted or moldy ingredients did nothing to improve their popularity, making them the Christmas fruitcake of Chinese cuisine. It's a shame because moon cakes are actually quite delicious.

In villages, farmers may try to travel to larger towns to see street fairs and performances of opera, stilt performers, and the like. The point is to take a rest from the hard physical labor that the harvest entailed.

Festivals Honoring the Dead

Qing Ming (Clear Brightness Festival, also called Tomb Sweeping Day)

The festival of Qing Ming (pronounced "ching ming") occurs on April 4, 5, or 6 and is celebrated throughout the Chinese diaspora although it never caught on with the non-Chinese population and thus does not have a standard English name.

The most important aspect of Qing Ming is to care for the graves of one's ancestors. Traditionally this meant sweeping the dirt away and weeding the cemetery plot. Now that most Chinese on the mainland are cremated, the festival mainly is about visiting the mortuary and placing symbolic offerings of food before the names of deceased relatives. In the past, family members also burned ghost money (i.e., paper meant to represent money) and paper replicas of material goods that the dead might like in the afterlife (cars, homes, cell phones even). There should always be an even number of dishes set before the grave and a bowl of rice with the two chopsticks sticking upright. Family members bow before the grave and also burn incense to show their respect.

Ghost Festival

Ghost Festival, which occurs on the fifteenth day of the seventh month of the lunar calendar, is a day set aside to make offerings for any wandering or hungry ghosts that may not have been properly buried by their own families or were somehow forgotten by their ancestors. Now they have become wandering spirits and can

cause mischief and harm. Although Chinese may not believe in ghosts per se, the day is similar to All Soul's Day or Halloween in its origins.

Buddhist monks and Daoist priests mark the day by performing ceremonies meant to appease the souls of these wandering ghosts. People may also burn ghost money in large metal trash barrels on the sidewalk so that the poor abandoned wandering ghosts might be able to bribe the officials of the underworld and become reincarnated as humans. Sometimes the money is meant more as an outright bribe to encourage any hungry ghosts to cause trouble somewhere else. Often businesses will set out large displays of fruit and food in addition to incense.

This tradition is widely practiced in Taiwan, Hong Kong, and throughout southern China and rural areas but is not so widely visible in northern Chinese cities.

Film

C hina's film culture has come a long way since the days of the Cultural Revolution when Chairman Mao's wife, Jiang Qing, herself a former actress, took over the entire film industry, so that only one movie was made during the entire decade of the Cultural Revolution. (The film was long and horrid, as one might imagine, and the lead actor was rumored to be Madame Mao's lover. Certainly his acting skills alone did not seem to justify his starring role.)

Since the 1980s, Chinese films have reemerged in the world of cinema, winning awards from the Venice Film Festival to Cannes to the Oscars. To provide a comprehensive list would take an entire book—and a long one at that—so here we've provided a list of some of the most famous, beautiful, useful, and easy-to find movies so that travelers can acquaint themselves with Chinese history and culture quickly before visiting the country.

Historical Themes

(We have arranged the films according to the time periods they depict, beginning with imperial times and ending in the present.)

The Last Emperor (1987). Starring Joan Chen and John Lone, this movie by Bernardo Bertolucci was the first film production directed by a non-Chinese to be allowed to shoot within the actual walls of the Forbidden City. The film beautifully brings to life Chinese imperial history, showing the reign of the last emperor, Pu Yi, his overthrow in 1911, then his acquiescence to the Japanese during World War II to serve as head of the puppet state of Manchuguo. The film shows life in China from 1903 to 1966 when, during the Cultural Revolution, the last emperor of China died, working as a common gardener.

To Live (1994). Starring Gong Li and Ge You (who won the Best Actor prize at the Cannes Film Festival for his performance), this masterpiece by director Zhang Yimou shows the political turmoil the average Chinese citizen has faced from the 1940s to the 1980s. Sumptuously photographed, this film poignantly traces the ups and downs of one family's quest to survive through the Sino-Japanese War, the civil war, then the political campaigns of Chairman Mao, the Cultural Revolution, and finally the reform era.

Farewell, My Concubine (1993). Starring Gong Li and directed by internationally acclaimed director Chen Kaige, this film reveals the inner workings of Beijing Opera troupes, and the jealousy between a beautiful woman (Gong Li) and a gay actor vying for the attention of the same male opera star. The film has especially poignant scenes of chaos during the Cultural Revolution.

The Blue Kite (1994). Although the scale is smaller than *To Live*, this well-acted movie, directed by Tian Zhuangzhuang, depicts a mother's attempt to raise her son through various marriages that parallel China's political upheavals from the 1950s to 1960s.

11 Flowers (2010) is a coming-of-age story set at the tail end of the Cultural Revolution. The drama is shown from the point of view of an eleven-year-old boy living in a small town, in which his father dreams of being a painter and his mother barely makes ends meet. When the boy wins the honor of being the class monitor, his mother uses the family's ration coupons for cloth to make him a new shirt, cautioning him to take good care of it so that it can be passed down to his younger sister. An accused murderer ends up snatching the shirt in a wry action sequence straight out of early Spielberg, setting up the quest of the boy and his buddies to get his shirt back. This superbly cast film depicts the deprivations and unfairness of life in the early 1970s through a boy's-eye view of the world, and viewers are all the richer for it.

Balzac and the Little Chinese Seamstress (2001). Based on an internationally bestselling novel and directed by the author himself, Dai Sijie, this depicts the vast social changes in China by contrasting the waning days of the Cultural Revolution with the glitter of contemporary Shanghai. The story focuses on the travails of two young men sent to the countryside under Mao's anti-intellectual policies. However, the movie belongs to the young actress who portrays their love interest (and seamstress of the title), Zhou Xun. Miss Zhou (whose name is pronounced "joe shün") is considered to be one of China's best new actresses and is actually quite a bit more popular in China than Ziyi Zhang.

Electric Shadows (2004) is a charming and unusual film for China in that it celebrates the history of Chinese filmmaking. Although the ostensible plot involves a mysterious young woman who attacks a bicycle deliveryman for no apparent reason, the main story is told in flashback, involving two children who both love movies. The film shows how movies helped them to overcome difficulties in their lives, some related to China's political upheavals, others entirely personal in nature. The performances are stellar (the children in particular are outstanding) and the film clips a delight. The film is also unusual as it is one of the rare Chinese movies directed by a woman, Xiao Jiang, to make it into international distribution.

Social Themes

(We have again arranged the films according to the time periods they depict.)

The Wedding Banquet (1990), directed by Ang Lee (of Taiwan). Although the movie is set in New York City in 1990, this comedy reveals the family dynamics still very much in play in Chinese families around the world, as a gay Taiwanese man hires a recent immigrant from mainland China to pose as his wife in an attempt to appease his parents who don't realize he's gay.

Not One Less (1999), directed by Zhang Yimou, reveals the incredible contrast between urban and rural life in China today. Featuring a cast of mostly nonprofessional actors, especially children, and filmed in a quasidocumentary style, the movie shows actual street scenes in which unsuspecting people go about their daily lives while the "actors" move about them.

Shower (1998). This gentle comedy directed by Zhang Yang was a big hit in China. It too depicts generational clashes and the fast pace of change in China's cities while focusing on a traditional-style bathhouse that is set for demolition.

Beijing Bicycle (2000). This jarring contemporary film, directed by Wang Xiaoshuai, portrays the powder keg that exists when urban poverty and wealth mix together. The film evokes a *Lord of the Flies* sensibility as urban teens fight over a fancy bicycle and the status it can bring them.

Quitting (2003). A low-budget but very well acted film, directed by Zhang Yang, this is one of the best films to portray the generational clash in China today. The story, based on the real life of the lead actor (Jia Hong Sheng), depicts a young man's descent into heroin addiction and his family's attempt to bring him back to their idea of a respectable lifestyle.

Martial Arts Films

(In alphabetical order)

Crouching Tiger, Hidden Dragon (1999), directed by Ang Lee, and winner of the Best Foreign Film Oscar (2000), is arguably the most lyrical and psychologically real martial arts film as well as the highest-grossing Mandarin language film ever made. This film made Ziyi Zhang a star. It's based on book two of a five-book series of martial arts novels written during the Republican Era

(1911–49), all of which have now been optioned by the Weinstein Company (owned by the former heads of Miramax), so sequels are definitely in the works.

Hero (2002). Directed by Zhang Yimou, this sumptuous Chinese production was a smash hit in China and stars most of the biggest-name actors in China and Hong Kong, including Jet Li, Tony Leung, Donnie Yen, Maggie Cheung, and Ziyi Zhang. Western critics panned the film's nationalistic theme—the story is based upon the legend of an assassin sent to kill the man who would become China's first emperor, founder of the Qin dynasty. However, for anyone who is interested in seeing the famed terra-cotta warriors from Xi'an come to life, this is the movie for you!

House of Flying Daggers (2005). Directed by Zhang Yimou and starring Ziyi Zhang, Andy Lau, and Takeshi Kaneshiro, this film is meant purely for entertainment value. It follows an absurd story line involving a blind courtesan who throws a mean set of hooked knives, a brave soldier who goes undercover to infiltrate a rebel group of green-clad knife-wielding superwomen, and the officer who was once the courtesan's lover and now must hunt her down.

Iron Monkey (1992). Directed by Yuen Wo Ping (aka Woo-ping Yuen), starring Donnie Yen, and produced by the legendary martial arts director/producer Tsui Hark, this delightful martial arts extravaganza also features extreme stunts and was wildly popular throughout China and the rest of Asia. The story is based on a true historical character who was known to fight on behalf of the poor during the Qing Dynasty.

Jackie Chan movies. This martial artist/comedian is best known in the United States for his comedies like *Shanghai Noon* (with Owen Wilson) and *Rush Hour* (with Chris Tucker), but in Asia he became a superstar on his early action movies. Check out *Drunken Master* (1977), for example, or *Police Story* (1984) to see the young Jackie work his magic and marvel at the incredible stunts, which he is famed for performing himself.

Kung Fu Hustle (2005). Directed by, choreographed by, and starring Stephen Chow, this film mixes comedy, action, and a lot of violence. A huge hit in Asia with respectable box office in America, this film showed a new daring in the martial arts genre.

Once Upon a Time in China, I–III (1990–92). While *Crouching Tiger* succeeded in the West, many Chinese martial arts fans felt the film was too slow. This series of films, directed by Tsui Hark and starring Jet Li, packs more punches per minute and is one of the most successful martial arts series ever filmed in Hong Kong.

Documentaries

Ai Weiwei: Never Sorry (2012). First-time director Alison Klayman's stunning documentary gives viewers an excellent account of China's most famous artist/dissident. The film includes footage of the aftermath of an attack on Ai at the hands of Chinese police in Chengdu and interviews at Ai's studio in Beijing, giving viewers an intimate portrait of a fascinating man living in interesting times.

Last Train Home (2010). Lixin Fan's film gives an up close and personal look at China's migrant workers. By focusing on one family, Fan shows the economic stakes that drive them to leave their farm to work in the city and the toll it takes on the children they leave behind. The shots of the rush of throngs of migrant workers struggling to make their way through the Guangzhou train station during the Chinese New Year holiday give an unforgettable sense of the "world's largest human migration."

Up the Yangtze (2007). Chinese-Canadian filmmaker Yung Chang gives an upstairs/downstairs view of life aboard a luxury cruise ship on the Yangtze River. Cross-cut with visits to the family of one of the kitchen workers, who never realized her rural family was poor until she left home, the film shows the hopes and dreams of China's youthful workers. From scenes of the ship's teenage workers shopping for the first time in the city to an unforgettable karaoke number by a clearly spoiled "Little Emperor" who dreams of superstardom, the documentary reveals the complexity of China's youth.

Food

It's often been said that food, family, and money are the cornerstones of Chinese culture. During Mao's three decades of authoritarian rule, food was rationed and supplied by communal kitchens. Now that China has thrown off Chairman Mao's shackles, food as an art form has returned to China.

Regional Cuisine

Every region of China has its own delicacies. When traveling you can ask what's the local specialty and most restaurants will only be too happy to accommodate your curiosity.

Certain regional flavors and styles of food are so commonplace, everyone should be aware of them:

Northern Chinese tend to favor wheat products, especially noodles, over rice. If you want rice while traveling north of the Yangtze River (or Chang Jiang, as it's called in Chinese), you'll probably have to ask for it, as it is no longer automatically served with a meal.

Southern Chinese, on the other hand, prefer rice to noodles in general. These preferences reflect the fact that rice is grown in the south and wheat in the north.

Sichuan Province in the southwest is famous for hot, spicy food flavored with red peppers that cause a burning feeling that soon turns into a numbing sensation. As a result of this unique numbing ability, unlike Indian spices, Sichuan spices generally do not grow in intensity once you've eaten them. However, if you find you've bitten directly into a red pepper and your mouth is on fire, ask for white sugar. A spoonful will stop the burn.

Sichuan is also famous for hot pot, which is a metal bowl filled with spiced oil and heated over an open flame. You are supposed to dip raw foods into the boiling hot pot to let them cook and absorb the spice, then remove the cooked item, dip it in sesame oil, and enjoy. True hot pot is very spicy and oily indeed. It's also delicious. Often at the fancier hot pot restaurants, tiny pieces of cake or other sweets are served in between courses so that the sugar will reduce the numbness and hot feeling in your mouth and restore your palate so you can taste the remaining courses.

Beijing is most famous for its roast duck, which is served on thin wheat tortilla-like pancakes with plum sauce, a scallion, duck meat, and crispy duck skin. The whole tortilla is rolled up and it is perfectly acceptable to eat this dish with your fingers.

Northern Chinese also are fond of a kind of meat- or vegetable-filled dumpling that is boiled in water. These are called *shui jiao* (pronounced "shway jow"), which literally means "water dumpling." Traditionally they were such a rare treat that they were served as festival foods for Chinese New Year (called Spring Festival in China) and weddings. Now you can order them year-round. However, many fancy restaurants consider *shui jiao* to be a home-cooked specialty and not worthy of being served as haute cuisine. Try to find a restaurant that does serve them; they're worth looking for!

Yunnan Province, on China's southwestern border, has many ethnic minorities who have their own cuisine. For example, in the autonomous region of Xishuang Banna, you can eat sticky purple rice balls dipped in various spicy sauces including a peanut one or a tomato-based salsalike one. Other delicacies include leaves fried tempura style, which can only be found in this region, stunning papayas and other fruits (the climate is quite tropical), and meat dumplings.

Shanghai is an international city that has absorbed the influences of all the different peoples who have lived there—including the French, English, Americans, and Japanese, as well as Chinese from all over the country. (Shanghaiese are proud to announce, "We are a city of immigrants!") Just as Shanghai dialect reflects all these different influences, Shanghai cuisine has become a mosaic of tastes. It's possible to have a banquet where Japanese sashimi, American-style salad with dressing, steak with gravy, steamed mitten crabs, and all manner of stir-fried dishes are served at the same dinner.

Nanjing has a rich diet, as Jiangsu Province is known as the breadbasket of China. Also, because Nanjing lies on the Yangtze River, it has a mix of northern and southern cuisines. You can get noodles as well as stir-fried dishes with rice; dumplings and *baozi* (a light airy dough that is stuffed with meat or vegetables or sweet pastes then steamed). Locals especially praise Nanjing fried eels and congealed duck blood soup.

Yangzhou, a small city near Nanjing, is perhaps best known as the *baozi* capital of the world. During early dynasties Yangzhou was the prosperous home to many salt merchants who traded along the Grand Canal. Avant-garde artists were invited to paint directly on the walls of their villas, and chefs were encouraged to create the most incredible *baozi* on Earth. You've not eaten *baozi* until you've eaten *baozi* in Yangzhou.

Guangdong in southern China is the food laboratory of the world, and the Guangzhou people (generally called Cantonese in America after the former English name of the capital) are the most daring foodies in the country if not the world. The Chinese outside of Guangdong have a saying that mocks the Cantonese spirit of adventure: "If it has four legs but isn't a table, if it has wings but isn't a plane, if it moves but isn't a car or bicycle, Guangzhou people will eat it." Yes, dogs, baby rats, monkey brains, civet cats (which are thought to be a source of the SARS epidemic in 2003), snakes, snake blood, snake bile, chicken feet, duck feet, fetal chickens still in the egg, and animals without names have all been served at some point on somebody's table here.

However, Guangdong also has exquisite food that doesn't scare the hell out of everyone else, including other Chinese people not used to such gourmandise. For example, dim sum dumplings are a Cantonese specialty. They may be steamed, fried, or boiled, and filled with all manner of delicious stuffings, including seafood, meats, vegetables, seeds and nuts, sweets, and combinations thereof. Traditionally, dim sum is served on carts that are pushed through restaurants so that patrons may see the dumplings and choose for themselves what to eat. (Dim sum is such a beloved food that the characters literally mean "little heart.")

Kaifeng, the city in Henan Province that was the former center of life for Jewish merchants who had come to China to trade along the Silk Road and decided to stay, is renowned for its mutton dishes. It is also one of the few cities in China where pork is not the most commonly served meat.

Xinjiang Province in far western China also relies heavily on mutton-based dishes because of its large Muslim population.

Vegetarian cuisine is widely available in Chinese cities, and many Buddhist nunneries have small restaurants where they allow guests to join them for meals. Traditionally, Chinese Buddhist dishes often actually look and taste as though they are made of meat, but in fact no animal products are used. Skillful artistry and a great variety of tofu (pronounced "dou fu" in Mandarin Chinese) make this illusion possible.

Chopstick Etiquette

1. Never stick your chopsticks upright in your rice bowl. (This action is used only to honor the dead at a family altar or gravesite.) Place them on the chopstick holder—usually a small ceramic or metal oblong by your plate—when you are not using them.
2. Don't lick your chopsticks if you're in public.
3. Try not to let the tips of your chopsticks touch your tongue or lips if you are also using them to remove food from a communal plate, as this is unsanitary behavior.
4. Don't stab your food with one of your chopsticks as though it were a giant toothpick.
5. Don't dig around in the food if you are eating "family style" from common bowls or platters of food. If your chopsticks touch something, it's yours.

Restaurant Etiquette

(These pointers refer to everyday eating situations. For more formal affairs, turn to page 11, "Banquets.")

While buffets are becoming more popular in big cities, most restaurants still serve food "family style." That means you are not given an individual plate of food, but rather the dishes are placed in the center of the table—often on a revolving round tray called a lazy Susan in English—so that everyone can try a little of each dish.

Fresh fish is a wonderful treat in China and if you are inviting Chinese out to dinner or are being treated by Chinese friends, fish is usually an essential dish. However, fish is served whole, head still attached. You can ask your waiter or waitress to "please divide the fish for us" and he or she will cut it up into equal portions, but still bring the head back on a separate plate and put it on the table. If the head faces you, this traditionally means you are considered the guest of honor. You don't have to eat the head; it's just the restaurant's way of showing you that the fish is fresh. Also, don't be surprised if the waiter or waitress actually brings out a plastic box containing the live fish for you to examine before it is cooked. This may be alarming to some people, but it's a good way to tell if your fish is indeed fresh. It should flop around heartily once the lid of the box is opened. If not, feel free to order a different fish and tell the server you want one that's fresher. You can also ask the server to recommend which fish is freshest that evening.

One big difference between Western and Chinese restaurants is that it is perfectly acceptable in China to make special requests. While a Western chef might be offended that you dare question his or her recipes, Chinese chefs are proud of their ability to make just about any dish requested. You can ask for dishes that are not on the menu or for certain cooking styles or for certain ingredients to be put in or left out. For example, if you are allergic to MSG, tell your waiter or waitress, and the cook will leave it out. The only time special requests are denied is if the ingredients requested are not available. Because Chinese chefs make everything on the spot rather than in advance, this kind of personal service is possible.

Forbidden City

Beijing's most famous tourist attraction is without a doubt the Forbidden City, where China's emperors for five hundred years resided until the last emperor, Pu Yi, was deposed in the 1911 revolution.

The Forbidden City was first constructed in 1407 by the third Ming emperor (Yong Le) after he decided to move the capital of China from Nanjing in the south to Beijing in the north. Since that time, the 180-acre site became home to not only the remaining Ming emperors but also the Qing emperors who succeeded them in 1644.

The palace, really more like a city within a city, lies at the heart of Beijing. Aligned on a north-south axis, the buildings all face south, which according to the principles of feng shui is supposed to provide protection from negative yin influences, such as cold winds, wandering ghosts, and barbarian invaders, all of which were associated with the north. The Forbidden City was also surrounded by walls, some thirty-two feet high, and wide drainage ditches 165 feet wide (although these moatlike ditches no longer exist), all meant to protect the imperial palaces from attack.

The architecture is resplendent, comprising a series of marble courtyards leading toward the inner sanctum of palaces, throne rooms, and the various living quarters of the emperor, his wives, his many children, and of course the bureaucracy of eunuchs who ran the day-to-day affairs of the Forbidden City. The buildings are brightly painted, and even the ceiling beams of the halls are decorated with scenes painted in resplendent reds, greens, blacks, whites, and blues. The tiles of the dwellings are a golden yellow, a color reserved for the emperor and which commoners were forbidden to wear.

Inside the palace, the treasures of the Chinese empire lay in its many rooms. Today many of these treasures reside in the National Palace Museum in Taiwan because Chiang Kai-shek carted them off with him when he fled the mainland for the island in 1949. However, enough opulence remains to give visitors a sense of the splendor and eerie seclusion that came with life within the palace walls. It is not difficult to see why China's emperors and the Empress Dowager Cixi eventually became corrupt and detached from the problems facing the Chinese people and also came to ignore the world outside China, until Western powers were literally blasting their way into China's ports.

The Forbidden City now offers visitors many informational films and displays, as well as tour guides dressed in traditional Manchu embroidered robes and elaborate coiffures. If not for the myriad tour guides blaring directions to their groups through bullhorns—and the Starbucks that was permitted to set up shop inside—visiting the palace compound really can feel like traveling back through time.

Bernardo Bertolucci's epic film *The Last Emperor* was filmed within the actual Forbidden City. Although the movie was controversial in China when it first appeared in 1986, as it took various liberties with imperial history—and provided scenes of sexy threesomes with actors John Lone, Joan Chen, and Vivian Wu—it remains one of the most artistically beautiful depictions of what life for the Chinese emperor might have been like.

Gang of Four

The Gang of Four refers to four Communist Party leaders who were charged with hijacking party control and creating the Cultural Revolution (1966–76). They were Wang Hongwen, a young Shanghai textile factory worker who was elevated to the number three position in the party, beneath Mao Zedong and Lin Biao; Jiang Qing, Mao's wife; Zhang Chunqiao, a propaganda specialist; and Yao Wenyuan, an ideological theoretician. All four were arrested after the death of Mao in 1976.

Could only four people truly have "hijacked" the enormous Communist Party apparatus, with its vast bureaucracy and tens of thousands of members? Of course not. The Cultural Revolution with all its excesses was the brainchild of Mao himself. However, in order to maintain control (and to exonerate themselves), party officials decided a show trial of four scapegoats would enable the party to continue to function and hold power while acknowledging that the Cultural Revolution had been bad indeed and somebody should be punished for it.

As for the Gang of Four, three died in jail (Mao's wife hanged herself) while Yao completed his term and was released in 1996 to live out the rest of his life in obscurity in Shanghai. He died in December 2005.

Gay and Lesbian Culture

China has had a long and relatively tolerant history of gay and lesbian culture, which unfortunately began to erode when contact with the West and especially Western missionaries' prejudices against homosexuality caused the government to curtail the freedoms long enjoyed by gay and lesbians in the so-called Self-Strengthening Movement of the 1860s to reform and "modernize" Chinese society.

Historically, China was more tolerant because there were no religious beliefs that flatly stated that homosexuality was a sin, such as in the Judeo-Christian tradition. The greatest problem from a religious and cultural point of view historically—and certainly to a very great extent today—was the importance of sons producing heirs to carry on the family surname, work in the fields, take care of elderly parents and grandparents, and continue the rites necessary to worship deceased ancestors. As marriage was not originally conceived of as a romantic relationship between the husband and wife but rather an arrangement between families conducted by the couple's parents so as to continue the family line, it didn't matter if the couple actually were in love or even particularly attracted to each other. So long as they fulfilled their filial duty and created heirs for the family, that was what counted.

In this sense, lesbians—historically and in the present—were more readily tolerated by society than gay sons. Since girls were expected to leave their home family and become part of someone else's family, it wasn't devastating if they ultimately did not marry a man. In fact, "sisterhood societies" often developed in which girls and women who worked together—in the silk industry, for example—and sent money home decided not to marry and pledged themselves to their sisters instead. Such women could form sexual relationships within their societies and even participate in marriage ceremonies. Ruthanne Lum-McCunn's richly detailed historical novel *The Moon Pearl* describes one of these "girls' houses" established by nineteenth-century silk workers.

The oldest term for homosexuality among men is the euphemistic "cutting the sleeve" (*duan xiu*) or "the passion of the cut sleeve." This term refers to an act of love by a Han dynasty emperor, who cut off his sleeve so that he could leave without waking his young male lover, who had fallen asleep upon it. Stories of male sexual relationships abound in Chinese classical histories, and it was not considered unusual for emperors in the Han, Song, Ming, or Qing dynasties to have male lovers in addition to female wives and concubines, who were necessary to continue the family line. It was never stated whether these men were gay or bisexual. Classical historians seemed to feel no need to explain that a man might love another man. However, they often mocked and criticized leaders who showed excessive love—to either male or female partners—if they were seen to be neglecting their duties to the state.

There are also vivid depictions of male sexual relations in classical Chinese literature and in paintings, dating from at least the eighteenth century during the Qing dynasty. Ironically, the first known law passed prohibiting homosexual relations occurred in the Qing dynasty in 1740, although it is not known how zealously this law was enforced.

Since the founding of the People's Republic of China in 1949, the sex life of all citizens came under scrutiny of the state. As a result of enforced prudery to control the population, gay and lesbian culture went completely underground during the Mao years. After Deng Xiaoping began his Open Door Policy in 1979, many restrictions on Chinese citizens' personal lives slowly began to lift. However, homosexuality was considered a mental illness until 2001.

In the 1980s, as Chinese society as a whole began to experience a kind of sexual revolution, gay and lesbian culture reemerged as well. By the mid 1990s gay and lesbian clubs were opening in most of China's major cities, including Beijing, Shanghai, Guangzhou, Shenzhen, and Nanjing. By the twenty-first century, openly gay and lesbian themes were being written about in government-controlled magazines and gay-themed magazines themselves came to be published. Gay blogs abound.

Opinion polls conducted in 2000 showed that less than 31 percent of Chinese disapproved of gay and lesbian relationships, and a Chinese scholar tried repeatedly to persuade the National People's Congress to change the constitution to allow for gay marriages, although he was not successful. Polls conducted by Western media showed much less hostility in the general population of China toward gays and lesbians than in the West and especially America, where the increased political power of the religious right made antihomosexual rhetoric a hot political issue and where violence toward gays was not uncommon. In contrast, when many Chinese men were asked by Western reporters if they ever felt like "beating up a gay man," they responded with outright shock: "Why would I want to do that?" Whereas Chinese men might respond with anger—or even violence—if their own sexuality were questioned in what they perceived to be a negative or mocking fashion, there is not the same feeling that homosexuality per se is an affront to God, and therefore it is not justifiable to attack gays and lesbians.

That being said, the government has been ambiguous as to how much freedom of expression it wants to grant when it comes to representations of homosexuality in the media. Every gay-themed movie from *East Palace, West Palace* (1996) to *Lan Yu* (2001; based on a Chinese Internet blogger's own story) to Ang Lee's *Brokeback Mountain* (2005) has officially been banned from China's theaters. (Of course, illegal pirate VCDs, DVDs, and downloads are available.)

While organizers were able to put together an independent lesbian film festival in Beijing with more than six hundred attendees in 2008 and a large conference for LGBT bloggers in a southern Chinese city in 2012, the government ultimately put a stop to attempts to bring that conference to Beijing. Officials said the problem was not the content so much as the potential of any mass gathering to become a threat to government control.

Furthermore, as many LGBT activists point out, while homosexual *behavior* has traditionally been tolerated, homosexual and lesbian *identity* is not necessarily accepted nor understood. What is the difference? While families may recognize that their son or daughter is gay or lesbian, they still expect them to enter into a heterosexual marriage and produce a child in order to continue the family's bloodline.

The burden to produce an heir has only grown since the One Child Policy created a generation of only children. Parents of gay sons and lesbian daughters still want their children to marry so that they can have a biological grandchild. As a result, many in the LGBT community remain closeted to their families and marry under parental pressure. If China eventually eases the One Child Policy so that gay children have straight siblings to carry on the family line, their burden will be greatly eased. However, such a policy change will already be too late for the current generation.

In the meantime, LGBT couples are increasingly turning to *xinghun* marriages, a term coined in the twenty-first century meaning a "cooperative marriage" between a gay man and a lesbian woman to fool their relatives and prevent them from being forced into marriages with unsuspecting straight partners. One online matchmaking service for gay and lesbian individuals looking for a *xinghun* match had more than 160,000 registered users and claimed to have facilitated nearly twenty thousand such cooperative marriages between 2005 and 2013.

Although male homosexuality was officially illegal in Hong Kong until 1991, in reality gay and lesbian culture thrived in Hong Kong. Gay and lesbian directors, actors, singers, writers, and other individuals grew increasingly open about their sexual orientation and did not experience loss in their popularity.

Taiwan has experienced the greatest increases in freedoms for gays and lesbians. Under Chiang Kai-shek, when martial law was a way of life, homosexuality was illegal on Taiwan. Since the death of his son and successor, Chiang Ching-kuo, in 1988, society became more and more free. By 1993, Ang Lee's *The Wedding Banquet*, which openly depicted a gay Taiwanese man's relationship with a white male New Yorker, became the highest-grossing film in Taiwan's history. The next year, famed screenwriter Chu T'ien-wen's novel *Notes of a Desolate Man*, about gay men living under the threat of AIDS in Taipei, won the island's most prestigious literary prize. Since then gay themes have appeared in many Taiwanese films, including Ts'ai Ming-liang's depiction of Taipei's gay bathhouses in *The River* (1997). In 2005, the Taiwanese legislature considered legalizing gay marriage. The issue was put on hold, but not outright rejected on a permanent basis.

For foreigners visiting China, it is wise to remember that many older Chinese find all public displays of affection—even between a married man and woman—somewhat shocking and uncouth. It is best to be aware of one's surroundings before engaging in such acts. Also, people in the countryside and smaller cities tend to be more conservative and therefore more alarmed by open displays of affection between members of the same sex. And while homosexuality has officially been declassified as a mental illness, less well educated rural police may not be aware of the change.

Gifts

In Chinese culture, it is very important to give gifts on far more occasions than is usual in the West. For example, when you visit an institution, company, or school, it is normal to give a gift to the highest-ranking person you meet as well as smaller gifts to your guides, interpreter, and anyone else who may be helping you. If you are starting a business, you should expect to give out symbolic gifts to any officials who may be helping you as well as company executives that you meet. Gifts do not have to be expensive lest they be viewed as bribes. (And in the bribery department, Westerners will never be able to compete with Taiwanese and other Asian business-people, who can routinely give out diamond jewelry, gold watches, and the like whereas in the West giving out bribes is illegal.)

For example, if you are starting an exchange program with a university, souvenirs with your home university logo on it are entirely appropriate small gifts that show you are being polite but not trying to bribe anyone for special favors. Wallets and watches are also very popular gifts.

When visiting a Chinese family, fruit and other edibles—including foreign wines or liquors—are considered acceptable gifts. If you know the family very well, you might consider giving them Western vitamins, which are very popular in China, especially among older people.

Be sure to wrap your gift in cheerful, colorful paper. Red or pink is a safe choice. Never use white as it is traditionally associated with death. Although many younger Chinese find white giftwrap to be chic for its clean and thus pleasing, even avant-garde, appearance, most older Chinese still believe white is a bad-luck color. Chinese generally do not open gifts in front of the givers, but will wait to open them in private.

For business travelers or travelers on official exchange programs and the like, the best time to give a gift is at the beginning because it shows a relationship of friendship is being established, commemorated by the gift. If you are staying for some time, remember that inevitably you will be given a farewell banquet and most likely will also be given a gift at that time. You may want to prepare accordingly with another symbolic gift.

When visiting a home or school or someplace you will not be returning to, offer the gift immediately to your hosts.

If you are assigned a driver while you are in China, it is considered appropriate to give the driver a gift of money in an envelope, the same as you would tip a driver in the West. However, if that feels awkward, a carton of American cigarettes is still generally appreciated, even though such a gift may feel politically incorrect for Americans coming from our newly antismoking culture.

Government

The Chinese government operates one of the largest bureaucracies in the world and also one of the least transparent. Sometimes it is evident, when corruption is unveiled, that the central government has little idea what is occurring at the provincial level and thus can have limited control. Conversely, when the central government in Beijing passes new laws, there is little explanation given to the rest of the nation as to the process that went into their drafting, which leads to many rumors, speculation, and guesswork as people try to understand why a new law has been put into effect and how it will impact their lives.

The Chinese government differs from other governments of the world, especially Western governments, in that it comprises three separate yet interrelated systems (the Chinese Communist Party, the government per se, and the military), which form six different institutions that operate on three to five different levels.

How does the bureaucracy function?

It operates under a so-called Leninist principle of organization:

1. The individual is subordinate to the majority as represented by the party.
2. A lower level (such as county) is subordinate to a higher level (such as city).
3. The entire population is subordinate to the decisions made by the Central Committee of the Chinese Communist Party as

The Chinese Government

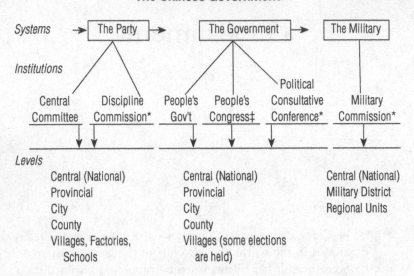

Systems → The Party → The Government → The Military

Institutions

| Central Committee | Discipline Commission* | People's Gov't | People's Congress‡ | Political Consultative Conference* | Military Commission* |

Levels

Central (National)	Central (National)	Central (National)
Provincial	Provincial	Military District
City	City	Regional Units
County	County	
Villages, Factories, Schools	Villages (some elections are held)	

* These only exist on three levels. (The Political Consultative Conference was designed to give a voice to non–Communist Party members, although it is headed by Party members, with nonmembers as deputies.)
‡ This congress exists on four levels.

governed by the twenty-five members of its Politburo, with daily decisions made by its Standing Committee of seven to nine members.

The Standing Committee of the Politburo of the Central Committee of the Chinese Communist Party was appointed at the end of the Eighteenth National Party Congress, held in November 2012. These men will hold the future of China in their hands for the next five years: Xi Jinping, Li Keqiang, Zhang Dejiang, Yu Zhengsheng, Liu Yunshan, Wang Qishan, and Zhang Gaoli. In 2017 another Party Congress, the nineteenth, will either select new members or else reappoint these seven men to power.

Some of the Standing Committee were also appointed to key positions in the government by the annual National People's Congress held in March 2013. For example, Xi Jinping was appointed president of China, Li Keqiang was named premier, Zhang Dejiang chairman of the People's Congress, Yu Zhengsheng chairman of the Political Consultative Conference, and Wang Qishan secretary of the party's Discipline Commission (a very important post to monitor and punish corruption).To understand the power of these men, imagine that the United States had only one political party. That party would hold a secret meeting to decide its leadership, then every five years would announce in November who would be the leaders of the party's key posts, and the following March it would announce which governmental positions these party leaders would also be assuming.

Clearly, the most important factor in China's system is the party, which controls both the government and the military. Within the government, for example, there are organizational units, known as cells, that represent the viewpoint and bureaucracy of the Communist Party. These cells function like an American union within a company. However, while a union is supposed to look after the rights of its members, a Communist Party cell observes the people in its territory to make sure that party dogma and policy are being observed. There are 6,869 "primary party organizations" at the urban neighborhood level; 34,000 at the town and township level; and 82,000 at the community level (which is considered the lowest level of organization). Even Walmart has Communist Party cells within its retail outlets in China. In addition, the party has 202,700 cells at all state-owned enterprises and 548,000 at privately owned enterprises. Finally, within the Chinese government, there are 235,000 cells in all the levels of the bureaucracy and 498,300 in public, educational, and religious institutions. For example, a public middle school will have a school principal and a party chief, both of whom oversee the running of the school. While this double bureaucracy may seem cumbersome—and it often is!—this system allows the party to control every aspect of life in China.

To eliminate possible personality conflicts within the political system, and to prevent intra-institutional competition (such as the party versus the government), the top leader may occupy both party and government positions simultaneously. For example, Xi Jinping is the party general secretary, president of the People's Republic, and chairman of the Military Commission. However, Xi is not an all-powerful dictator (as Mao Zedong was); he must make his decisions with the concurrence of members of the Standing Committee of the Politburo.

At lower levels, whenever there are two separate individuals with similar responsibilities, the party leader will hold seniority when it comes to deciding differences. This also applies to the military.

Under the current setup, there is no possibility of a military coup because of the multiple layers of bureaucracy and the resulting connections (*guanxi*) that a military leader would need in order to gain the backing of the rest of the military apparatus and the other parts of the bureaucracy. In fact, since the founding of the PRC in 1949, there has been only one attempted military coup. It occurred during the Cultural Revolution and was reportedly led by Lin Biao, formerly the defense minister, who tried to overthrow Mao. The attempt failed (and Lin later died under mysterious circumstances).

The current bureaucracy is so complicated, even within China, that many branches of the government are not sure what other branches at different levels (village versus provincial, city versus provincial) are doing. This allows corruption to flourish as it takes a very long time to unwind the threads of any corrupt dealing and figure out who is responsible. However, anyone attempting to do business in China must have a sponsor from any of the six institutions to help ease the bureaucratic snafus possible. Naturally, the bigger the business, the more influential that member of the bureaucracy will need to be in order to have a success.

One of the oldest Chinese conceptions of Hell was a vast bureaucracy governed by corrupt and inept bureaucrats. (Conversely, one of the oldest concepts of Heaven was also a vast bureaucracy; however, Heaven was presided over by a wise and benevolent emperor . . . with many bureaucrats in his employ.) Obviously, the Chinese have had to endure so many bureaucracies for so many millennia, it became impossible to conceive of life or death, Heaven or Hell, without a corresponding set of bureaucrats.

For a quick primer on some of the intricacies of the bureaucracy, watch the DVD of *The Story of Qiu Ju* (1993), directed by Zhang Yimou and starring Gong Li. While the story of a peasant woman seeking justice is compelling in and of itself, the documentary-style shots of actual street scenes and the depiction of the incredible lengths that ordinary Chinese must go to in order to seek "justice" and work within the bureaucracy will give viewers a new appreciation of China's vast differences from the West. (The word *Kafkaesque* may also come to mind.)

Great Leap Forward

The political movement known as the Great Leap Forward (1958–61) was perhaps the greatest political and economic disaster to hit China until the Cultural Revolution began in 1966. During this period, Mao attempted to restructure the entirety of China's economy in order to "catch up with the West" in five years' time. He forced massive collectivization of farmers, establishing "People's Communes" instead. He promoted rapid industrialization through incredibly wrongheaded policies such as "backyard furnaces," in which all residents of villages and towns were forced to melt every piece of metal they owned in an attempt to smelt steel. During this time the People's Liberation Army was also dispatched to Tibet to suppress a revolt against Communist rule and the Dalai Lama fled to India.

The tragic results of Mao's incompetent policies are hard to fathom even today. By collectivizing all peasants into twenty-four thousand communes then insisting they meet a set quota of agricultural production, he succeeded only in causing widespread famine. No one could possibly meet the high quotas under the best of circumstances, yet not meeting your quota meant official censure and punishment for local cadres. So the communes overstated how much grain and produce they grew. Industrial plants, operating under the same impossible set of quotas, lied as well. As a result, the central government in Beijing had no idea how much food or coal or steel, for example, was actually being produced anywhere. And the backyard furnaces, of course, could not produce steel but only slag. Meanwhile, peasants had lost not only their farm implements but cooking utensils as well.

For decades the official death toll given by historians showed that some 30 million people died from the resulting famines, floods, and disease. New research in provincial archives opened by the government since the 1990s paints an even grimmer picture, as mass killings and torture to punish "class enemies," suicide, human trafficking, and plots to cover up mass starvation were revealed. In some villages as many as one in ten people starved to death. In one county, the death toll was reported to the central government in Beijing as eighteen thousand, but was actually eighty thousand. Historian Frank Dikötter wrote in his 2010 book *Mao's Great Famine* that internal party documents estimate the toll between 43 million and 60 million deaths, and research is still under way.

Great Wall

        lthough the Great Wall is now a revered symbol of the Chinese nation, for many years the Great Wall was seen as a sign of oppression. Although there have been many kinds of walls built since China's earliest known history, large-scale construction on what would become known as the Great Wall did not begin until the first Qin emperor (known as Qin Shi Huang Di) unified China in 221 BCE. The Qin emperor conscripted labor to "complete" the many walls along China's northernmost border in order to keep out the "barbarian" tribes that lived to the north. He forced hundreds of thousands of male farmers off their land and moved them (as well as political prisoners) north to spend their lives building connecting walls and guard towers and reinforcing the walls that had already been constructed. If a worker died, his body was not returned to his home village but rather was interred in the wall. This act was a great sacrilege according to Chinese religious beliefs at the time, which dictated that these men should have been buried in their home villages with their ancestors, lest the soul become lost and forced to wander the earth as a hungry ghost. By the time the Qin emperor died (207 BCE) the wall was never actually completed although it had been lengthened. Later, during the Ming dynasty (1368–1644 CE), a hundred-year effort was made to restore and complete sections of the wall. Today nobody knows exactly how many workers died building the Great Wall.

Traditional folk sayings report that it is ten thousand *li* long (*li* being an ancient unit of measure roughly equal to one-third of a mile). Actually the wall is about fifteen hundred miles long and stretches from Shanhaiguan in Liaoning Province to Jiayuguan in Gansu Province (in the Gobi Desert to the west). It was never fully continuous but had sections that were not connected. The Great Wall also proved fairly ineffective as a means of defense as the so-called Northern Barbarians were able to climb over it, ride around it, or knock sections down.

Still, the Great Wall without a doubt is one of the ancient world's engineering marvels and a testament to the labor of the men forced to give their lives to build it. The wall is mostly made up of bricks or stones, with some sections made of tamped earth. The width varies from fifteen to forty feet at the base and twelve to thirty-five feet wide on top, where troops were meant to patrol and look out for invading armies. It ranges in height from twenty to fifty feet. Watch towers with narrow windows from which weapons, such as arrows, could be fired were constructed at regular intervals, and additional troops could be summoned in times of war by lighting beacon fires atop the wall.

Most major hotels for tourists in Beijing sell tickets for the many daily bus trips to the wall, which passes roughly forty-five miles from the city center.

The wall is built on extremely hilly terrain and walking atop the wall can be akin to climbing a mountain, hence the popular T-shirt slogan: "I climbed the Great Wall." The most popular areas for tourists are the sections north of Beijing known as the Badaling section and the Mutianyu section. Here it is possible to see for oneself the famous vistas of the wall snaking across the countryside like a giant dragon in repose.

From this vantage point,

President Richard Nixon's famous quote indeed rings true: "The Great Wall is a great wall."

True or False?

The Great Wall is the only man-made object that can be viewed by the human eye from space.

Answer: False. Although this tidbit was taught in Chinese textbooks for decades and occasionally in America as well, the Great Wall cannot be viewed by the naked eye from space.

Guanxi
(Connections)

Guanxi (pronounced "gwan shee") refers to social connections or one's network of friends and partners. Such connections are the single most important factor for success in China today. Without *guanxi*, it doesn't matter how intelligent or talented you are or how wealthy, you won't get ahead. People with better connections can block you at every move, just like the round discs in the ancient game of Go.

At one middle school in Nanjing, for example, the three seniors who made it into college had not actually scored the highest on the nationwide entrance examinations. One was a star basketball player and had been admitted to a very prestigious university because that school was going to be hosting the Asia Games (similar to an all-Asia, collegiate form of the Olympics) in four years. He would be a senior then and be able to play on the university basketball team, giving them a good chance of winning and saving face as hosts. His coach used his *guanxi* with the university coach to get his star player a berth at the school. The other two students had used family connections to get into their universities. This was not considered corruption. It was widely known and the teachers discussed it openly. They weren't necessarily pleased, but they understood that this was how the world worked.

Similarly, one of the biggest tech companies in China is a joint venture between the son of a top pro-independence politician in Taiwan and the son of a former president of China, Jiang Zemin. Even though China has vowed to "take back Taiwan," even by force if necessary, in reality, the joint venture between these two political princes is not unusual and was regarded widely throughout China as a sign the company would be a success. With the two heads' political connections, they would have the *guanxi* to get whatever permission they needed from the local, provincial, and national government to carry out their business, unimpeded by the kind of bureaucratic holdups that can plague many other businesses.

This pragmatic realization, that private entrepreneurs and government officials make for the best partners, enabled Jiang Zemin to declare as new party dogma that the Communist Party could now, as of 2002, represent capitalists as well as workers. Jiang promulgated this new concept of the "Three Represents" to augment Deng Xiaoping's theory of building "socialism with Chinese characteristics."

Connections can also play an important role in something as simple as treating food poisoning. If you are living in China for an extended period of time and become ill, it is a good idea to ask your Chinese friends or hosts if they have any personal connections to a doctor who might be able to help you. Even if you have food poisoning and their connection is to a cardiologist, it doesn't matter. Their friend can use his connections with other doctors in his hospital to make sure you get superior care.

Guomindang
(Kuomintang or KMT)

The Guomindang is the Mandarin Chinese word for the Nationalist Party, which was founded in 1894 by Sun Yat-sen. At that time, he put together a "China Regeneration Society" in Honolulu to foment revolution in China and overthrow the corrupt Qing dynasty. The revolution finally took concrete form in October 1911 and succeeded in overthrowing the Manchu-led dynasty. In 1912, Sun's Nationalist Party became the ruling party of China, first with Sun as its head then Generalissimo Chiang Kai-shek. The Guomindang was defeated by the Chinese Communist Party in 1949. Chiang then fled with his remaining troops to the island of Taiwan, which he proclaimed the new home of the Republic of China.

The Nationalist Party remained in power on Taiwan until the 2000 presidential election. By that time, a faction of the Guomindang had formed its own party, known as the Independents. The vote was nearly a three-way tie but ultimately the Democratic Progressive Party (DPP) emerged victorious. In subsequent elections, Taiwan has remained a multiparty democracy; the KMT regained power in the 2008 and 2012 elections.

The Guomindang was practically a curse word in China during Mao Zedong's twenty-seven-year reign. However, since the mid-1990s the Nationalist Party has won China's favor as its members still espouse the pre-1949 belief that Taiwan is irrevocably part of mainland China, while the DPP is officially pro-independence for Taiwan.

From a practical point of view, China has not discriminated in business dealings with Taiwanese regardless of party affiliation.

Hand Gestures

Because Chinese cities have been very crowded and very noisy for more than a thousand years, hand gestures have become an important way for Chinese to communicate with each other, as simply trying to shout above the fray can be impossible.

Street vendors naturally are some of the most practiced in using gestures to communicate.

Chinese do not say "Come" the American way, by extending a hand palm up and curling up one finger. They will instead extend a hand palm downward and curl their fingers toward themselves. While to Western eyes this gesture can resemble a wave good-bye or a way to call to a small child, it is not a sign of disrespect. This is simply normal and neutral.

Other useful hand gestures are the signs for numbers one through ten, all of which can be made with one hand, depending on the way you hold up your fingers. This system developed because markets tend to be so noisy. Sometimes if a merchant can't hear how many of something you want, he or she will hold up a hand, fingers arranged just so, as a way of asking you if that's the correct number.

See the following illustrations for the numerical hand signs six through ten. (One to five are self-explanatory, so not shown here, but six through ten are based on the shape of the Chinese characters for these numbers.)

Other differences in hand gestures include pointing. When referring to themselves Chinese point to their noses to mean "I," not to

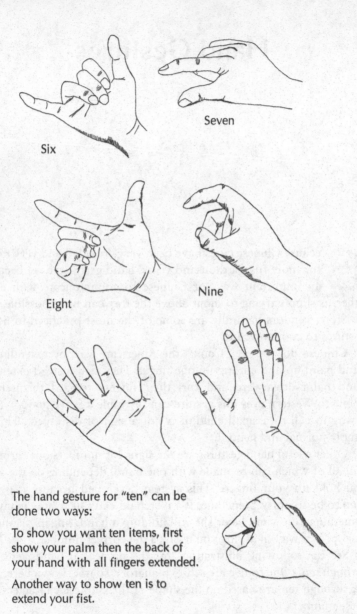

Seven

Six

Eight

Nine

The hand gesture for "ten" can be done two ways:

To show you want ten items, first show your palm then the back of your hand with all fingers extended.

Another way to show ten is to extend your fist.

their chests as Americans do. Similarly, when pointing to another person, they will point at that person's nose rather than the chest area. Again, this is not meant in a disrespectful way.

Southern Chinese will knock their bent fingers of one hand (sometimes just two fingertips) on the tabletop when you refill their teacup. This means both "Thank you" and "Stop pouring, that's enough." The gesture is rumored to have originated when an emperor wanted to go out in disguise as a commoner to survey the countryside. When he refilled one of his courtiers' teacups at an inn, the man could not bow without blowing the emperor's cover. So instead he bent his knuckles as though they were his knees then knocked them on the table in a symbolic kowtow (pinyin: *ketou*), which is the act of a commoner kneeling and knocking his forehead on the ground before the emperor to show respect.

This gesture is most common in Guangdong Province, Hong Kong, Taiwan, and Fujian Province. However, wherever southern Chinese have settled, set up businesses, and made their presence felt, this gesture can be seen. You can use it to show that you have enough tea (or other kind of beverage) and the pourer can stop refilling your cup.

Shaking hands when you meet someone, just as in America, is now a common practice in China.

As for obscene gestures, because of the popularity of American movies, a raised middle finger is recognized for what it is in China, even if it is not a traditional Chinese gesture. The older Chinese form of this nearly universal insult is a raised little finger. (However, the implication is slightly different. The raised pinky means "You have a small penis.")

Obviously, you don't want to raise your pinky and wave it in someone's face unless you like getting beat up.

Finally, when men are about to fight, they don't generally form fists as they do in America. Rather they might raise their unfolded hands before their faces, palms to the sides. Yes, Chinese actually do use martial arts in street fights, not just in movies.

History

Perhaps nothing is as important to understanding how Chinese people view themselves and the world as their sense of their history. They are extremely proud of China's five thousand years of history, its cultural sites, inventions, art, and continuity. However, the turmoil of the 150 years of Western imperialism and Communist political campaigns from roughly 1840 to 1989 have left the Chinese with a sense of shame, destiny unfilled, sorrow, and ambition that may be hard for the West to comprehend.

The following list of major conflicts and losses suffered by the Chinese from the decline of the Qing dynasty into the present will give you a sense of this part of China's humiliation and suffering.

1839–42   Opium War, fought between Britain and China. Result: Chinese forced to sign the Treaty of Nanjing, opening five treaty ports to unrestricted British trade (including the dumping of opium onto the Chinese market as a way to addict the populace); the loss of Hong Kong to Britain; the payment of 21 million taels (ounces) of silver to Britain as indemnity.

1843   Treaty of the Bogue. China must grant Britain "most favored nation" status, meaning any privilege granted by the Qing government to any other nation automatically will also be granted to Britain.

1844	Treaty of Wanghia. China must allow U.S. citizens the "principle of extraterritoriality," meaning they are exempt from Chinese law and cannot be tried in a Chinese court.
1858	Treaty of Tianjin. After Britain sent troops to the northern port city of Tianjin and threatened to attack, China was forced to grant Britain the right to open ten more port cities for trade, unrestricted freedom to preach Christianity, and the right to establish a British ambassador in Beijing.
1860	Sino-Russian Conflict. Russia gains control of Manchuria, Mongolia, and Chinese Turkestan.
1884–85	Sino-French Conflict. France gains the protectorate from China over Annam (present-day Vietnam).
1886	Loss of Burmese Territory. China coerced to give up sovereignty over Upper Burma to Great Britain.
1887	Loss of Macau. Portuguese formally obtain possession of Macau, where it had previously had informal ties and trade.
1894–95	Sino-Japanese War. Japan claims control of the Ryuku Islands by defeating Chinese forces in Korea, which comes under Japanese control as well.
1895	Treaty of Shimonoseki. China must give up Taiwan, the Pescadores Islands, part of Manchuria, and four more treaty ports and pay an indemnity of 200 million taels.
1900	Boxer Rebellion. Impoverished peasants, armed only with martial arts skills (called "boxing" in English in those days, hence the name), in northern China attack foreigners and Chinese Christian converts in an attempt to drive the foreigners out of China. A combined effort of eleven Western and Japanese military forces defeat the Boxers.
1901	Boxer Protocol. The Qing government is forced to agree to open more territory to Western and Japanese powers, allowing them to exploit the natural resources and trade there, as well as to pay an indemnity in silver greater than the Qing government's annual income.

1911   Chinese Republican Revolution. Chinese reformers
            gather forces with warlords and overthrow the corrupt
            Qing dynasty, forming the Republic of China.

1919   Treaty of Versailles. Although China supported the Al-
            lied forces, German-controlled territories in northern
            China are handed over to the Japanese rather than given
            back to China.

1921–28   Period of Warlordism. China disintegrates into regional
            armies run by warlords and is reunited under the Re-
            public flag only in 1928 by the Nationalist Party led by
            Chiang Kai-shek.

1932   Invasion of Manchuria. Japan takes over most of north-
            ern China and sets up the puppet nation of Manchuguo,
            under the nominal leadership of the former (and final)
            Qing emperor, Pu Yi.

1937–45   Sino-Japanese War. Japan invades China, starting in the
            north outside Beijing at the Marco Polo Bridge, then in-
            vades Shanghai, Nanjing (leading to the infamous Rape
            of Nanjing), and continues to move inland and south-
            ward, taking over territory as the Japanese Imperial
            Army progresses.

1945–49   Chinese Civil War. Chinese Communist Party forces and
            Nationalist troops fight, with the Communists ulti-
            mately winning and the Nationalists fleeing to Taiwan.

Following are the major political campaigns the Chinese people endured during the first four decades of life under Mao in the People's
Republic of China.

1950   Group Study (indoctrination into Communist Party
            ideas)

1951   Thought Reform (anti–U.S. imperialism campaign)
            Three Anti's Campaign (against corruption, waste, and
            "obstructionist bureaucracy")

1951–52   Five Anti's Mass Movement (against Chinese capitalists,
            entrepreneurs, and businesspeople who had stayed in
            China after 1949)

1952	Land Reform Movement (abolishment of private property)
1953	Agricultural Cooperative Movement (beginning of collectivization of farms)
1954	New Cultural Movement (purges of "anti-Party" writers)
1955	Reform of the Written Language Movement (official adoption of simplified Chinese characters and pinyin system of spelling)
1956	Hundred Flowers Campaign (to encourage intellectuals to critique the Communist Party)
1957	Anti-Rightist Rectification Drive (to punish intellectuals who critiqued the Communist Party in the previous campaign)
	Three Red Flags (term used by Mao to justify this campaign)
	Xia Fan Movement (policy to send intellectuals down to the countryside for "reeducation")
1958	People's Communes (continued efforts at collectivizing agriculture)
1958–61	Great Leap Forward (attempt to fast-track production leading to a three-year famine that killed more than 40 million Chinese)
1959	Anti-Tibet and Anti-India Movement
1960	Anti-Soviet Movement
1961	Cultural Renaissance Movement (brief liberalization movement promoting the study of traditional Chinese literature)
1962	Socialist Education Movement (reaction against the previous year's campaign)
1963	Study Maoist Thought
1964	Emulate the PLA (People's Liberation Army) Movements
1966	Cultural Revolution begins
1973	Anti–Lin Biao and Anti-Confucius Campaigns (movements to criticize so-called feudal aspects in society but really meant to purge Mao's rivals)
1976	Mao dies and the Cultural Revolution ends

Post-Mao political developments and movements:

1978–79	Democracy Wall Movement (spontaneous movement by Chinese people putting up posters in Beijing calling for political reform including democracy)
1982	Anti–Spiritual Pollution Campaign (movement to limit allegedly Western-inspired "decadence" in writing and the arts)
1989	Tiananmen Square Pro-Democracy Movement (a million Chinese students and workers demonstrate at Tiananmen Square in Beijing, calling for political reform and an end to corruption)
1989	Tiananmen Square Crackdown (aka "Six Four" in China; demonstrations in Beijing are stopped when the army shoots protesters and clears them from the capital on June 4)
1997	Deng Xiaoping dies.
2000–2002	Jiang Zemin introduces the concept of "Three Represents," which states that the Chinese Communist Party represents advanced social productive forces, advanced culture, and the interests of the overwhelming majority of the people. This concept essentially allowed capitalists to become members of the CCP. It was accepted by the Sixteenth Party Congress as the guiding ideology of the Chinese Communist Party in 2002, officially signaling China's shift toward state-controlled capitalism.

Many Western pundits have criticized young Chinese today for their lack of discernible political goals and seeming interest only in earning a lot of money, but perhaps it is easier to understand this generation's apparent political apathy after examining the horrific political campaigns their parents and grandparents were forced to endure.

Hong Kong

For most of the twentieth century, until 1997, Hong Kong was a colony of the British Empire. Hong Kong was originally ceded to Great Britain in 1842, after the Opium War, when the British used their superior military might to force the Qing dynasty–led government to open up China's ports to British traders. (It is called the Opium War because one of the products the British were most interested in selling to China was opium, which they then proceeded to dump on the Chinese market. After tens of thousands of addicts developed, they naturally raised the price.) Kowloon, the part of Hong Kong that is attached to mainland China, was annexed in 1860, and the New Territories, also on the mainland, were leased from China to Britain in 1898 for ninety-nine years. (For three years and eight months during World War II, Hong Kong was under Japanese control but was returned to Great Britain in 1945 after Japan was defeated by the Allies.)

When the New Territories' lease expired in 1997, all of Hong Kong (Hong Kong Island, better known as "Central" after its business district, as well as Kowloon and the New Territories) was returned to China under an agreement called "one country, two systems." That policy meant China would permit Hong Kong to continue its political and economic autonomy for fifty years. Thus, Hong Kong—capitalist haven—became part of the People's Republic of China.

Although Hong Kong is relatively small compared to China—measuring roughly 423 square miles with a total population of some

7 million residents—it became an economic powerhouse in the twentieth century, known as one of the "four tigers" of East Asia. Its population enjoyed the highest standard of living in Asia, second only to Japan's.

While much of Hong Kong's reputation has focused on its central position as a great place to shop, Hong Kong culture is rich, diverse, and one of the most exciting in the world. Hong Kong filmmakers such as Wong Kar-wai (director of such acclaimed films as *Days of Being Wild, Happy Together, In the Mood for Love,* and *2046*), John Woo (A *Better Tomorrow, Face/Off, Windtalkers, Mission: Impossible II*), Stanley Kwan (*Rouge, Centre Stage*), Stephen Chow (*Kung Fu Hustle*), Mabel Cheung (*The Soong Sisters*), Ann Hui (*Boat People, A Simple Life*), and many others have proven that they can compete artistically and commercially with the rest of the cinéaste world with art-house dramas and action-packed movies.

Hong Kong actors, artists, singers, designers, doctors, scientists, and academics have all made their mark not only in Asia but the world. And Hong Kong's unique blending of Chinese and Western culture is now cited as a model for development for most of China's major cities. (In fact, Hong Kong is a blend of *world* cultures, as its residents and businesspeople include people from every continent.)

Hong Kong people also enjoy considerable freedoms denied their mainland counterparts. The Falun Gong religion is not banned in Hong Kong, under the "one country, two systems" rules, and all residents can practice any religion they choose—or none at all—without registering with the government. The anniversary of the June 4, 1989, bloody crackdown is annually observed on Hong Kong, whereas its mention is still banned in China. Furthermore, English is the de facto second language of most educated Hong Kong people (behind Cantonese) although the mainland government did require all middle schools to begin instruction in Mandarin Chinese (a foreign tongue to most Hong Kong people) after the 1997 handover.

Hong Kong's gay and lesbian community has also enjoyed more openness than on the mainland. For example, many openly gay stars and directors have continued to work and write without suffering prejudice. One significant example was pop star and actor Leslie Cheung. Although he was openly gay and played two gay roles in very well known films (*Farewell, My Concubine* in 1992 and *Happy Together* in 1997), he continued to play macho kung fu stars, hetero lotharios, and other "straight" roles that would have been denied handsome but openly gay actors in the West.

Hong Kong people take pride in their unique, hybrid identity. In a 2012 survey only 16.6 percent of residents self-identified as Chinese, an all-time low since the 1997 handover. Meanwhile, protests against mainland-backed changes have been on the rise. In 2012 tens of thousands of people protested against proposed changes to the school curriculum, which would introduce mainland-style textbooks that include chapter titles like "The Destruction of the Bourgeois and the Victory of the Proletariat Are Inevitable." Other protests have erupted because of overcrowded maternity wards in hospitals where mainland mothers pay large sums so that their babies can have Hong Kong residency permits while local mothers are left to scramble to find a room.

Hong Kong's past glory as the capitalist center of Greater China has been gradually replaced by the rise of Shanghai as well as the movement of Asia's billionaires to Singapore. It is still a much freer place than any other city in the mainland, and citizens value their access to a free media, better education system, freedom to worship and to travel and to protest against and to criticize the government. Hong Kong still has an independent judiciary not subject to control by the Chinese Communist Party. Some observers believe this could eventually influence Chinese behavior on the mainland, but that remains to be seen.

Whether Hong Kong will be able to retain its unique place in the world in the coming decades is impossible to ascertain, but today it remains a gorgeous city of futuristic skyscrapers juxtaposed with traditional Chinese single-story shops, a population well versed in modern science and banking with a strong faith in feng shui, and some of the most hardworking people in Asia. Six-day workweeks of ten-to-fourteen-hour days are not uncommon for Hong Kong people—not just in sweatshops (which are increasingly rare as the real estate has become too pricey for low-end businesses) but for managers, businesspeople, actors, waiters, barmaids, and, well, just about everyone.

And, of course, Hong Kong is still known for its quintessential brunch, serving the best dim sum in Asia.

Human Rights

Every year Amnesty International issues Human Rights Reports detailing problems in countries around the world, and the report on China always details "serious and widespread human rights violations" throughout the country. China annually responds to the report with its own protest, citing everything from a lack of understanding of China's culture to China's nascent but underdeveloped legal system to the "hypocrisy" of the West for attacking China for practices that occur in many Western nations. That being said, serious human rights violations do occur in China, and the Chinese are well aware of these problems. In fact, the Chinese government does not necessarily condone many of the violations reported by Amnesty International but has not yet succeeded in finding a way to control the corruption, bureaucratic miscommunications, misinterpretation of laws, and sometimes outright lawlessness that leads to many of the abuses, such as detaining and beating at the local and provincial levels of human rights workers, AIDS workers, lawyers, grassroots peasants' rights activists, and members of religious groups.

Some of the continuing human rights problems include:

- Government crackdowns on Uighur activists in Xinjiang Province under the name of fighting "the war on terror" (the Chinese government disagrees that this is a human rights violation and insists the activists are proto-terrorists at best or terrorist cell builders who seek a separate Muslim state apart from China).

- A riot in Urumqi in 2009 was labeled "the most deadly episode of ethnic unrest in recent Chinese history" and ended in 156 deaths and more than one thousand people injured. Hundreds of ethnic Uighurs were later detained with reports from activists of prisoner abuse and no access to legal representation.
- Forced evictions and land grabs against farmers who are not adequately compensated (the government has stated that cracking down on such illegal and corrupt practices is a priority, yet it seems unable to control the practice, which leads to more than two hundred farmer-led protests per day in China)
- Restriction of freedom of expression (the government reserves the right to ban and censor news and the Internet and still controls all the media, which it considers an essential act to prevent anti-government attacks, although Chinese journalists and bloggers continue to raise the bar on free speech)
- Restriction of freedom of religion, especially in Tibet (again, the Chinese government justifies its policies in Tibet as necessary to prevent separatist movements from gaining ground)
- Use of torture on prisoners (denied by the government or blamed on "untrained" local police)
- Use of the death penalty after unfair trials (the government denies the trials are unfair and points out that the United States also uses the death penalty in its penal code)
- Violence against women (a problem the government acknowledges but has not been able to solve, especially in rural areas, where women may even be kidnapped and sold as brides due to a shortage of women and unwillingness of many to move to the countryside, where life is very harsh)
- Detentions and enforced disappearances of human rights defenders and their family members, such as the house arrest of Liu Xia, wife of imprisoned Nobel Peace Prize winner Liu Xiaobo. Other activists such as lawyer Gao Zhisheng simply disappeared and are suspected of being in official custody.
- Periodic crackdowns on political critics, especially Internet users (the government asserts its right to prevent what it calls conspirators trying to overthrow the government)

While these reports highlight many problems, the Chinese people and government are not necessarily ignorant of these issues nor do they necessarily disagree that they are problems. Certain issues, such as the use of the death penalty and the crackdown on what they view as dangerous separatists in Xinjiang, are not considered human rights violations by the Chinese, and they feel Amnesty does not understand the extent to which they need to act against what they perceive to be criminal and terrorist elements in society.

The Chinese people, especially activists, also have a definition of human rights violations different from Amnesty's. For example, many Chinese would list the huge disparity in income, access to health care, and education between rich urbanites and poor migrant workers as a huge human rights problem that they are trying to solve, and middle-class Chinese are increasingly worried about environmental pollution, official corruption, and the difficulty of their grown children to find jobs. Many human rights groups such as Amnesty do not emphasize such economic class issues per se, but anxiety about being left behind in China's fast-paced economy ranks very high among ordinary Chinese as a human rights issue. As such, the Chinese people have been willing to cede many of their political rights in the belief that only a strong centrally controlled government will be able to keep China stable and thus keep the economy growing. As to whether their faith will be borne out, only the future will tell.

Inner Mongolia Autonomous Region

Inner Mongolia remains the last reminder of Mongolian rule in China, when during the Yuan dynasty (1206–1368) the fierce Mongols led by Genghis Khan first conquered China, then ruled the nation for more than a hundred years. Today Inner Mongolia is part of China, although as an "autonomous region" it is afforded more political self-determination than a Chinese province. After the 1911 Nationalist revolution overthrew the Qing dynasty, Inner Mongolia became separated from Outer Mongolia, which became an independent state called the Republic of Mongolia.

The Chinese consider Inner Mongolia to be an important strategic buffer for the Chinese state, as it borders Russia and Mongolia proper, which is now a democracy. It is a vast region of 454,633 square miles, but is sparsely populated by the traditionally nomadic Mongolians across expansive grass steppes, with the Great Gobi Desert in the west.

Many native Mongolians still practice their traditional way of life, eschewing cities to live in tents (known as *ger* in Mongolian) and moving their animals to different pastures as needed.

Once known for their superior horsemanship (which allowed Genghis Khan to overtake the Song emperor's armies in the thirteenth century), today motorcycles are becoming more popular with young people, and the elderly fear that Sinicization will eventually eradicate Mongol culture. In fact, Mongolians are a minority in their homeland, comprising only 15 percent of the population, which is now 85 percent Han Chinese. Furthermore, the enticement of the city lifestyle, with its more lucrative jobs and easier way of life along with increased access to world culture via satellite TV and DVDs, draws the young away from the old traditions.

Interracial
Relationships

If you are a Chinese male and your wife is not Chinese, you're not generally going to have to worry. You're a majority person; you can do as you please. Your wife, however, may feel at times alienated. (It's important to help her build up a support network of friends, Chinese and non-Chinese, to improve her situation.) If the situation is reversed, and an ethnically Chinese woman is with a man of a different race or ethnicity, the onus may fall on her to justify the relationship if people have problems with interracial dating. (Some new religious cults in fact outright preach against interracial dating.)

What to do? For a short trip with a tour group, let your guide know immediately your concerns. Your guide and the tour company are responsible for your safety and your enjoyment. They will do their best to keep bigoted people at bay. If you are a student, make friends with as many Chinese as you can. Ask their advice. Find out from other students in similar relationships where are the safest clubs and restaurants, friendliest businesses, and so on to frequent. Build a safety net of friends for yourself so that individuals with chips on their shoulders will have a hard time—and socially unacceptable time—harassing you and your partner. Similarly, if you are planning an extended stay, such as for business, research, or long-term study, let your Chinese hosts know your concerns early on. You can put this in a tactful way, such as, "I wanted to let you know that my wife and I are of different races. Is this going to be a problem?" Of course your host will say no, but now the burden is on your host to make sure it won't be a problem for you.

In the 1920s and '30s, many leading intellectuals in China openly advocated interracial relationships as a means of improving the Chinese race. They felt China had become too insular and thus to make up for lost time, they urged Chinese to marry foreigners. Nonetheless, as back then, many Chinese still remain deeply suspicious of interracial relationships.

Images on television and in Chinese-made films may show a Chinese man with a white woman, but they will rarely show the reverse. (This perhaps is not as odd as it seems, as American movies and television shows often show white men with Asian women but also rarely show the reverse.)

During the 1980s there were numerous anti-African riots on campuses across the country, often sparked by images of African students dating Chinese women.

Today the situation is somewhat improved. African American sports stars, for example Shaquille O'Neal and Damon Jones, have been signed to represent Chinese-brand sneakers because of their enormous popularity and the fact they are seen as having more "street credibility" than Chinese basketball stars. Tiger Woods, who is well known in China for having an African American father and Chinese Thai mother, is enormously popular, too. Chinese newspapers have run many favorable articles on famous stars who have some Chinese in their background, including supermodel Naomi Campbell.

Therefore, in urban areas, interracial couples—black and Asian, white and Asian—as well as interethnic couples, are generally accepted and not considered shocking to people.

In general, Chinese people are very friendly. Race relations have improved vastly since the periodic racially motivated demonstrations of the 1980s as China has become increasingly open to the world and exposed to more kinds of people. Also, as China's economy has improved, the Chinese have become more self-confident and less threatened by the sight of, say, a Chinese woman with a black man. However, the world is never perfect; there will always be a few rotten apples. There's no need to fear loving someone of a different race in China nor should fear of others' reactions be so great as to prevent you from taking a trip of a lifetime or a great business opportunity or a study abroad program in China. Just remember: surround yourself with friends and people friendly to you. Individualism is not necessarily valued in China. Making a group of friends is always a good idea.

Jiang Qing

Jiang Qing (1914–49) was the last of Chairman Mao's three wives and by far the most notorious. (The others died before Mao and Jiang married.) Jiang was a member of the infamous Gang of Four who participated as leaders of the disastrous ten-year-long Cultural Revolution (1966–76).

In her youth, Jiang (whose name is pronounced "jahng cheeng") was a minor film star in Shanghai. She married Mao Zedong in 1938 during the early years of the Communists' civil war against China's pre-1949 leader, Generalissimo Chiang Kai-shek. Later, she used her film connections to oversee the production of propaganda films and plays for Mao's army.

Jiang was arrested after Mao's death in 1976 and sentenced to life in prison for her role in promoting the Cultural Revolution. Unrepentant to the end, she famously harangued the judges at her trial and denounced them all for hypocrisy to the "revolution." She hanged herself in the summer of 1991.

Jiang Zemin

Jiang Zemin, as China's first president after Deng Xiaoping's death, presided over the fastest expansion of China's economy and increase in personal wealth of the entire twentieth century. Although he could not officially assume power until Deng's death in 1997, he in fact enjoyed much power throughout most of the 1990s as Deng's health was failing.

Jiang was born in Yangzhou, Jiangsu Province, in 1926, and graduated from Shanghai Jiaotong University in 1947 with an engineering degree. He also studied in Moscow in 1955. He worked as a technocrat in various ministries before becoming the mayor of Shanghai from 1985 to 1987.

He was handpicked by Deng to become premier in Beijing after the Tiananmen Square pro-democracy protests ended in bloodshed in 1989, in large part because Jiang had handled earlier student demonstrations in Shanghai without ordering a single shot to be fired at protesters. This combination of pragmatism and savvy was seen as appropriate for leading China into the new decade.

Jiang is considered exceptionally cosmopolitan for a party member of his generation. He has a gregarious personality and avid interest in the West. He once bragged that he'd memorized Lincoln's Gettysburg Address. He is credited with improving U.S.-China relations after the horror of the Tiananmen Square bloody crackdown, and famously appeared on U.S. television, speaking in English, with interviewer

Barbara Walters. He also was known to recite poetry and even break into song while entertaining foreign diplomats.

More reticent party members privately expressed some alarm but chalked up Jiang's behavior to all the years he'd spent in cosmopolitan Shanghai.

Jiang made several innovations to Chinese Communist Party doctrine. In 1997 he first introduced his new concept of the "Three Represents" to augment Deng's theory of "socialism with Chinese characteristics." Under the "Three Represents" policy, the party could "represent the development trend of China's advanced production forces; the orientation of China's advanced culture; and the fundamental interests of the overwhelming majority of the Chinese people." What this boiled down to in practical terms was that capitalists and business entrepreneurs could join the Communist Party. Marx and Mao might have been spinning in their graves, but the party enshrined the doctrine into its constitution in 2002.

Also breaking with precedent, Jiang actually stepped down from power in 2002, allowing Hu Jintao to take over as president and general secretary of the party, rather than clinging to power until he died, as Deng and Mao had done.

Jiang reemerged as a powerbroker leading up to the 2013 change in leadership, working behind the scenes to push his protégés to power. He had been so quiet for years that there were periodic rumors both in the Chinese blogosphere and in the international press that he had died. However, all rumors were put to rest in 2011 when he was seen and photographed at party events in Beijing. Rumors about his political irrelevance were also quashed when five of his protégés were appointed to the most powerful ruling body in China, the seven-member Politburo Standing Committee including, most significantly, Xi Jinping, who was named general secretary of the Communist Party in 2012 and president of China in 2013.

Kunming

Kunming, the capital of Yunnan Province in southwestern China, is known as the City of Eternal Spring because of its temperate climate. However, visitors should remember that spring is a fickle season in general and plan accordingly. Brief but chilly snow showers can still occur in the winter months.

Kunming is also one of China's most unusual cities because of the large number of ethnic minorities who maintain a highly visible presence there. Visitors will encounter not only Han Chinese but dozens of other ethnic groups, who can be differentiated from the Han by their traditional attire, including brightly embroidered clothing, unusual tribal markings, and body piercings. Kunming truly looks like a global market with its mix of urbanites sporting Western high fashion, minority women in tall black headdresses, men and women with unusual facial tattoos, people with their teeth stained bloodred from chewing betel nut, ethnic travelers from inner Yunnan and its autonomous region (Xishuang Banna) coming to trade or look for work in the capital, and large numbers of foreign tourists and businesspeople.

The history of Kunming is similarly diverse. When the Mongols captured Kunming in the late thirteenth century (after overthrowing the Song dynasty and founding their own Yuan dynasty in 1279), Muslim traders from along the Silk Road came to Kunming in large numbers. Thus, ethnic Chinese who practice Islam, known as the Hui (pronounced "hway") people, form a large presence in the city into the present. Later, Kunming became the refuge of last resort for the Ming imperial family after the Ming capital in Beijing was overtaken by the Manchus in 1645. More recently, in World War II, Kunming played an essential role for the Allies fighting against the Japanese. The famed Burma Road was built to connect Kunming with Lashio, Burma, in an attempt to create a land route to bring in supplies to the Chinese forces after the Japanese cut off access to all China's seaports. The U.S. volunteer air force called the Flying Tigers flew out of Kunming to bring supplies to the Allied forces stationed in Chongqing, a perilous journey dubbed the Hump Air Route as the pilots had to navigate over many mountains. A memorial in honor of the Flying Tigers is located in suburban Kunming. And in honor of U.S. general Joseph Stilwell, who trained Chinese ground forces, the first China-to-India highway, which originates in Kunming, has been named the Stilwell Highway.

Kunming is a beautiful, verdant city with many parks filled with subtropical plants including camellias, magnolias, azaleas, and roses. There are many sparkling lakes and the city is surrounded by mountains with caves open to exploration and tours.

Travelers should note that because southern Yunnan borders Burma, Kunming is part of the famed Golden Triangle and heroin smuggling has returned to the city. Furthermore, areas outside Kunming become very rural very quickly and there are traffickers who resort to kidnapping to sell brides to inland farmers. While white and black tourists need not fear kidnapping, Asian women of childbearing age should be forewarned it is not terribly safe to wander by oneself far from the city or outside the sight of groups of other people. If you should find yourself in a dicey situation, the most important thing is to convince your attackers that you are not a Chinese citizen. It might be worth your time to learn to say in Mandarin, "I'm an American!" (You can ask your tour guide or a Chinese friend to teach you this simple phrase with proper tones.)

Li Keqiang

Li Keqiang was named China's premier in March 2013, becoming one of the most powerful leaders of the Chinese government, second only to Xi Jinping, the president and general secretary of the Communist Party. Li was born in 1955 in Anhui Province, and came of age during the Cultural Revolution. After he graduated high school in 1974, he was sent down to the countryside like many educated and urban youths of the time, but perhaps because his father was already a Communist Party official, he was allowed to join the party and moved back to the city to study at Peking University where he eventually received his Ph.D. in economics.

Like many high-ranking Chinese cadres, Li had much experience governing before rising in rank. He served as governor of Henan Province from 1998 to 2002, where he was officially credited with improving economic development. Some of his actions weren't as admirable: during this time he also helped to cover up an AIDS scandal that had resulted from a previous governor's policy of promoting blood sales as a way for the province's 100 million impoverished farmers and coal miners to earn extra income. On the more positive side, as governor of Liaoning Province in 2004, Li reduced massive unemployment and built huge tracts of housing for millions of poor farmers and workers.

The American media have characterized Li fairly favorably. The *New York Times* noted that he came from a "liberal background" at

Peking University, where he demonstrated an avid interest in Western ideas and law, and even went so far as to compliment him: "Arguably China's best-educated leader, Mr. Li speaks confident English." Meanwhile the BBC cited an American diplomatic cable that called Li "engaging and well-informed." Whether his educational background will make him a more effective premier than his predecessor, Wen Jiabao, remains to be seen.

Long March

The Long March (1934–35) refers to the near-mythic retreat of Chinese Communists and what was then called the Red Army across the country to escape persecution by the Nationalists led by Generalissimo Chiang Kai-shek. As a result of the trek, Mao Zedong rose within the Communist Party to become its helmsman. His later allies and the next generation of party leaders all participated in the Long March, including Deng Xiaoping.

According to Western journalist Edgar Snow's famous account, *Red Star Over China*, the Communists covered some 6,000 miles in 235 days on foot, crossing eighteen mountain ranges, twenty-four rivers, and eleven provinces. Originally, the Communists numbered about 100,000 men and women. However, when they finally arrived at their new base in Yan'an in remote, northern Shaanxi Province, only 10,000 people had survived. A Soviet adviser to the Chinese Communist Party, Otto Braun, also survived the journey.

Some contemporary scholars have cast doubt on some of the statistics of the Long March, including its exact distance, the number of fatalities, and even its duration. For example, Yale historian Jonathan Spence writes that the Long March lasted 370 days and estimates that there were between 8,000 and 9,000 survivors out of a total of 80,000 participants. Nevertheless, it cannot be doubted that the march served as a crucible for the party. While in Yan'an, Mao began to solidify his base and to work on creating his image as the leader of

New China. He had former leftist filmmakers from Shanghai film him practicing calligraphy—an important propaganda image as it proved he was not illiterate but a worthy successor like the emperors of old. Other propaganda images included shots of a unified People's Liberation Army holding mass exercises, men and women performing drills together (although in fact, they were so ill-equipped the soldiers often had to scrounge weapons from the dead following battles between Nationalist forces and Japanese troops). He also began working on his philosophical treatises, known as Mao Zedong Thought, and began censoring critics. At one point, he even banned the use of irony by writers (as party censors had great difficulty picking out these stories and articles).

Mao's propaganda efforts paid off and he attracted more and more intellectuals into the party as many Chinese grew disgusted with the corruption that they had witnessed under Chiang Kai-shek. He also insisted his army would "serve the people" and soldiers were required to pay local peasants for any items—whether cooking oil or chickens—that they might need whereas desperately underfunded Nationalist troops and warlord-controlled armies were often terrifying to the local populations where they fought battles, as they would steal whatever food and weapons they could find in the villages. Sometimes they also kidnapped young men as new "recruits" and reports of rape were common. Mao, who himself came from a peasant background, absolutely forbade his troops from kidnapping or raping the peasants. Many images were created, both drawings and photographs, showing Mao eating with his troops and with peasants, laughing and smiling, a man of the people.

As a result, Mao was able to increase army ranks from 180,000 in late 1938 to an estimated 500,000 in 1940. Party membership swelled to 800,000 by 1940. He was also able to gain more territory, promising to protect the villages that pledged allegiance to him, so that while he controlled an area of only 1.5 million civilians in 1936, that number grew to 96 million people by 1945. It was only four years later, in 1949, that Mao was able to take control of all China from Chiang Kai-shek by convincing warlord after warlord to join his forces and abandon the corrupt Nationalists.

For nearly six decades the Long March was lionized in Chinese textbooks and all its survivors treated as heroes. Two generations of Communist Party leaders emerged from the Long March, and it was long considered a liability for party members if they did not have direct ties to the Long March. It was only in 2006 that new textbooks in elite Shanghai schools began to deemphasize Mao's revolutionary heroics, relegating the Long March to a few paragraphs in junior high and emphasizing more modern, technological achievements in China. However, the mythos of the Long March will not be completely over until all those Chinese schooled in its history have died.

Macau

Macau, a small area roughly ten square miles in size near Hong Kong, is the gambling capital of the world, generating $34 billion in gambling revenue in 2012, more than five times what rival hot spot Las Vegas earned in the same period.

How Macau went from a former Portuguese colony made up of sleepy fishing villages to a glitzy gambling paradise is a particularly late twentieth-century story, possible only after Macau reverted back to Chinese control in 1999. As part of the agreement with Portugal, which had made Macau a colony in 1557, the Chinese government agreed to guarantee that Macau's capitalist economic system would remain in place for at least fifty years.

Macau, which consists of a peninsula and two small islands, was made a Portuguese colony in 1557. However, in 1999, Macau reverted back to Chinese control. As part of the arrangement, the Chinese government agreed to guarantee that Macau's capitalist economic system would remain in place for at least fifty years.

During World War II, Portugal's neutrality made Macau a haven for southern Chinese and Hong Kong residents fleeing Japanese occupation. After the Chinese Communists won the civil war on the mainland, Macau remained a capitalist enclave under Portuguese rule. As a result, Hong Kong capitalists turned Macau into a gambler's paradise—replete with rival gangsters fighting for control, frightening assassinations, and a fairly open business in prostitution and other vices.

The economy of Macau had been flailing for years before the 1999 takeover by the Chinese government, in large part due to these mob wars, which scared away tourists. In an effort to revitalize the local economy, China spent $20 billion to build some twenty-five new casinos and hotels, including ventures with many American gambling resort giants.

The Chinese government's investments more than paid off as Macau's fortunes have risen steadily since the takeover. Within a decade, Macau had surpassed Las Vegas in gambling revenue, attracting 18 million tourists and generating $8 billion in gambling revenue compared to Vegas's roughly $6 billion.

Unfortunately, Macau's more unsavory elements have prospered as well. Macau's organized crime gangs have now moved into mainland Chinese cities, and Macau is believed to be a major center of money-laundering. While mainlanders flock to Macau's casinos, they are barred by Chinese law from taking more than $50,000 out of the country per year, yet high-stakes players have been known to go through $10,000 to $40,000 *per hand*. Most of these players depend upon "junkets," middlemen in Macau who loan money to gamblers then collect the debts in mainland China. There are as many as ten thousand people working in the junket industry in Macau, which was responsible for 75 percent of the gambling revenue in 2012. Meanwhile, U.S. government reports estimate many junkets were connected to organized crime gangs known as "triads."

The Chinese government has vowed to crack down on corruption in Macau. A high-profile lawsuit filed in 2012 by an American working for the Macau branch of an American casino has shed light onto the often shadowy world of junkets, casinos, and triads. The ongoing investigation has caught the attention of Nevada gaming officials and the scrutiny of the Justice Department and the Securities and Exchange Commission. While the Chinese and U.S. government struggle to put a damper on Macau casinos' ties to crime, Macau continues its reign as the center of the gambling world.

Mao Zedong

Mao Zedong (1893–1976) remains a complex figure, both reviled and beloved by different sections of the Chinese population. Although most intellectuals decry his wrong-headed economic policies, paranoia, and endlessly destructive political campaigns, which kept China isolated and impoverished from 1949 until his death, many peasants still revere him. As the economic boom of the reform era has left many in the countryside further and further behind the urban nouveaux riches and emerging middle class, Mao's slogan "Learn from the peasants!" creates nostalgia for the days when at least someone in China's government considered them important. In fact, shrines and small temples built in honor of Chairman Mao have appeared throughout the countryside, where impoverished farmers go to pray to Mao for help, such is their hopelessness and despair in contemporary times.

As a result, while Mao is generally demonized in the West, it is wise for visitors to China to remember he is still an important symbol and he should not be publicly denigrated. Some Chinese may criticize him because they suffered under his policies, but unless you're speaking with close friends, a foreigner's criticism of Mao can be mistaken for condescension toward China in general and even a kind of insouciance about the suffering caused by his policies.

Mao was born in 1893 in Hunan Province to a peasant family that was wealthy enough to educate their son. At the end of World War I, he traveled to Beijing, where he found work as a librarian at Beijing

University, where the May Fourth cultural movement originated. He became a founding member of the Chinese Communist Party in 1921.

From 1927 to 1935, Mao rose through the ranks of the party to emerge as its leader. This was a period of great turmoil, as Chiang Kai-shek decided to destroy the Communist Party in 1927 and had five thousand of its members in Shanghai killed, even though he had before that time joined forces with them in order to unite China, which had disintegrated into regions controlled by warlords between 1912 and 1928. After the massacres in Shanghai, the Chinese Communists began to form secret cells throughout other cities. By 1934, they were forced to retreat on foot to a remote northwestern part of Shaanxi Province. The six-thousand-mile journey, known as the Long March, was initially devastating for the party, as only one in ten of the original marchers survived. After establishing a new base in Shaanxi, in an area called Yan'an, Mao emerged as the leader of the party for his charisma, endurance, and political views.

Mao's reinterpretation of Marxist-Leninist thought paved the way for Communism to take further root in China. He believed that China could not follow the Soviet model, which depended upon a large urban worker, or proletariat, class. Instead, he felt China's huge peasant class could be used to form the basis of the party. Most party intellectuals knew little about the countryside. Here Mao's peasant background became essential to recruiting new members from the disenfranchised and impoverished farmers, who made up more than 80 percent of China's population. For one, he insisted his army, named the People's Liberation Army, treat the local population with respect. While Chiang's impoverished forces often "requisitioned" provisions by simply stealing from the nearby and nearly starving villages where they were stationed, Mao forbade his soldiers from stealing from the peasantry. Rape, pillage, looting, and banditry were forbidden and punishable by death. He created a well-disciplined force, even if they were not particularly well armed, but more important, he created an image of a new Chinese leader whose goal was to "serve the people" rather than exploit them.

By 1945, after the Japanese had been defeated and were forced to leave China, Mao could launch his attack against Chiang Kai-shek's Nationalist government in earnest. Sickened by the corruption of Chiang's regime, many generals decided to side with the charismatic and seemingly plain-living and honest Chairman Mao. In 1949, Chiang fled the mainland, and on October 1, Mao declared the founding of the People's Republic of China in Beijing, the former capital of the Qing dynasty.

However, the rest of Mao's achievements are more ambiguous and some downright despicable. Mao launched a series of nearly endless political campaigns to remake Chinese society. He collectivized farms, banned individual landownership, punished intellectuals and capitalists, purged the party of leaders who might oppose him, and most famously launched the Cultural Revolution in 1966, which disrupted the entirety of China for a decade until he died in 1976.

Books published since his death, including a two-volume biography written by his personal physician, have painted a new portrait of Mao, this time as despot, not savior. According to his doctor, he knowingly spread venereal disease to hundreds (if not more) of unsuspecting young girls from the countryside who were chosen for the "honor" of satisfying the chairman's perverse sexual needs. Far from being the patriot who fought bravely against the Japanese army during its invasion of China from 1937 to 1945, he secretly tried to broker a ceasefire between the Communists and the Japanese Imperial Army, even offering up Chinese territory if Japan would recognize his government over Chiang Kai-shek's. His wrongheaded policies of the Great Leap Forward (1959–62) led to the deaths of an estimated 40 to 60 million Chinese. No one knows even today how many Chinese died during the Cultural Revolution. Estimates range from hundreds of thousands to millions. His environmental policies of deforestation are still felt today every time dust storms blow across the city of Beijing.

Mao's wife, Jiang Qing, was imprisoned for life in 1976 for her role in the Cultural Revolution as part of the infamous Gang of Four. His only known child, a son, died fighting during the Korean War.

Today, Mao's preserved body is entombed on Tiananmen Square, and foreign tourists may view it as well as Chinese. Long lines of Chinese, mostly from the countryside, still queue up to view the chairman. Men remove their hats before his glass-enshrouded corpse and many weep.

As a visitor to China, it is essential to maintain an air of respect before his body regardless of your personal feelings about the man. To the suffering Chinese farmers who still revere him, a sign of disrespect to Mao would only be another wound to their already heavy hearts.

Martial Arts

When Russian president Vladimir Putin visited China in 2006, he had one special request. He asked to see the famed Shaolin Temple, thus becoming the first head of state to formally visit China's most famous school for martial arts. Putin, like many people around the world, is fascinated by Chinese martial arts and is, in fact, an accomplished practitioner of the Japanese martial art of judo.

In China, martial arts are known as *wu shu* (pronounced "woo shoe"), which means literally "martial methods" but was historically called *wu yi*, "martial arts," which demonstrates the esteem with which the Chinese regard the discipline. (The more familiar American term, *kung fu*, derives from the Chinese term *gong fu*, which refers to talented practitioners in any physical skill, not just martial arts.)

Far from being viewed as simply a sport or a means of fighting, in China *wu shu* is considered an art form, a philosophy, and a means to cultivate unity of the body, the soul, and the universe. The true goal of *wu shu* is not to beat up somebody, but to attain spiritual enlightenment for oneself through the strict physical and mental discipline that *wu shu* requires. Buddhist and Daoist monasteries are often the centers of martial arts training. The Shaolin Temple, for example, teaches the Chan school of Buddhism (known as Zen in the West), which emphasizes long periods of meditation to purify the mind. The meditation sessions also help the monks to keep focused during their *wu shu* practice, which helps them to sustain themselves physically during their meditation, a circular process considered essential to attaining their spiritual goals.

Altogether the official Chinese Wu Shu Association recognizes 129 different forms of martial arts. Eleven are allowed to be used in athletic competitions.

Despite the diversity in styles, there are a few general factors that are used in categorizing martial arts:

- Internal versus external
- Southern versus Northern
- Shaolin, Wudan, or Ermei schools

Internal martial arts emphasize the strength in the upper body and legs whereas external refers to very specific training of the arm and leg muscles. Northern and Southern styles refer to regional differences. For example, director Zhang Yimou said when he made the film *Hero* he wanted to emphasize northern martial arts schools as opposed to what he saw as the southern and "softer" (some might say more fluid) style exhibited in director Ang Lee's film *Crouching Tiger, Hidden Dragon*. The Shaolin school refers to the style taught to the Buddhist monks in the Henan Province temple, which was established some 1,500 years ago. Wudang refers to the style originally developed by Daoists in Hubei Province, and Ermei is named after the famed mountain, a Buddhist holy site, in Sichuan Province.

Competitions divide practitioners into six categories:

- Empty hands forms (meaning no weapons allowed)
- Weapons forms
- Choreographed routines (two or more people)
- Group practice
- Sparring competition
- Qigong power demonstrations

Each category involves very complicated demonstrations of one's skills. For example, the so-called empty hands form can be subdivided into myriad styles. One form, known as Long Fist, is associated with the Shaolin monks and can comprise up to thirty different forms of fighting. Southern Fist is a separate division that developed largely in Guangdong Province, with more than four hundred forms originating in the city of Guangzhou (Canton) alone. Other forms include those based on imitating the movements of animals, such as Praying Mantis, Eagle Claw, Monkey, Tiger, Leopard, and even Duck form. There is even one very fluid style called Drunken style because the practitioner's weaving motions, although highly controlled, appear similar to those of a drunk man.

In weapons competitions, traditionally more than four hundred types of Chinese weapons could be used but now only eighteen standard weapons are allowed in competition, including the broadsword, straight sword, various spears and staffs, double swords, double hook swords, double-ended spears, nine-section whips, rope-darts, and daggers.

Qigong competitions are unique in that they emphasize the strength that their practitioners' intensive breath training as well as physical workouts have given them.

Elements that apply to all the martial arts styles include kicking, striking, throwing, hitting, thrusting, and something called "controlling," which actually includes rather nasty-sounding moves like joint locks, striking of nerve points, the painful extension of muscles and tendons, and the obstruction of breathing or the flow of blood in one's opponent.

Martial arts can be practiced by men and women. In fact some of China's earliest written histories describe a *wu shu* contest in the Western Zhou dynasty (1122–771 BCE) in which a woman beat three thousand contestants to become China's master swordsfighter. Her methods were thus studied for thousands of years.

Many forms of martial arts in other Asian countries originated in China, including the Japanese styles known as karate (which is derived from southern Chinese schools of *wu shu*), jujitsu (which developed in the sixteenth century based on the writings of a Chinese martial artist), and judo (which was codified by a Japanese man in the nineteenth century based on Chinese wrestling or "throwing" methods). However, over time these forms developed their own unique points and training methods, so they are no longer technically considered Chinese martial arts.

Nowadays, foreigners are welcomed to participate in Chinese martial arts competitions and schools. In fact, more than two thousand competitors from sixty-six countries and many Chinese provinces have gathered for the World Traditional Wu Shu Championships in Henan Province. The renowned Shaolin Temple has accepted more than three hundred foreign disciples to study martial arts.

People who want to study martial arts in China can contact schools and temples directly. People who would rather watch can find tours specifically geared toward martial arts displays. The Shaolin Temple routinely holds festivals where its monks and as many as fifteen thousand local martial arts disciples display their skills. The temple opens in the morning for visitors but closes by 5 p.m. Visitors may stay in the small town of Dengfeng, where the temple is located, or the larger cities of Luoyang and Zhengzhou in Henan Province and take tour buses from their hotels to visit the temple.

Medicine
(Traditional)

Traditional Chinese medicine has always operated on very different principles from Western-style medicine. From the earliest forms of Chinese medicine to the present, these remedies have sought to restore balance to the body and work systemically rather than taking the Western, twentieth-century approach of trying to attack one disease and cure it. Much of Chinese medicine involves boiling herbal mixtures for long periods of time, then drinking the strained liquid that's left behind. Other remedies include acupuncture, which requires the practitioner to place needles along the meridians of the body that control the flow of qi (that is, the person's life force); moxibustion or cupping, which involves placing glass cups onto the back of the patient (the air is first sucked out of the cup using a match or similar lighted object, so that the cup attaches to the skin through suction); diagnosis by examining a person's iris or ear or pulse; and, mostly in rural areas and often among minority peoples, shamanistic-type rituals.

The goal of Chinese traditional medicine remedies is to restore the balance of yin and yang (negative and positive forces) within the body so the body can heal itself. This concept shows the early Daoist influences in Chinese medicine as the Daoists experimented with herbs, roots, and ground-up bones and antlers while searching for the elixir of immortality. In the course of their hundreds of years of herbal cataloging, they found combinations of ingredients useful for treating a great variety of illnesses.

Today in China people use a combination of traditional and Western medicine. Many Chinese still swear by traditional medicines; however, many fake brands using inferior products have sprung up, making it essential to go to a reliable herbalist. Some traditional medicines also use animal products such as snake bile (excellent for curing a chest cold and sore throat), as well as ground tiger bones, rhinoceros horns, and elephant tusks. Many of these latter potions are of doubtful efficacy but are sold as Viagra-like products to cure impotency. As a result, tigers, rhinos, elephants, and varied other animals have been hunted mercilessly to fill the market for these drugs. For the last fifteen years the Chinese government has been trying to crack down on traffickers in illegal animal parts, with uneven success.

Chinese herbal medicine is growing in popularity in the United States but this is hardly a new phenomenon. In the late nineteenth century and the first three decades of the twentieth century, Chinese herbalists were some of the only doctors on the West Coast as Caucasian doctors trained in East Coast medical schools saw little profit in the small prospecting towns and far-flung ranches and farms that dotted the Western states. However, Chinese herbalists would travel from site to site, earning quite a decent living. When East Coast doctors first began coming to California in large numbers in the early twentieth century, they were shocked to discover that white settlers refused to come to them and still preferred the Chinese immigrant herbalists. Many Western states passed laws trying to reduce "competition" from Chinese herbalists by requiring onerous English-language-only exams to become licensed. However, as court cases and newspaper accounts of the era prove, even when it was obvious that a Chinese herbalist was technically running an illegal practice, all-white juries refused to convict him. Such was the case of Dr. Ing Hay, whose renown was great for healing patients in Idaho, Oregon, and Washington State, and who was credited with curing one boy's blood poisoning, saving all his patients during the flu pandemics of 1915 and 1919, and providing cures for meningitis. Although he was later charged with practicing medicine illegally, no jury would convict him.

It was only when the importation of herbs became nearly impossible due to restrictive state laws and the disruption of trade due to the Chinese Civil War of the 1940s, that Chinese medicine fell largely by the wayside for the West Coast's non-Chinese population. However, by the 1980s Chinese herbal remedies were once again in vogue and today in the twenty-first century even Stanford University offers acupuncture clinics to pregnant mothers as a normal therapy course to combat depression and other ills.

Many American insurance plans and HMOs offer acupuncture as a routine part of their coverage, especially in California, where access to trained and licensed acupuncturists is common. Today acupuncture in both the United States and China is widely used to treat pain, repetitive stress injuries, infertility, and many other imbalances in the body.

Hotels in China often offer access to both Western and traditional Chinese doctors and medicine. Generally, herbal medicine bought from these hotels' on-site pharmacies will not be counterfeits. If your hotel does not have an acupuncturist on duty, ask at the front desk or the concierge for a referral. (Even if you are not a guest, you can pretend that you are. Most staff members will not demand ID from a foreigner for this type of request.) You can also ask your Chinese hosts, friends, or guide to give you advice or even accompany you if you want to buy medicine or see a traditional doctor, to ensure that you receive the proper herbs and treatment. This will not be seen as an imposition as they will feel responsible for you anyway should you become ill.

Migrant Workers

Who are they? About 252 million people in China.
What do they do? Make everything that people in other countries buy: clothes, purses, shoes, toys, furniture, tools, solar panels, smart phones, computer pads and netbooks, computer tablets, e-readers, printers, and much, much more.

Unlike migrant workers in the United States, these people are not foreigners coming to work seasonally in another country. They are Chinese citizens, born in the countryside, who have left their hometowns to find work in the cities. However, like many migrant workers in the United States, China's migrant workers are treated like "illegal aliens" in the cities in which they live. They do not have the right to live in the city in which they work except temporarily, which is why factories build dormitories, hospitals, and even recreational centers for their workers.

Since the 1950s, all Chinese are required to live where they were born, or where their household registration (known as a *hukou*) is, unless they can change their registration. If you're born in a village, your *hukou* is that village. If you're born in Shanghai, your *hukou* is Shanghai if both your parents are official city residents. However, if the mother is a migrant worker and the father a city resident and they are not married to each other, then by law their baby's *hukou* is the same as the mother's. As a result, this policy does very little to discourage some unscrupulous bosses from having affairs with or sexually harassing the young women from the countryside who work for them as the young women have very few rights.

Migrant workers do not have the right to social services in the city—such as welfare, medical care, or housing benefits—nor can they put their children in public schools. Therefore, many migrant workers leave their children behind in their villages. If they can save enough money, they will try to send their children to private schools in cities near their hometowns, where the teachers and educational resources are believed to be better than in the countryside. The children often live at the schools, but these schools are far from the rich environment of traditional Western boarding schools. In the 2008 Sichuan earthquake these schools for migrant workers' children collapsed first whereas city government buildings right beside them were left standing, as the schools were built of substandard materials. Some five thousand students were believed to have been killed; the Chinese government never released an official list of the dead.

Migrant workers are generally allowed only one vacation per year: the traditional lunar new year holiday that can fall sometime between January and February. This may be the only time they get paid as well, as some factories save up the workers' wages for the end of the year so they won't quit and leave earlier. During this month-long holiday period hundreds of millions of workers return to their villages in the countryside, bearing gifts they've bought in the cities for the families they've left behind. This period is known as the largest annual human migration in history because of the sheer number of people traveling at one time. For example in 2013, a record 3.4 billion journeys were made: 3.1 billion via long-distance bus, 240 million trips by rail, 42.5 million trips by ship, and 38 million trips by plane.

This discriminatory practice of forcing China's factory workers to live and work on factory grounds on a non-permanent basis has fueled China's economic boom in the cities for thirty years. However, even the Chinese government recognizes this policy is no longer tenable as a model for growth. Young migrants are protesting their unequal status and many young people are no longer willing to accept these jobs.

Before leaving office in 2013, Premier Wen Jiabao called for reform of the *hukou* system that would allow China's migrant workers to move permanently to the city, purchase apartments, put their children in the public schools, and have access to hospitals and police protection. These changes would unleash the migrants' spending power in the city, boosting consumption in China and helping China to move away from an export-driven economy. While there have been efforts at reform on a city-by-city basis, nationwide reforms have not yet been enacted in a meaningful way for China's hundreds of millions of rural residents and migrant workers.

Music

The Chinese music scene is as diverse as it is popular. Neo-punk girl bands spring up in Beijing every year while classical pianists like Lang Lang can sell out a concert hall as quickly as the latest boy band from Taiwan or Korea. Although the popularity of Chinese music stars changes rapidly, the following three musicians have withstood the test of time, and their music is readily available both inside and outside China.

Cui Jian is China's rock 'n' roll king, whose throaty voice and poignant lyrics have caused him to be compared to American superstar Bruce Springsteen. Cui Jian (pronounced "tsway jen" with a hard "j") is perhaps best known for his song "Yi Wu Suo You" (I Have Nothing), which became the unofficial anthem of the pro-democracy demonstrators at Tiananmen Square in Beijing in 1989. Because of his iconic status, *Rolling Stone* chose to feature his silhouette on the first Chinese edition of the magazine in 2006. As a result, the Chinese government banned *Rolling Stone* from publishing another issue. Although Cui Jian is allowed to perform concerts, record CDs, and run his famous jazz club in Beijing, he is still considered a somewhat controversial figure although the government has never officially condemned him or his music. His CDs are available in Chinatown CD and DVD stores, online, and in some large urban music superstores in the United States.

Faye Wong is one of the most successful pop stars in China, enduring where others have come and gone, in part because she simply has an amazingly beautiful soprano voice. She also likes to experiment with different sounds and genres, and has starred in high-profile films, including *2046* and *Chungking Express*. Her work is available in most Chinatown CD and DVD stores and online. (In China she is known by the name Wang Fei.)

Tan Dun, the avant-garde composer, won an Oscar for his haunting score for *Crouching Tiger, Hidden Dragon*. His score for *Hero* is also available in the United States. For his more avant-garde work, which mixes traditional Western opera, Chinese opera, Chinese folk music traditions, jazz, and rock influences, check out his scores for *Bitter Love* (commissioned for a modern update of the sixteenth-century Chinese play *The Peony Pavilion*); his collaboration with Kronos Quartet called *Ghost Opera*; or his original operas, such as *Marco Polo*. In 2006 he collaborated with Zhang Yimou to create the score for the New York Metropolitan Opera's production of *The First Emperor*. His myriad CDs can be found in the classical music section of most large music stores.

Traditional Music

Once banned during the Cultural Revolution, appreciating Western classical music is now seen as a sign of sophistication. Lessons in everything from piano to violin to Western opera voice training are growing in popularity in China's cities for the children of the nouveaux riches and nascent middle class.

The unfortunate side effect of this trend is that traditional musicians and troupes are struggling to survive. However, in the countryside you can still find an elderly man playing an *erhu* while the other men wade through the paddies guiding plows being drawn by water buffalo.

China's indigenous music is as varied as China's dialects, and regional performances of folk songs and folk tunes are a special treat (even if they increasingly are appreciated mainly by the elderly, musicologists, and foreign tourists).

Before the 1949 Communist revolution, Chinese music was not

just for farmers. An educated man was not considered truly refined unless he could also play a musical instrument. These are some of the major instruments that are part of this scholarly tradition:

The *qin* (pronounced "cheen") is a long, wooden zitherlike instrument very similar in appearance to the Japanese *koto* that can be played by plucking, strumming, and occasionally beating for a drumlike effect.

The *dizi* ("dee dzih") is a wooden flute that produces a haunting, breathy sound.

The *erhu* ("R hoo") is held like a miniature banjo across the lap but sounds more like a violin. It is played with a bow drawn across the strings, which lie in front of a snakeskin-covered drum.

The *pipa* ("pee pah") looks similar to a Western lute and is traditionally played by women, often as they sing a story in dialect or classical Chinese. (The DVD of *The Peony Pavilion* production that was performed at New York's Lincoln Center in 1999, and in London, features a scene with two excellent *pipa* players.)

Drums, bells, gongs, and various horns also make up traditional Chinese "orchestras" that often accompanied operas, shadow puppet plays, and even funerals.

Today avant-garde composer Tan Dun and Western-trained cellist Yo-Yo Ma have both made efforts to preserve Chinese musical traditions as well as combine them with Western and other musical forms. Their CDs can be found in many stores in the United States and online.

The best way to find traditional performances in China is to ask to visit a music conservatory where the old ways are still taught or to happen upon a local festival in the countryside. Many so-called traditional performances for tour groups are in fact highly Westernized, Vegas-like shows that bear little resemblance to actual classical Chinese music.

Names

Chinese names are written in reverse order of Western names, that is, with the surname first and the personal name second. This order shows the traditional respect accorded to one's family or clan; the individual is not as important as the family from which he or she comes. For example, the famous Chinese director of *Hero* and *House of Flying Daggers*, Zhang Yimou, should be referred to as Mr. Zhang. Similarly, the famous Chinese actress Gong Li is Miss Gong. Her "first name" in the American sense is Li. However, Chinese who have only two syllables in their names never are called by a single syllable name. Thus Gong Li is always referred to as Gong Li, never as simply Li.

Most Chinese surnames have only one syllable. A very few, historically important surnames, such as Sima, and surnames of ethnic minorities have more than one syllable.

In workplace situations, Chinese tend to be more formal and title oriented than Americans. For example, Zhang Yimou is never referred to by his first name by the actors who work with him in public news conferences. They always call him Director Zhang (pinyin: Zhang Daoyan). Even when Gong Li was openly living with Zhang Yimou, she still referred to him as Director Zhang in public. It is best to follow this formality at work or at school. Teachers and professors are not called Miss Bai or Mr. Zhu. They are called Teacher Bai and Teacher Zhu (pinyin: Bai Laoshi and Zhu Laoshi).

In many Western-oriented hotels and businesses, Chinese employees have been given Western first names and their name tags will reflect the Western order of first name/last name, such as Shirley Wu or Henry Lin. Again, it's best to refer to people by their title or Miss Wu and Mr. Lin unless Shirley and Henry specifically ask you to call them by their Western first names.

Chinese often add family terms to people's personal names to show familiarity and friendship. Even Ronald McDonald has become Uncle McDonald in China. (He has also been given a wife, called Auntie McDonald.)

Using family terms to address a total stranger is not unusual. Out of politeness—and a desire to get better service—some shoppers might refer to a store clerk as Little Sister (Xiao Mei) or Older Sister (Jie Jie), for example, even though they are not at all related. Similarly, young people may refer to senior citizens as "Ye Ye" (grandfather) or "Nai Nai" (grandmother) as a sign of respect. It is now common to refer to nannies and female household help as "Ayi," the traditional term for "Auntie." It is also common for Chinese to have their children refer to any woman of the same generation as their mothers as Auntie (Ayi—pronounced "ah-ee"), and men of the same generation as their fathers as Uncle (Shu Shu for younger men and Bo Bo for older men). Young people—college age or slightly older—may refer to their classmates as sisters and brothers or cousins, again as a sign of closeness. As a result, it can actually be very confusing to figure out who is actually related to whom.

Among very close friends, Chinese often add diminutive terms before the surname or to their friends' personal names. The two most common diminutives are *lao* (which rhymes with "plow" in English) or *xiao* (which sounds like "shao"). *Lao* literally means "old" and *xiao* means "young" or "little." However when used before names, they do not refer to age so much as familiarity. For example, you might hear someone refer to a longtime colleague as Lao Li (the word *Lao* plus the surname *Li*). While the literal translation, Old Li, sounds offensive to American ears, it actually means that the speaker has known Li for a long time and it does not mean that the speaker thinks Li is literally old. Similarly, *Xiao* plus a surname refers to a junior colleague or sometimes a slightly younger colleague with whom the speaker is also on very familiar terms. It is not a put-down. (If you are familiar with Japanese, *lao* is similar although not as formal as the Japanese term *san*, which is placed at the end of a surname; and *xiao* is roughly equivalent to the Japanese term *chan*, which shows affection and is similar to the Spanish ending *-ita* or *-ito*.)

Another important difference with the West is the fact that Chinese women do not take the surname of their husbands but keep their maiden names throughout their lives.

Children generally take the surnames of their fathers. However, under special circumstances, such as that a family line would die out if the child did not take on the mother's surname, some families do use the maternal surname. This is more likely to occur if the family has more than one child (meaning they were born before 1979 when the One Child Policy was enacted). In these cases, usually one child keeps the father's surname and the second child takes the mother's.

In pre-1949 China and in the Chinese diaspora, it is common for personal names of two syllables to be hyphenated. However, in mainland China under the official pinyin alphabetic writing system, personal names no longer contain hyphens.

Nanjing

The beautiful city of Nanjing, located about three hours by train from Shanghai and bordering the Yangtze River, has been the capital of nine dynasties. In fact, the name Nanjing means "Southern Capital." The most famous archaeological remains of the city's illustrious path is the Ming Tomb of the dynasty's founder, Hongwu, which is located just outside the city limits. Lining the road to the tomb are large paired statues of animals—some mythological, some real—in what is known as a Spirit Path (in Mandarin: *shen dao*). The Spirit Path was meant to guide the soul of the departed back toward the tomb should it wander away and get lost.

The remains of the Ming dynasty city wall can be visited. Each brick is signed by the name of its manufacturer, and the fascinating turrets, gutters for rolling flaming balls of pitch, and deep recesses for hiding from enemy arrow-fire make for a true journey back in time.

The city was also the capital of the Kingdom of Heavenly Peace, so named by the nineteenth-century revolutionary Hong Xiuquan, who believed he was the younger brother of Jesus Christ and nearly succeeded in overthrowing the corrupt Qing dynasty. Unfortunately, after settling with more than 100,000 followers in Nanjing, Hong became ill with fever and militia groups combined with Western forces in 1864 were able to defeat his acolytes, all of whom were killed in a nearly citywide inferno. Today there is a museum dedicated to the history of the Taiping Rebellion, as it came to be known.

In 1912, Sun Yat-sen declared the end of the Qing dynasty and the birth of the Republic of China in Nanjing. However, the capital was soon moved to Beijing and warlordism reigned until 1928, when Generalissimo Chiang Kai-shek reunited China and reestablished the capital of the Republic of China in Nanjing. Sun Yat-sen's tomb (called Zhong Shan Ling in Chinese) is located on Nanjing's famous Purple Mountain. The elaborate marble structure is breathtaking, as hundreds of steps lead up to the mausoleum's main building, which is covered in lapis blue roof tiles that contrast with the stark white stone and the green of the surrounding pine trees.

In December 1937, the infamous Rape of Nanking occurred, in which an estimated 300,000 Chinese civilians were killed and tens of thousands of women and girls were brutally raped before being murdered by Japanese soldiers. A memorial to what the Chinese call the Nanjing Massacre contains a museum, rock garden dedicated to the memory of those killed, and other historical information about this atrocity.

Today Nanjing is also known for its many universities, including its most famous school, the eponymous Nanjing University. The sycamore-lined streets still teem with bicycles as students cannot yet afford cars, and the city has a young feel to it, much like a college town in the United States, even though Nanjing is also an industrial center with a total population of more than 5 million people.

Visitors should be warned that the summers are notoriously hot and humid, earning Nanjing the title of one of China's "three furnaces" (the other two are Wuhan and Chongqing). However, autumn is beautiful, and the trees on the hills surrounding the city are bright red. The Qi Xia Monastery, with its intricate thousand Buddha statues carved into the hillside, is resplendent this time of year. In late winter and early spring, when

there may still be snow on the branches, the plum blossom trees on Mei Hua Shan (Plum Blossom Hill) bloom, and Nanjing residents flock to view the delicate pink and white flowers that announce the imminent arrival of spring. Not coincidentally, the plum blossom is the official city flower of Nanjing.

National Holidays

January 1   New Year's Day

January 2   New Year's Day Holiday

January–February Spring Festival (Chinese New Year)

During the thirty-to-forty-day holiday period, migrant workers in the cities return home to their villages. Due to the extremely crowded travel conditions, this period is known as "the largest annual human migration in history." The exact dates will vary according to the traditional lunar calendar.

April 4, 5, or 6   Qing Ming ("Clear Brightness" or "Tomb Sweeping Day"; date varies according to lunar calendar.)

May 1–May 3   Labor Day

June   Dragon Boat Festival (Date varies according to the lunar calendar.)

July 1   Founding Day of the Chinese Communist Party

October 1–3   National Day Holiday

Note: Banks, government offices, and any official offices will be closed.

Private businesses can choose to remain open. Hotels will remain open.

(See "Festivals" for traditional festivals and their approximate dates according to the lunar calendar.)

Novelists

Despite official censorship, Chinese novelists have reemerged from the nightmare of the Cultural Revolution, when only so-called revolutionary texts were published and contraband books—i.e., literature—were burned. A comprehensive list of Chinese authors would be impossible for one book to provide, as new Chinese writers emerge every day, some in China, some overseas, some as bloggers who may post under pseudonyms on the Internet to tens of thousands of followers. One of the most popular genres in China, dubbed "bureaucracy lit" or "officialdom lit" because it features tales of government officials and their dirty work, is similar to Western mystery or detective novels but has no real equivalent. The tales do not feature detectives per se, and some of them are read as "how-to" books on how to get ahead in the bureaucracy. Furthermore, while official censorship about "sensitive topics" can seem arbitrary at times, a thriving black market keeps Chinese readers in the know of even banned books. China is the largest publishing industry in the world in terms of sheer number of volumes, with 7.7 billion books published in 2011.

Listed below is a sampling of the many writers whose work has won acclaim and whose books are available in English.

Da Chen is not particularly well-known in China because he writes in English, but his memoir *Colors of the Mountain*, detailing his life of hardship growing up in a small town during the Cultural

Revolution, gives English-language readers a good sense of that time period.

Dai Sijie writes in French, but his bestselling novel (also available in English) *Balzac and the Little Chinese Seamstress* was made into a movie in China, directed by Dai himself. The book depicts the hardships endured by two young Chinese men who are sent to the countryside in the early 1970s because they come from educated families and who fall in love with the same girl. A secret stash of French novels leads to intellectual freedom and a sexual awakening for the three protagonists.

Gao Xingjian may have won the Nobel Prize in Literature in 2000 but the Chinese government refused to embrace this Chinese-language author, mainly because Gao sought asylum in France after the crackdown at Tiananmen in 1989 and later became a French citizen. Gao's most famous novel, *Soul Mountain*, is a sprawling mix of memoir, erotic fantasy, reportage, and experimental writing about a man traveling through rural communities in southern China after the Cultural Revolution.

Ha Jin was born in China and joined the military, but became an American citizen after the killings of student demonstrators outside Tiananmen Square. His novel *Waiting*, which won the National Book Award (though it is not especially well-known in China), provides a poignant and lyrical look at traditional Chinese values, in which a man must wait decades to marry the woman he loves because his wife refuses to grant him a divorce. (In today's China, divorce is far more common and easily obtained, and the sexual revolution has been under way for two decades now, but the novel depicts a time and yearning that many older Chinese still remember quite well.)

Mo Yan is arguably the favorite author of the Chinese establishment. His 2012 Nobel Prize in Literature was lauded across China's official press and media (although human rights activists were disappointed by his official statements before the Nobel awards ceremony that seemed to condone some instances of censorship). Many Chinese intellectuals find his violent and surrealist tales of rural life thrilling, and point to his depiction of official corruption as a sign of his true sympathies. Most of his books are available in English and many of his novels have been made into films. *Red Sorghum*, one of Zhang

Yimou's first films starring the incredible nineteen-year-old Gong Li, depicts the life of a family of winemakers as they fight the Japanese invasion during the Sino-Japanese War (1937–45). The book has been translated well and is available in paperback. His collection of short stories, *Shifu, You'll Do Anything for a Laugh*, deals quite openly with China's recent sexual revolution, and the title story was (very) loosely adapted by Zhang Yimou into the film *Happy Times*.

Su Tong is a bestselling author whose fast-paced, plot-driven novels are very popular in China. His novella about a man and his four wives who must fight for his attention was translated as *Raise the Red Lantern* in English. It was also made into a movie (starring Gong Li) and a ballet. Other popular novels include *Rice* and *My Life as Emperor*.

Wang Shuo is considered the "bad boy" of Chinese fiction, for his often bawdy, very funny novels that satirize politics and everyday life. His work is full of puns and inside jokes, which make them very difficult to translate, but you can check out his style in the one English translation currently available: *Please Don't Call Me Human*.

Yiyun Li came from China to America on a scholarship to study immunology and ended up writing an award-winning collection of stories, *A Thousand Years of Good Prayers*, while still a graduate student. Although she is now a U.S. citizen like Ha Jin, she continues to write about China's changing society as in her novel, *The Vagrants*, set in the aftermath of the 1978 pro–Democracy Wall movement and in her second short story collection, *Gold Boy, Emerald Girl*.

One Child Policy

In 1978, Deng Xiaoping promulgated what has become, at least in the West, China's most controversial family planning policy. The One Child Policy is exactly that: as of 1979, all Chinese families (with exceptions for ethnic minorities) could have only one child. The reason Deng felt the need for such a policy was the astronomical growth in China's population under Mao Zedong, who at one point had advocated and rewarded "model mothers" who gave birth to the most number of children. Mao believed that a more populous China would offer the nation protection, famously declaring that even if a U.S. nuclear attack killed 300 million Chinese, there would still be 300 million more Chinese whereas America could never survive such a war of attrition.

The problem with promulgating a rewards system for very large families, and making birth control difficult if not impossible to obtain, was that China's population soon outgrew its ability to feed itself. China simply didn't have enough arable land, flood control measures, pesticides, herbicides, fertilizers, and the like to grow enough food reliably, nor was its economy strong enough to provide a high standard of living for such a large population. Everyone was becoming very poor and underfed.

By 1971, even Mao began to realize China had a population problem. In 1949, when the PRC was founded, China had roughly 450 to 500 million people. By 1964, the population had reached nearly 700 million. In his new "Five Year Plan," Mao included a proposal for later marriages, longer spacing between births, and fewer children. However, the policy was seen as too little too late and so, after Mao's death, the One Child Policy was formulated and adopted into the constitution in 1978. By 1979, 90 percent of Chinese couples signed one-child certificates pledging to have only one child. Those who signed the certificates were awarded with benefits—such as health care, extra food ration coupons, the right to send their child to school, and other rather basic necessities. Those who failed to sign faced harsh penalties ranging from large fines to forced abortions and even forced sterilization. (Still, the 1982 census revealed the population had surpassed the 1 billion mark.)

By 1981 the State Family Planning Commission was established. Women were forced to reveal the dates of their periods to their "work units," that is the party apparatus that every employed person belonged to. Work units provided you with housing, permission to marry, permission to have a child, and they could also report you to authorities if you did not obey the law, including the One Child Policy. Furthermore, "neighborhood committees," often run by retired, elderly women, would patrol the apartment complexes in their neighborhood blocks, essentially spying on residents to make sure everyone obeyed the laws. Not everything the neighborhood committees did was bad, of course. They could also mitigate domestic disputes and help women suffering domestic violence, they kept crime down to a minimum, they looked after neighborhood children, they helped the sick, the weak, and the elderly. But they also ensured that no one had much privacy.

The policy did effectively slow China's population growth, although with 1.3 billion Chinese, China remains the most populous nation on earth. However, it also brought about many unintended consequences and much suffering. Rural Chinese in particular did not like the policy, as the traditional Chinese preference for male children—as well as farmers' need for a son to work in the fields and to take care of parents when they aged—caused many desperate, poor couples to commit female infanticide. Today there is already a shortage of women in the countryside and many male farmers fear they will never find a bride. This has led to a billion-dollar industry in the trafficking of women from one part of China to another, as well as Asian females from poor, rural parts of Southeast Asia who are kidnapped and sold by traffickers as wives to Chinese farmers.

The policy also led many local officials to commit draconian human rights violations in order to meet their population quotas. For example, activist lawyer Chen Guangcheng was sentenced in 2006 to more than four years in prison after he exposed an illegal campaign of forced abortions and sterilizations that had occurred years earlier in rural Shandong Province. By the time these measures had been inflicted upon the population, the central government had in fact eased up on enforcement of the One Child Policy in rural areas, realizing its futility. Alas, this did not help Chen, a self-taught lawyer who has been blind since birth.

Today, the One Child Policy still exists but its enforcement is uneven. Many wealthy urbanites simply bribe officials now so that they can get a birth certificate for a second child (or even a third). They can pay for private schooling and health care as well, so they no longer need to worry if the government tries to forbid an additional child from attending publicly financed schools and hospitals. The government allows more official exceptions as well—for example, when either spouse is an only child, the couple is allowed to have two children, as the burden of one child taking care of so many elderly parents and grandparents would be too great.

In the countryside, the government has already allowed farmers to have two children, and many officials look the other way when families end up having more (although their female children are often not sent to school, as it is too expensive, but are made to work at a young age). Many families make use of ultrasound machines that allow them to determine the sex of the fetus. If it's a girl, they'll abort and try again for a boy. Female infanticide has decreased now that it is easier to drop off an unwanted baby girl at one of the government's "orphanages." As foreign adoption of these girls has increased (and become more lucrative for the government), local officials no longer are pressured to force pregnant mothers to have late-term abortions or to become sterilized. (However, foreign adoption of Chinese girls has not solved the ever-growing problem of the skewed sex ratios, something the government is aware of but has not yet acted to fix.)

Finally, as China grows more prosperous, the government has been weighing the idea of allowing all families to have two children.

When the government announced it was merging the National Population and Family Planning Commission into the Ministry of Health in 2013, many Chinese took this to mean that the government would be backing away from enforcement of the One Child Policy in preparation for abandoning it someday. However, while a group of social scientists has been petitioning Beijing since 2004 to abandon the policy, the government has thus far refused.

Meanwhile, the social effects of the One Child Policy can no longer be ignored. A survey of 489 people by the official Xinhua News Agency in 2013 revealed that 72 percent of respondents did not know how to address members of their own extended families. The Chinese language has very specific kinship terms. Unlike English where "uncle" or "aunt" can cover relatives on both sides of the family, Chinese use terms specific to the age and paternal/maternal line of each member. For example, your father's older brother is your *bo bo*, his younger brother is your *shu shu*, whereas your mother's brothers are called *jiu jiu*. The terms get even more complicated for a paternal elder great uncle, *bo gong*, and so on. One universal term like "uncle" simply doesn't cut it. However, members of this new generation of only children are not used to hearing extended kinship terms as many of their fathers and mothers don't have siblings.

Even more alarming are the skewed male-to-female birth ratios. While typically there are about 106 boys born for every 100 girls, in China there are 122 boys born for every 100 girls. Sociologists predict there will be some 30 million "extra" Chinese men by the year 2020; extra meaning men for whom there are no single female partners. Social scientists say this could lead to major unrest: from a rise in crime to civil disorder to perhaps even war as societies with a large pool of single, young men have generally been more unstable historically.

It is important to remember that many Chinese support the One Child Policy as they believe it is necessary in order for China's economic prosperity to continue. Not all Chinese couples want to have more than one child, and in a new trend, many young urban couples now say they'd rather not have a child at all. It has grown increasingly expensive to raise a child in the city with a good education, clothing, tutoring, and all the advantages that parents feel they need to give their child in order for him or her to succeed in the ever-competitive market-driven economy. Parents often sacrifice greatly for their child and many young people are beginning to question whether the sacrifices are worth it. As the concept of retirement communities grows in popularity and in practice in urban areas, couples realize they will not necessarily be dependent on their child in their old age but can provide for their own care. Thus, having a child is becoming a choice rather than a necessity. However, in the countryside, having a child—and a son, at that—can still mean the difference between life and death for a farming family.

One Country, Two Systems

The "one country, two systems" principle was devised by Deng Xiaoping in the 1980s in order to convince the British, who controlled Hong Kong, to allow for its reunification with China. Deng also espoused the policy to promote reunification talks with Taiwan.

Hong Kong was a capitalist colony of Great Britain for 150 years, with a British-style legal system, freedoms of speech and religion, and many other rights guaranteed to its population that were not enjoyed by the people of mainland China. When Deng negotiated with the British in 1985 for Hong Kong's return (the lease on a part of Hong Kong known as the New Territories was due to expire in 1997), he promised the British that China would allow Hong Kong to maintain its capitalist system, as well as economic and political autonomy, for fifty years. (The idea was that the mainland would be able to catch up economically with Hong Kong and evolve politically, eventually making full political integration feasible.) During this time, the Chinese mainland, however, would maintain its system of "socialism with Chinese characteristics" under the Chinese Communist Party. The British agreed and the "one country, two systems" policy was implemented into the so-named Basic Law for Hong Kong in 1997.

Deng and his successors have also tried to use the concept of "one country, two systems" to persuade Taiwan to reunify with China. Taiwan currently is an independent state that separated from China as a result of the Chinese Civil War of 1945–49. In 1949, Chiang Kai-shek fled to Taiwan and reestablished his Nationalist Party–led government, the Republic of China, on the island. Since that time, Taiwan developed into a capitalist, free-market, and democratic state under U.S. protection and aid. Thus far, Taiwan's leaders and people have not agreed to reunify with China. Members of the Democratic Progressive Party (the other major political party in Taiwan) have openly espoused independence, the Nationalist Party has never ruled out eventual reunification, and the majority of the Taiwanese people, according to opinion polls, prefer to maintain the status quo of de facto independence without provoking China into war by openly declaring independence.

Peking Opera

Peking Opera is generally the Western generic term not only for Beijing Opera but other traditional Chinese opera styles as well.

Beijing Opera enjoyed its greatest popularity beginning some two hundred years ago during the Qing dynasty. In fact, this style of Chinese opera has its origins in two different provinces, Anhui and Hubei. However, scholars estimate that there are thousands of forms of Chinese opera, as many as there are dialects. Some forms allow only male singers, others only female, and nowadays many have mixed casts. While there are many subtle differences in each style, for newcomers to the genre the most obvious differences will be how Chinese operas differ from Western ones.

First of all, the singing is completely different and involves a different musical aesthetic. To Chinese opera aficionados the rising and falling cadences of the trained Chinese opera singer are as nuanced as that of Luciano Pavarotti or Beverly Sills, even if the harmonic scale is completely different. To the novice, the singing may in fact sound more like crying or wailing.

Second, the acting is not meant to be naturalistic but is highly stylized and very difficult to learn. One does not portray love, hate, longing, fear, and so on through facial expressions so much as long-established gestures and body movements, which can vary from the way a foot is raised or a step taken to the flip of a sleeve to a full body cartwheel.

Third, the costumes and makeup are essential to understanding who is the hero, the villain, the clown, the warrior, the lovers, and so on. Here color plays an extremely important role. For example, red or black face paint signifies a good character, white represents evil. There are myriad variations of the coloring, all of which add to the audience's appreciation of the characters.

Fourth, traditional sets are very plain without elaborate props. The musicians are clearly visible and seated to the side of the stage. Unlike the orchestra of a Western opera, Chinese opera musicians use fewer instruments, including the *pipa* (Chinese lute), *erhu* (a tiny stringed instrument with a snakeskin drum played with a bow), *qin* (a long zitherlike instrument), drums, and gongs.

Fifth, audience members (in nonimperial performances) are not expected to remain quiet or even in place. Often they may come and go and even shout out their approval at an especially skilled performance by rising to their feet and calling out, *"Hao! Hao!"* (which is similar to "Bravo!" and literally means "Good!").

Finally, the most notable difference is the use of acrobatics and martial arts displays such as spinning, leaping, and swordfighting for certain martial operas. These operas are among the favorites in contemporary China as they are accessible to opera buffs and novices alike, as well as to young people.

Unfortunately, the ancient art of Chinese opera may be dying. Young people in China prefer rock or pop music, and opera troupes have seen their audiences dwindle. Attempts are being made to revive the art form by shortening some of the plays and adding more contemporary elements such as combinations of Western and Chinese music and more naturalistic acting, and mixing elements of contemporary play-acting spoken in vernacular Chinese with the traditional singing parts. One example of this was the highly successful run of the classic sixteenth-century play *The Peony Pavilion* in New York City's Lincoln Center in 1999. (Censors in Shanghai had delayed the production for a year, refusing to let the costumes leave the country, because they felt the young Chinese director had taken too many liberties with the text and styling.)

Another modern interpretation, also of *The Peony Pavilion*, was overseen by British avant-garde opera director Peter Sellars, with the music composed and conducted by Tan Dun (who wrote the Oscar-winning score for the film *Crouching Tiger, Hidden Dragon*). Sellars combined traditional *kunqu* opera singing and dance moves with a Western ballet pas de deux as well as modern dance. Tan Dun combined traditional folk music, *kunqu* opera music, and Western rock 'n' roll, jazz, opera, and ecclesiastic music. This version of *The Peony Pavilion* debuted at the University of California at Berkeley's Zellerbach Hall to sold-out crowds in 1998. The CD of an adaptation of the score is available under the title *Bitter Love*.

For those unfamiliar with Chinese opera, two excellent films are available on DVD that feature dramatic story lines that also show the difficult world of opera training and its stars: Chen Kaige's masterpiece *Farewell, My Concubine* (1993) and Huang Shuqin's *Woman Demon Human* (1987).

Peng Liyuan

Following decades of invisible First Ladies who made nary a public appearance, the arrival of Peng Liyuan on the world political stage in 2013 marked a new phase in China's governance. Not since Jiang Qing (Chairman Mao's wife) has a wife of a Chinese Communist political leader garnered any media attention, but Peng is not a typical political spouse, by Chinese or Western standards.

Born in 1962 in Shandong Province, Peng was famous long before her husband Xi Jinping became president of China. Since the 1980s she has been a popular folk singer, appearing on Chinese central television's Chinese New Year spectacles, which are watched by hundreds of millions of people each year. Appearing in glamorous shiny red ball gowns or ethnic minority costumes, Peng commanded the stage with the confidence of an old showbiz pro. In fact, she often toured the country, singing patriotic songs as a member of the People's Liberation Army's musical troupe. As such, she earned the title of major-general.

Peng also broke with precedent when she gave personal interviews about her relationship with Xi. She told interviewers that when she first met Xi in 1986 when he was deputy-mayor of the port city of Xiamen, she found Xi "rustic and old-looking" but intelligent and that he won her over by conversing intelligently and showing an interest in her singing. She is, in fact, Xi's second wife. He was married for three years in his youth but divorced without having a child. Peng and Xi have one daughter, Xi Mingze, who enrolled at Harvard under a pseudonym.

When it became clear that Xi had been picked to become president, she started toning down her public performances, and in her first foreign tour as First Lady of China to Russia in March 2013, she appeared in a tasteful, dark coatdress with a bright turquoise scarf and chic leather satchel. Pictures of the outfit soon appeared online and spurred sales of knockoffs across China. As one netizen proclaimed, "Finally we have a beautiful First Lady!"

Not since Mao has the wife of a Chinese political leader been given press in China (or abroad), and it was apparent the Chinese government fully intended to allow Ms. Peng to assume a modern role for a political spouse—appearing in public on state trips with her husband, and promoting good causes at home. She is a World Health Organization Goodwill ambassador for AIDS and promotes charitable giving in China, still a relatively new activity for China's growing middle class.

All was not completely rosy for Ms. Peng's emergence as a modern First Lady. Despite praise for her poise and intelligence, rumors appeared online and in the press that she was behind one of the controversial decisions during the 2008 Beijing Olympics opening ceremony. It was said she urged director Zhang Yimou to replace the little girl who sang the opening anthem with a "prettier" child model who ended up lip-synching to the first little girl's actual voice. Whether the anecdote is true, it reveals what political spouses in the West have long known: celebrity is not all glamour and adoration.

People's Liberation Army (PLA)

I n 1946, the Chinese Communist Party's militia and guerrilla forces became a regular army known as the People's Liberation Army (PLA). It defeated the Nationalist forces in the Chinese Civil War (1945–49) and fought the United States in the Korean War (1950–53) and engaged in a number of border clashes with India, the USSR, and Vietnam, all between the 1950s and 1979. Most notoriously, perhaps, the PLA was used by the Chinese government against its own citizens in 1989 to put down the student-led pro-democracy demonstrations at Tiananmen Square in Beijing.

Today the PLA is a modern army with a formidable air force and navy and ICBMs armed with nuclear warheads that can reach the United States.

The PLA is unlike the American military in that it owes its allegiance to both the party and the state. (Imagine if the Democratic Party and the Republican Party both had to have their own militaries and you'll see just how unusual this arrangement is.) However, it is the Communist Party that controls the PLA, not the other way around. As Mao famously remarked, "Political power grows out of the barrel of the gun, but it is the party that controls the gun."

Party control is exercised by the party bureaucracy within the military at the central, provincial, and local "unit" levels, and party bureaucrats with military ranks supervise the activities of military commanders. Furthermore, every member of the military, from privates to generals, is a member of the party. However, the PLA also has its own bureaucracy. For example, it has its own auditing system, which is not part of the nonmilitary government.

Another difference from the American military is that the PLA's activities are not limited to military affairs. The PLA can operate economic, educational, medical, agricultural, and scientific enterprises for its own profit. For example, one of the fancier hotels in Beijing, the China Palace, is owned by the military, open to the public, and employs civilians to run the hotel for profit. Many of China's technical and computer companies are also owned and operated by the military's bureaucracy. The military grows its own food. And some of China's best hospitals are run by the military. Senior party officials with the proper connections may also use them.

Currently, there are 1.6 million ground force soldiers in the PLA, making the army one of China's largest employers; this number of soldiers also ranks as the world's largest ground force. Altogether there are 2.3 million members of the PLA when the air force and navy personnel are included in the mix. The PLA also has a reserve force of roughly 1.2 to 1.5 million personnel.

Once considered an army made up largely of semiliterate peasants under Mao, today's PLA is highly trained, technologically advanced, well equipped, disciplined, and considered to be an important regional military power.

Since 2000, China has been embarking on the largest military buildup in the world, with defense budget spending growing by double digits, from just over $30 billion in 2000 to nearly $120 billion in 2010. The goal has been to improve China's high-tech capabilities. Military specialists say that China wants to develop and deploy the following within ten years: satellites and reconnaissance drones; surface-to-surface and antiship missiles; stealth and nuclear attack submarines; stealthy manned and unmanned combat aircraft; and of course space and cyberwarfare capabilities, including antisatellite weapons.

Despite the PLA's buildup, analysts in the Chinese military predict it will take thirty to fifty years for China's forces to catch up with America's. In the meantime, China has many domestic issues that take precedence over military development, including more internal threats than external, an aging population that will put a strain on health care costs, and domestic demands to move more poor people into the middle class.

Pinyin Spelling System

After the Communist victory of 1949, the government decided to reform the way Chinese was transcribed into the Roman alphabet. Previously, many different systems coexisted, most invented by Christian missionaries but some haphazardly created by Chinese living abroad. The most common romanization system was known as Wade-Giles, named after the two men who created it, and is still used in the Chinese diaspora and in Taiwan. That is why in America we have a tennis star named Michael Chang instead of Michael Zhang and ice skater Michelle Kwan instead of Michelle Guan.

However, the People's Republic decided to use the pinyin system, which literally means "spell sound." Thus, all official Chinese signs that are written in "English" will appear with the pinyin alphabet, which looks like the English alphabet but does not correspond exactly to the English alphabet, leading to some confusion.

That being said, many Chinese do not pronounce words uniformly or in any way resembling what the proper pinyin pronunciation would suggest. Even when they are speaking Mandarin (and not an entirely different dialect of Chinese), most Chinese have regional accents that do not correspond to the pinyin pronunciation of Mandarin, despite the government's efforts to standardize the language.

Chinese in northeastern provinces are the most likely to speak standard, textbook Mandarin. Beijing residents tend to add an *r*

Most Confusing Pinyin Sounds for English Speakers

C	pronounced "ts" like the end of "bats," never like "kuh"
G	always pronounced as a hard "g," never like "juh"
J	always pronounced as a hard "j"
Q	pronounced "ch," never "qwuh"
X	pronounced "sh"
Yi	pronounced "ee," not "yee"
Z	pronounced "dz," like the end of "buds"
Zh	pronounced like a hard "j," never a soft "j"

sound to the end of words, making them sound like nothing your Mandarin class would ever teach you. For example, the word for *door*, written *men* in pinyin but actually pronounced more like "muhn" in English (with a rising tone so that it sounds like a question) is pronounced "muhr" in Beijing-accented Mandarin. This can take some getting used to.

Southern Chinese don't usually put the harsh *r* sound at the end of words. They also tend not to retroflex their tongues (that is, touch the tip of their tongue to the back of the palate at the roof of the mouth) when pronouncing "ch," "sh," or "zh" the way northerners do. Therefore, these three consonant clusters can sound almost exactly alike when spoken by people who've grown up below the Yangtze River. This will be most noticeable when trying to hear a price, as the word for four (*si*) and the word for ten (*shi*) will differ only in tone. So forty-four, instead of sounding like "sih sure sih," can sound like "sih sih sih" to an English-trained ear.

Other quirks of accents (and we're not even talking differences between dialects here) are the tendency among southern Chinese to transpose "l" and "n" when they appear at the beginning of a word; "f" and "h" sounds are also often transposed.

Fortunately, most businesses that cater to foreigners will have trained their staff to speak standard Mandarin and English.

Qi

While even some Chinese are skeptical if qi (pronounced "chee") actually exists and if feng shui can actually affect and measure how qi moves through the universe, others will point to what they consider concrete evidence. For decades, a government-sponsored institute in Shanghai has been using purportedly scientific methods to study the effects of qi. In fact the institute released a video showing a test subject, a rather ordinary-looking man, radiating qi from his hands. At first the institute's meter registered very little energy coming from the subject. Then the man performed a number of breathing exercises combined with hand gestures, known as qigong. When he held up his palms the next time, the needle on the meter jumped forward.

This may not definitively prove the existence of qi, often translated as "life force," but it does testify to the degree to which many Chinese do believe in qi and its powerful qualities. For example, acupuncture needles are used to unblock the flow of qi when a person is ill, and tests in China have shown that acupuncture can even be used in place of anesthesia in some operations. Traditional Chinese herbal medicine was also conceived to correct qi when it becomes unbalanced. Meditation also is believed to improve the flow of qi.

Two forms of exercise—tai ji quan (known as "tai chi" in English) and qigong—are useful for promoting the flow of qi to promote good health. The Daoist priest Zhang Sanfeng is credited with creating tai ji quan in the fifteenth century. Daoists were concerned with being in harmony with the universe as a way of prolonging life. This gentle martial art promotes slow, rhythmic movements and awareness of one's own body. (Older visitors to China should not feel offended if they are offered advice and even DVDs on the practice. It simply means your hosts care about your health.)

Qigong experienced a resurgent popularity in China in the 1980s after being denounced as feudalistic during the Maoist era. This martial art uses meditation and stylized movements in combination with specialized breathing techniques. Unfortunately, because the Falun Gong religious movement also uses a unique form of qigong to attract followers, the Chinese government has been discouraging the practice. However, you can still see people, especially older men (as men were originally believed to possess qi and women were not), practicing various forms of qigong and DVDs of various qigong are widely available, although they generally lack English subtitles.

Practitioners of many forms of martial arts believe it is essential to harness your qi in order to perform their intricate moves, and all feng shui principles depend upon allowing qi to flow naturally through your work, home, and physical environment. While feng shui was scoffed at as superstition for many decades, it was widely practiced in Hong Kong and Taiwan. Since the 1990s, a renewed interest in feng shui has occurred on mainland China, perhaps spread by interaction with successful Hong Kong businesspeople and Taiwanese who insist upon following its principles and consult pricey feng shui masters—all to maximize the benefit of the environment's qi.

Qingdao
(Tsing-tao)

Qingdao (pronounced "ching dow") is well-known internationally because of its popular Tsing-tao beer, which uses the pre-1949 spelling of the city's name. The original Qingdao Brewery was created by Germany in 1903, making it the first beer brewery in China. (Traditionally Chinese preferred clear rice- or sorghum-based wines, which to the Western palate can give new meaning to the phrase "fire water.")

During the declining years of the Qing dynasty, China was forced to cede this port city in China's northeastern province of Shandong to Germany in 1898 after the killings of two German missionaries. After Germany's defeat in World War I, the Treaty of Versailles specified that all Germany's territories in China be given to Japan as a prize for Japan's participation with the forces allied against Germany. (This action naturally infuriated the Chinese, who had also sided with the Allies and who had fully expected their territories to be given back to China.) However, China's protests went unheeded and Japan was able to establish a strong naval base at Qingdao (much to the Allies' detriment in World War II). In 1945, Qingdao was at last returned to China. China now maintains its own naval base here.

Qingdao is an unusual Chinese city as it looks very European, due to the German influence in architecture. Delicious European-style breads, croissants, and pastries (even cream puffs!) are sold on the streets, in contrast to other Chinese cities where generally only Chinese bread products are available.

Qingdao is also a very popular tourist resort because of its location on the ocean and its fine, white sand beaches. However, it is generally jammed full of tourists during the summer months. Off-season can be a lovely time to visit; although it is too cold to swim in the ocean, the crisp sea breezes are both bracing and refreshing.

Visitors should not be startled by the presence of women in ski masks. Chinese women have not embraced the American concept of a "healthy tan," as tan skin still connotes a life of hard labor. While the new middle class flocks to the beach for vacation, women protect their skin from the sun's rays with more than sunblock: umbrellas, sun hats, goggles, ski masks, lace gloves, and long-sleeve shirts are de rigueur for locals.

Religion

Officially, the Communist Party of China is atheist and all its members must also be atheists. However, the constitution allows all other Chinese citizens to practice five officially recognized religions: Buddhism, Daoism, Islam, Protestant Christianity, and Catholicism. Practice of a religion comes with one very important caveat: members must belong to a state-sanctioned church or temple. As Chinese society has opened up and people can move about more freely without the state monitoring their work and personal lives, many unofficial religious groups have sprung up in China. In fact, the fastest-growing religion in China in the twenty-first century has been Protestant Christianity, with thousands of new converts estimated to join churches every day. Most of the adherents are joining what are called "underground churches," in that they are not registered with the government but generally meet privately in people's apartments for services.

Many China watchers have pointed out the irony that the Communist Party with its strict rules has managed to usher in the greatest era of Protestantism in China while Western Protestant missionaries for some one hundred years, from the Opium War of 1842 to the Communist revolution of 1949, could barely make a dent in the Chinese population in terms of winning converts. Numerous factors are responsible for this religious tide change. One is that China with its freewheeling, winner-take-all brand of capitalism no longer provides any spiritual comfort to those who are left behind economically or who are simply appalled by the lack of moral virtues they see these days. Another important factor is that Chinese citizens have more access to the outside world, and Protestants from Korea, Taiwan, and the Chinese diaspora have managed to bring their religious beliefs to China in a way that seems less alien than when Protestantism was associated mainly with Caucasian foreigners and imperialistic policies that treated Chinese as second-class citizens.

However, Christians still make up only 5 percent of the population, which is equal to 65 million people. The vast majority of Chinese practice more homegrown religions, as rituals of many stripes are being revived all across China. Buddhist temples, Daoist sects, esoteric folk religions, and newly invented religions that cross ancient practices like qigong or tai ji with New Age spiritualism (such as the Falun Gong movement) have attracted millions of followers across China. Temples devoted to clan worship, Confucius, and even shrines to the deceased Chairman Mao have risen in the countryside. In fact, the four traditionally "native" Chinese religions—known in the West as ancestor worship, Confucianism (despite Confucius's ambivalence to religion, temples bearing his name developed over time), Daoism, and Buddhism (which took on a uniquely Chinese outlook over the centuries as folk traditions were incorporated into the original teachings of the Buddha)—are all flourishing again.

The Chinese central government is at present deeply ambiguous about the growth of religious groups in China. While without doubt there is more religious freedom in today's China than at any other time since the founding of the People's Republic in 1949, and the government has even made overtures to the Vatican (which still recognizes Taiwan as the "official" China), the government is insecure about the role of religion in Chinese society. As a result, there have been a number of well-publicized and violent crackdowns on so-called unofficial churches and religious groups, with members beaten and arrested. More famously perhaps, the Falun Gong movement was officially banned, and many diehard adherents claim physical abuse and harassment.

While this might seem like unbridled paranoia, in fact the Chinese government has good reason to fear religious movements, which throughout Chinese history have been a rallying point for the disenchanted to attack the government. In one of the most famous examples, known as the Taiping Rebellion (1850–64), a convert to Protestant Christianity named Hong Xiuquan read missionary-translated Bible tracts, decided he liked Jesus's populist message, and also recognized within himself a sense of déjà vu that he'd previously found inexplicable: that is, he decided that like Jesus before him, he too was God's son and was put upon this Earth to bring God's heavenly kingdom into fruition. The man managed to rally tens of thousands of Chinese peasants and ethnic minorities to his cause—opposing the excesses of the corrupt Qing empire—and then took control of much of southern China, from Guangdong Province to the former Chinese imperial capital of Nanjing. He advocated an end to footbinding, equality between men and women, and a vaguely socialist style of government rather than the Qing system of taxes that so onerously fell upon the peasantry. He and 100,000 followers were defeated in the city of Nanjing in 1864, by a coalition of Chinese clan militias loyal to the Qing emperor and Western military powers, who had no desire to see a strong and nationalistic China arise and thwart their colonialist aims.

More recently, the protest of ten thousand Falun Gong members at Tiananmen Square in 1999 scared the government by the rapid way the members were able to organize, assemble, and demonstrate without any government official figuring out the plan in advance. Although the protest asking for tolerance of Falun Gong was peaceful, the government could imagine a day when such a wide swath of the population might easily turn against government officials. Hence the crackdown on Falun Gong.

Tibetan Buddhists and Muslims in the western province of Xinjiang are generally treated with the most suspicion by the government as they are seen as harboring separatist goals.

Whether China will continue to allow religious freedom to grow is hard to gauge. It is equally hard to gauge if the Chinese government has the power to stop unofficial religious practices anymore.

Respect for Elders

Traditionally in Chinese culture, the oldest members of a family or clan were accorded the most respect. The grandfather's word was paramount in making decisions. The first—and eldest—wife's commands were more important than that of secondary wives or daughters-in-law. And a traditional blessing was "May you live to see five generations together under one roof." (In America, this might very well pass for a curse!) Also, China may be one of the few countries in the world where the constitution states that children are required to take care of their aged parents.

Today young people might still refer to an older man or woman by family terms, such as "Ye Ye" (grandfather) or "Nai Nai" (grandmother), even when they are not related to the older person, as a sign of respect. And a few young people are still willing to take hold of an older person's arm and help that person up or down difficult stairs or to board a bus. However, many older Chinese who have seen their benefits cut by the government and the fast pace of life increasingly geared toward the young feel the traditional respect for older people has decreased. They often blame the One Child Policy.

Nowadays, because most families are still only allowed to have one child (exceptions are made for minorities, poor farmers, and rich industrialists who can bribe their way to a larger family), the youngest member of the family rules the roost. Both sets of grandparents and the child's parents must invest their whole future on the success of just one child to succeed in school and thus take care of them in their old age. As a result, many young people have grown up quite accustomed to a lot of pampering with no siblings to have to share their parents' and grandparents' affection with. In the countryside where jobs are scarce for young people, entire villages can seem like a ghost town of old people, left to fend for themselves, while the youth have gone to the cities in search of work and a better life.

However, respect for seniority in rank is still very important in China. Junior-level government officials and company executives can never make a decision without consulting with the more senior- official above them. This situation can make the Chinese seem very noncommittal when you are trying to negotiate a deal or even change the itinerary of a travel plan, but China is a highly bureaucratized nation and the bureaucracy rests upon the notion of seniority. Not for nothing is the oldest conception of Hell in traditional Chinese culture a vast bureaucracy presided over by corrupt court clerks and a myriad of judges, all of whom can obstruct your path to being judged by the number one Judge of Hell. Without this judge's blessing or curse, you cannot reenter the cycle of birth and rebirth, you cannot go to the Western Paradise, you could end up wandering the earth as a hungry ghost, caught between worlds.

In practical terms, it is always important to greet the most senior-ranked official at a banquet, meeting, or even casual encounter first. Also, you cannot expect anything to be accomplished if you only talk to the most junior member of an organization. Usually the junior members tend to be younger than the senior members so this hierarchy can still give the impression of "respect for elders," but this hierarchy is changing and it is no longer unheard of to find CEOs or senior officials who are in fact younger than their more junior colleagues.

However, in general in China, ordinary Chinese people will tend to be polite to foreigners who appear older in age. Do not be offended if someone offers you a helping hand. The Chinese conception of "the active senior citizen" is not the same as in America and such help is not meant to suggest that you look feeble or incapable of getting around by yourself but is meant as a sign of respect. Even if you're still capable of climbing Mount Everest, you may be asked if you'd like to "take a rest" or "have a snack" before continuing a strenuous sightseeing tour or attending another meeting. Again, politeness requires this. You don't have to agree to rest or slow your pace in any way. If on the other hand, you are indeed feeling tired—or are completely bored by a certain activity and would prefer to do something else—you can always tell your host or guide that you would like to take a rest now, and very few Chinese would find this odd. (If you want to sneak out later on your own to pursue your own interests, you've actually saved the face of your host by relieving him or her of the responsibility of watching over you for the moment.)

If you are a young person, it is generally a good idea to offer your seat on a bus or monorail or even bench to an older Chinese person—male or female. Seniority is not a gender issue, and it is perfectly acceptable for a young woman to give up her seat to an elderly man.

Similarly, when seated at a formal dinner banquet, don't be surprised if the oldest members of your group are served first—even if they are men. Chinese notions of chivalry have traditionally been geared toward age rather than gender.

When you are attending a meeting at a university or school, company, or government office, if you are younger than the Chinese official sent to welcome you, be especially polite, even deferential by American standards. You will not come across as weak or unimportant but will be giving the older person "face," which will predisposition that person to like you. Brashness, bragging about oneself, or cutting into a senior Chinese official's speech—no matter how long or tedious—will come across as disrespectful and may even cause your host to lose face, which would be a disaster.

Shanghai

In its heyday in the 1920s and '30s, Shanghai was China's most cosmopolitan city. Called alternately the Paris of the East and the Pearl of the Orient, Shanghai was famed for its diverse population, where missionaries, capitalists, coolies, colonialists, soldiers, priests, pimps, opium addicts, drug runners, gangsters, gun molls, working girls (both the kind in factories and on street corners), Communists, and artists rubbed shoulders. The city was divided into concessions, each controlled by a different foreign power: the French, the Japanese, and the international settlement, which was largely British and American. The concessions were ruled by the laws of each foreign government and any Chinese could be tried in these foreign-run courts whereas no foreigner could be tried in a Chinese court. Such were the rules of the unequal treaties that the Qing government had been forced to sign when it first opened Shanghai to the West after the First Opium War in 1842. Signs on foreign clubs famously proclaimed: "No Dogs and No Chinese Allowed."

And yet, old Shanghai still holds a mystique today that many Chinese find irresistible. Despite the oppressive anti-Chinese laws, Shanghaiese were able to carve a niche for themselves and many of the best-educated Chinese returned from schooling overseas and settled in the city. They set up thriving factories, hospitals, even churches. Shanghai film studios produced movie stars more popular in terms of number of fans than Hollywood. Writers, male and female, began pathbreaking literary journals and their writing is still read and beloved today.

Today, Shanghai is still a city of extremes. Its residents are known throughout China for their fashion sense, business savvy, sophistication, and, yes, vice.

Much of the old city's famous architecture was slated for demolition, with city planners promising to take down 95 percent of the old buildings by 2010. However, luxury developers stepped in to save (or at least gentrify) some of Shanghai's historic neighborhoods, including the former French concession and the waterfront district known as the Bund. While historically the Bund (called the *waitan* in Chinese) was famous for its many financial banks facing the Huangpu River, today it is known for its chic nightclubs and high-end shopping, from Chanel to Prada to Armani. At least one hotel features a rooftop helicopter pad and a luxury fleet of Rolls-Royces.

One symbol of the mix of old and new is the refurbished Peace Hotel, which dates from the late 1920s, making it one of the oldest hotels in Shanghai. For decades the once-luxurious hotel looked its age, replete with water-stained carpets and gloomy interiors. Purchased by a Canadian luxury hotel chain in 2007, the hotel was remodeled to the tune of $64 million and reopened in 2010. The hotel's famed "Old Jazz Band" is made up of octogenarians who learned to play jazz before the Chinese Communist revolution in 1949. Although jazz was forbidden during the Cultural Revolution, they became the first jazz band to play again in the reform era beginning in 1980. Many Peace Hotel aficionados claim the hotel would not be the same without its legendary musicians, who still perform nightly.

Shanghaiese proudly proclaim they are a city of immigrants, and many Chinese from the provinces suspect that Shanghaiese already see themselves as an international city rather than a Chinese city per se . . . and they may well be correct. Yet one-third of Shanghai's current population of 23 million are from other Chinese cities, so obviously the sense of superiority is not a birthright but something that can be acquired.

From an American point of view, Shanghai, with its shining skyscrapers, floating monorail, dense traffic, diverse population, luxury stores, and enormous hanging billboards featuring some of the most glamorous models in the world may not seem like a typical twenty-first-century Chinese city so much as a twenty-second-century world metropolis. And most Chinese might very well agree with this assessment.

Shenzhen Special
Economic Zone

S henzhen is China's first wealthy city. Once known for its cheap knockoffs of designer goods, Shenzhen is now one of the world's largest markets for luxury items. For example, of the fifty Icelandic rare wigeon duck down comforters produced in the world in 2006, retailing for $14,000 each, all three stocked in Shenzhen's Sam's Club sold out for Chinese New Year. Another popular item was solid-gold bottles of Chinese rice wine (*bai jiu*) retailing at $11,000 per bottle. And these are just items sold in discount stores.

After Deng Xiaoping opened up China in 1979, he designated several areas as Special Economic Zones (SEZ), where market-driven capitalist policies would be put in effect first. Shenzhen, formerly a region of paddies and villages about 126 square miles in size in southern China not far from Hong Kong, was designated as the first. Its transformation into a megalopolis of skyscrapers, shopping centers, capitalism, drugs, prostitution, millionaires, and extremely fast economic growth has been the poster child—for better and worse—of the Special Economic Zone policy.

(Altogether four SEZs were established in 1979—Zhuhai, Shantou, and Xiamen are the other three—followed by fourteen additional cities plus the island of Hainan in 1986. However, Shenzhen remains the city with the most visible transformation of its fortunes.)

During the 1990s, Shenzhen was dubbed "the wild, wild East" by many Western journalists for its laissez-faire atmosphere. Some of the

SEZ policies included giving preferential tax exemptions to foreign firms looking to invest in China; massive investment in new infrastructure including office buildings, hotels, banks, schools, and residential high-rises (including de facto gated communities where foreign businesspeople and their families could live in luxury, separate from the hustle-bustle lives of the Chinese workers recruited to the city). Hong Kong residents soon flooded into Shenzhen as well, attracted by the relatively lower cost of living and housing.

By 1996, China's central government endorsed the Shenzhen SEZ model and authorized the establishment of new zones throughout China. New Special Economic Zones include the greater Chongqing metropolitan area in Sichuan Province (which encompasses 30 million people) and most recently Tianjin, a formerly affluent city now mostly associated with China's "rust belt" of aging state-run factories and laid-off workers.

Shenzhen continues to be a magnet for young Chinese from the provinces seeking work in the booming economy. As a result, Shenzhen is known as being the rare Chinese city with more people under the age of thirty than over thirty. As there were very few parental figures to look askance at the behavior of its young population, Shenzhen became infamous as a center of vice. The government has tried to crack down on some illegal activities, including drug use and prostitution, with varied success.

In the twenty-first century, Shenzhen has become one of the major centers for tech research and development. The Shenzhen Software Park was created to develop software in 2001 as part of the central government's National Plan for development. Many of China's top technology firms are now based in the southern city, including BYD, Huawei, Tencent, ZTE, and Skyworth. And by 2007, a full 20 percent of all China's Ph.D.'s were working in Shenzhen.

Shopping

China continues to be a shopper's paradise. However, one should not assume, just because many (if not most) items for sale in the United States that are made in China are cheaper than European or American products, that this will be the case in China. In fact, many things that are made in China for export are actually more expensive in China than abroad. For example, Western-style clothing in posh department stores in Shanghai and Beijing and other large Chinese cities can be much pricier than they would be in the United States. The same is true for foreign brands from America or Europe that are imported to China. So when shopping in China, it's very important to take into account where you are and what you want in order to find the best prices.

However, every Chinese city will have some unusual local specials that you won't be able to find anywhere else. These may be clay teapots in the town of Yixing or the famed pottery of Jingdezhen, Suzhou silks, or the fancy embroidered clothing of many of China's ethnic minorities in Kunming and other cities in Yunnan Province. In the case of these unique items, if you see something you like, buy it immediately. You can always ship it home. A good hotel should be able to provide shipping services and pack things well enough so that they do not break. (Of course, this will not necessarily be cheap so you must figure this into the cost of any item you purchase.) You shouldn't wait until the end of your trip when you're in another locale and may never be able to find that item again.

In most cities there are tailors who can make you clothes to size, but they will need at least twenty-four hours usually and perhaps a week for very complicated hand-embroidered designs.

Many kitschy trinkets can be purchased at major tourist spots at the Great Wall, the excavation site of the terra-cotta warriors, Yellow Mountain, and the like. If something interests you, you might want to consider buying it, as many of these items are selling on eBay for surprisingly large sums.

Antiques should be bought from reputable shops that carry government certificates of authenticity for two reasons: 1) There are many fakes out there. 2) If you buy a real antique from an unauthorized dealer, you may not be allowed to carry it out of the country without the proper certification and it will be confiscated from you and you will not be reimbursed. China has been plagued by art smugglers in recent years and the government has vowed to crack down on the illicit trade in "national treasures."

Original artworks are also for sale at very good prices. Many art students from local colleges will set up exhibits in city parks near their campuses on the weekends and this is a good time to stroll about and find a lovely original painting. Department stores often carry original but mass-produced designs. There are also hucksters who approach foreigners on the street and invite you into a home for a "private viewing" of artwork that they promise will be sold at a special price. Even the most unassuming-looking people who approach you in this way should be treated with great suspicion. We have heard too many stories of people being robbed or otherwise ripped off by such grifters.

If you are interested in buying famous contemporary artworks, Beijing and Shanghai have many modern galleries that represent well-known artists who are also represented internationally in New York, Paris, and London. The prices are not necessarily better in China unless the artist is still up-and-coming and not yet well-known. As for famous ancient artworks, Christie's and Sotheby's Hong Kong auction houses host numerous events, but be forewarned the prices go up very quickly as the Chinese nouveaux riches tend to buy such treasures for themselves more so than Western or contemporary works.

Many Chinese are increasingly turning to online marketplaces like taobao.com, which bills itself as an online shopping mall where consumers in China, Hong Kong, Macau, and Taiwan can buy new and used goods. At the same time big-box stores and department store chains from around the world, from Carrefour to Walmart to Apple, have been moving into Chinese cities to capture shares of this increasingly important market. All of these companies are finding that they must modify their goods and even their ethos to integrate themselves into the culture. For example, Home Depot discovered Chinese consumers prefer not to assemble things themselves, much less build things from scratch, as they often lack the space and tools to assemble or build furniture at home. After years of trying to fit into the Chinese market, the chain decided to close its big-box stores in 2012 and concentrate instead on specialty stores that focus on the home decor preferences of consumers in specific cities.

Meantime, luxury retailers have been successfully tailoring their products for the Chinese domestic market for years, which is the fastest-growing market for luxury goods in the world. For example, Chanel spent years educating Chinese consumers about the brand, including financing a show about the founder Gabrielle "Coco" Chanel that ran at the Museum of Contemporary Art in Shanghai. The marketing has paid off. When Karl Lagerfeld designed a limited-edition red leather purse for the opening of a Chanel boutique in Shanghai, the $4,000 bags sold out within forty-eight hours.

Sino-Japanese War

Every time a prime minister of Japan visits the Yasukuni Shrine, where Class A war criminals are buried, protests break out throughout the rest of Asia, including China. The bitterness Chinese feel about the Japanese government's apparent lack of remorse for the suffering Japan caused during its eight-year war in China manifests itself in street demonstrations, protests outside the Japanese embassy and consulates, and sometimes violence, rock-throwing, and destruction of property, depending on the timing of the prime minister's visit. Should you be in China when such a protest occurs, get off the street and into shelter as soon as possible!

A few facts about the war may help visitors to understand why this conflict still resonates so deeply with the Chinese.

- An estimated 33 million Chinese died during the war with Japan.
- Japan was the aggressor, yet many of its textbooks and the museum at the Yasukuni Shrine refuse to acknowledge this fact.
- The brutality of the Japanese occupation has only been vaguely acknowledged by Japan's leaders.
- The Rape of Nanjing (or the Nanjing Massacre, as it is called in China), in which an estimated 300,000 civilians were killed and more than 80,000 women raped, is downplayed at best, and openly denied by Japanese politicians at worst. (This despite photographic evidence taken by Japanese soldiers themselves,

film footage taken by an American missionary, a detailed diary of the horrors kept by a Nazi businessman, and Japan's own admission during the War Crimes Trial of 1946 to having killed at least 220,000 civilians.)

- Reparations to so-called comfort women, who served as sex slaves to the Japanese military and who were often brutally slain when they were no longer needed, have been consistently refused by Japanese courts.

The Sino-Japanese War officially began in July 1937, when the Japanese army attacked Chinese troops near the Marco Polo Bridge ten miles west of Beijing. Chiang Kai-shek decided to fight back rather than cede more territory to the Japanese, who had begun taking over parts of northern China, a major concession in Shanghai and the island of Formosa (now called Taiwan) since the late nineteenth century. The conflict spread to Shanghai in August, where Chiang hoped the large international presence would cause Western powers to intervene to stop Japan's aggression. Instead the world watched as China burned. Chiang's troops fought for three months in Shanghai, despite the fact they were outmanned and outgunned, and he eventually lost 10 percent of his best-trained officer corps and suffered 250,000 casualties. The Japanese suffered 40,000 causalities.

Chiang then ordered a retreat. The Japanese commanders were infuriated by their own losses and decided to march upon the Chinese capital of Nanjing to try to force Chiang into submission. Chiang had troops defend the capital for a mere ten days before withdrawing inland to buy more time, as his supplies were limited. The Japanese army then took out its frustrations on the civilian population. In her bestselling book, *The Rape of Nanking,* Iris Chang cites reports by Western eyewitnesses (as well as Chinese) that corpses soon littered the streets, the Yangtze River ran red with blood, Japanese soldiers raped girls as well as elderly women then bayoneted them, and babies were killed before their mothers' eyes. However, far from breaking China's spirit, this act of barbarism led the Chinese to despise and fear the invading Japanese army, making the army's task of subduing the countryside more difficult.

Despite China's pleas for help, and worldwide condemnation of Japan in the press, from the *International Herald Tribune* to the *New*

York Times to the *Manchester Guardian*, and censure in the League of Nations, Western nations did not militarily come to China's aid. Europe was grappling with the dilemma of how to react to the rise of Hitler, and the United States was staunchly isolationist at the time, despite the fact that the day before invading Nanjing, the Japanese had bombed the USS *Panay* in the Yangtze while the ship had been clearly marked with American flags.

Chiang Kai-shek in 1939 established a new wartime capital in Chongqing (spelled "Chungking" in that era). The mountainous terrain allowed myriad bomb shelters to be built in which the populace could hide and the foggy weather made it hard for Japanese bombers to accurately bomb the city. Nevertheless, the Japanese flew more than nine thousand sorties over the city, dropping more than twenty-two thousand bombs.

Finally, after the Japanese attack at Pearl Harbor on December 7, 1941, the United States declared war against Japan and came to China's aid, sending military advisers, money, and weapons. Retired air force flyer Claire Chennault became head of the famed Flying Tigers, which was at first a voluntary air force unit in China and later was incorporated as a unit of the U.S. forces. Chennault was granted the U.S. rank of lieutenant general. General Joseph Stilwell, who spoke fluent Mandarin, was sent by President Roosevelt to help train Chinese troops. Unfortunately, he and Chiang clashed, for Stilwell was disgusted by Chiang's corrupt government and seemingly little regard for the average Chinese foot soldier. Stilwell was then sent to Burma to take charge of Chinese troops along with the British in an effort to keep the so-called Burma Road open, so that supplies could be flown and trucked into China after the Japanese cut off all other routes by sea and river.

In the meantime, the Japanese embarked on the "Three Alls" policy as they moved across the countryside: loot all, kill all, burn all. Panicked civilians fled the advancing army any way they could—by train, sampan, and on foot. Many succumbed to fatigue, starvation, and disease on the way. The Japanese, taking a page from Dr. Josef Mengele, as they were allied with the Nazis during the entirety of World War II, began to conduct medical experiments on Chinese POWs as well as civilians—including children and babies—and foreign POWs. The most infamous of these medical camps was called Unit 731 in Harbin in northern China.

By 1942, Japan tried deploying anthrax, cholera, dysentery, typhoid, and plague germs against Chinese Nationalist troops in several Chinese provinces. The biological warfare plan failed, however, as diseases do not distinguish between nationalities, and some ten thousand Japanese troops ended up being infected as well.

The war ended in 1945 after America dropped atomic bombs on Hiroshima and Nagasaki.

The contemporary tragedy of the lingering resentments caused by the Sino-Japanese War is that Japan and China historically were not enemies. Japan's first writing system came from China, and Chinese characters (called *kanji* in Japanese) still are used in Japan. The kimono, ink brush painting and calligraphy, traditional architectural styles, Confucianism, Zen Buddhism (called Chan Buddhism in China), and many other cultural institutions in Japan originated in China and were brought to Japan by monks and other immigrants.

Unfortunately, right-wing politicians in Japan have hijacked the history of World War II for their own political purposes as they fear the growing economic clout of China and do not want there to be good relations between the two countries. They downplay China and Japan's traditional friendship, lie about the Sino-Japanese War, and spread vicious propaganda (dubbed "hate manga" when it occurs—ever more frequently—in comic book form) to try to stir up negative feelings toward China. Their behavior does nothing to help improve China's attitude that the Japanese government is not remorseful for its wartime atrocities.

While individual Chinese and Japanese people are generally on friendly terms in China, studying and working together, if politicians continue to play the hate card for their own gain, it is hard to say what the future of China-Japan relations will be.

The Soong Sisters

Once upon a time, there were three sisters who became the most powerful women in all the land. One loved money, one loved power, and one loved China.

So goes a popular saying about the three Soong sisters, who indeed were the most powerful sisters in the first half of the twentieth century and perhaps the entirety of Chinese history.

The Soong family first came upon its wealth when patriarch, Charlie Soong, made a fortune publishing Bibles in the nineteenth century. He became close friends with many American missionaries and the industrialists who funded their work in China and used these connections to build his family's empire. He educated all three of his daughters and raised them as Christians, ensuring that they would be able to maintain close ties with the United States.

The eldest, Soong Ai-ling (ca. 1880s–1973), became the wife of industrialist H. H. Kong, one of the richest men in China and a descendant of Confucius. Through her family's connections to the Nationalist government, her husband gained a position overseeing the treasury. After the Communist takeover of China, she and her husband fled to America. She is buried in a cemetery in Hartsdale, New York.

The middle sister, Soong Ch'ing-ling (1890–1981), married revolutionary hero and founding father of the Chinese Republic, Sun Yat-sen. After Mao won the civil war and established the People's Republic of China, she alone opted to stay on the mainland and served in a number of symbolic positions with the Communist government. For this devotion, she is considered the sister who loved China.

The youngest sister, Soong May-ling (1898–2003), married Sun's successor, the Generalissimo Chiang Kai-shek, who became the paramount leader of China from 1928 to 1949. In 1949, he and his wife fled to Taiwan, where he reestablished the Republic of China, vowing until he died to "take back the mainland" from the Communists, a vow his wife espoused as well.

Their brother, T. V. Soong, was educated at Harvard and became the foreign minister of the Republic of China through his sisters' connections.

The Soong sisters have been the subject of innumerable books, movies, and even television miniseries in China. Ironically enough, it is Soong May-ling (also spelled "Meiling") who became the inadvertent star of these accounts even as they ostensibly rebuked her politics (and certainly her husband). But while Chiang was a man who could not transcend his times, she has come to embody a certain louche glamour associated with an era when a woman could be powerful, educated, wealthy, and beautifully dressed.

Even if she has often been played by models-turned-nominalactresses, in reality Soong May-ling was always more a Condoleezza Rice than a Kate Moss. Soong May-ling was educated at Wellesley, spoke fluent English (with an accent and diction that eerily recalled Joan Crawford), and served as her husband's most important emissary to the United States during the years of the Sino-Japanese War (1937–45). She traveled across the United States, speaking before crowds and even Congress to draw public support for China, as well as funding.

It was this funding that came to be the undoing of the Soong family, as General Stilwell reported that much of it ended up in the family's private coffers rather than in the hands of the army it was supposed to supply or the starving civilian population. (However, Stilwell did not personally blame Soong May-ling for this and in fact praised her in his private diaries for her intelligence and diplomacy.) By the war's end, President Truman famously refused to meet with her, signaling the end of what writer Sterling Seagrave has dubbed "the Soong Dynasty."

The best film yet made depicting their extraordinary lives is *The Soong Sisters*, directed by Mabel Cheung of Hong Kong and starring Michelle Yeoh as Ai-ling, Maggie Cheung as Ch'ing-ling, and Vivian Wu as May-ling.

Spring Festival

Like English muffins in England and Belgian waffles in Belgium, Chinese New Year is not actually called Chinese New Year in China. It is most commonly referred to as Spring Festival (in Mandarin: *Chun Jie*) as it traditionally marked the end of winter and the coming of spring. Spring Festival is China's most important holiday and is marked by the largest annual movement of people on the planet. Because it is considered essential to be with your family for the lunar new year festivities, tens of millions of Chinese—mostly migrant workers from the countryside who've found work in the cities and college students—make their way to their hometowns, literally by plane, train, ship, and automobile, but mostly by train. The Chinese government estimates that annually some 4 million people travel by train every day during the holiday period.

According to the lunar calendar, Spring Festival can fall in January or February. Many migrant workers, hoping to beat the travel rush, will begin their long treks to their villages weeks before the actual dates of the holiday, which traditionally was a fifteen-day period beginning with the first day of the new lunar year and ending on day fifteen with a lantern festival. Now, however, the holiday period—and travel crunch—has stretched into a monthlong period.

Traditions

Traditionally, Spring Festival was a time when villagers celebrated the end of winter by visiting family and friends. Firecrackers were set off to symbolically chase away evil spirits. Everyone was considered a year older (individual birth dates were not celebrated in traditional society), and married couples gave children candy and red envelopes with money, symbolizing good luck and prosperity in the coming year. In fact, the traditional greeting in Mandarin, *"Gong xi fa cai!"* literally means to have "good fortune" and "become wealthy." To simply say "Happy New Year" was just not good enough in the old days.

The traditional celebration was quite complicated. A week before the new year was to begin, the Kitchen God would ascend to Heaven and report on the family's behavior over the year. Like a Santa Claus in reverse, instead of bestowing gifts on the family with whom he lived, the snitch of a Kitchen God instead would tell the Jade Emperor in Heaven about all the family's squabbles, troubles, and evil deeds—unless he was bribed with sweets, so that only sweet words could pass from his mouth. Thus Chinese families would set out a plate of sweet foods, then burn his image in the family stove, thus allowing him to ascend to Heaven. Thus bribed, the newly contented Kitchen God was supposed to bring prosperity to the family in the coming year after delivering his honeyed words in Heaven.

Then the family had to set about paying off its debts and cleaning house before the actual lunar new year began. It's considered extremely unlucky to start a new year without first solving your problems from the previous year. People were also required to bathe before the new year, sweep, and wash their hair.

A traditional woodblock print of a child with a kite to celebrate the start of the lunar new year

Decor

On the eve of the lunar new year, offerings are made to various gods and the family ancestors. These include setting out food before the family altar or bringing food to the family temple, and burning ghost money (paper imprinted with images from the "Bank of Hell" or with silver or gold dye to symbolize currency) for the ancestors to use in Heaven—the better to bribe officials with and help their still-living, earthly descendants. The house should be decorated with cheerful pictures. These include rhyming couplets in beautiful calligraphy pasted on both sides of the household's front door or gate; images of fearsome-looking door guardians to drive away unlucky or evil spirits; and the word for "Spring" in calligraphy on red paper, often pasted upside down on the front door. (The rationale for this is similar to the American habit of hanging horseshoes upside down: you don't want the luck to run out.) A family reunion dinner is held and traditionally people stayed up all night.

By the late nineteenth and early twentieth centuries, new year prints, including hand-colored woodblock prints and later commercially printed posters, also became very popular to give as gifts as well as hang in one's home. Many feature healthy—that is, chubby—children playing with giant fruits or vegetables, surrounded by gold coins or flying beautiful kites. These charming prints all represent wishes for prosperity in the coming year. Other popular images include the "One Hundred Children" prints showing multiple, if not exactly one hundred, children romping playfully through a landscape. Traditionally, plump children were always seen as a sign of prosperity and good luck, as they represent a family or a village's future.

Good Luck and Bad Luck

On the first day of the lunar new year it is forbidden to wash one's hair or sweep one's house. Why? Because the words for washing hair (*xi fa*) are a homonym for the expression "to lose wealth." Similarly, sweeping as an action suggests one is sweeping away one's good luck.

For the next three or more days, families visit with friends and neighbors, giving gifts, generally of lucky foods, which include candy, dried fruits (a traditional delicacy since fruit was hard to come by in the winter months) and nuts, and symbolic foods like oranges, pomegranate seeds, apples—anything reddish in fact—as they are considered good luck.

Food

Naturally food plays one of the most important parts of Spring Festival and every region, every city, every village has its own specialties. Traditionally, in northern China (and along the Yangtze River, which is considered to divide north from south), people eat dumplings called *jiaozi*, which are boiled in water and are similar to ravioli, except they are not served with a tomato sauce but rather soy sauce, vinegar, and sometimes hot red pepper powder. For many poor farm families in Chinese history, Spring Festival may have been the only time all year in which they would actually get to eat meat. For southerners, however, the first night's meal is vegetarian.

If you are invited to celebrate Spring Festival with a family, remember to bring a gift. Food is always appropriate, as are expensive wines, liquors, bright bouquets, small orange trees, and candies nowadays. Use bright-colored paper to wrap your gift—red is best for the new year.

Noisy lion dances and dragon dances—powerful, lucky animals—also mark the new year festivities.

Why is red considered good luck?

According to legend, an ancient monster called the Nian appeared in villages at the end of every year. The Nian monster attacked people and livestock. Finally the Chinese discovered the Nian had three weaknesses: it was terrified of loud noises, hated sunlight, and despised the color red.

Thus, the ancient Chinese set off firecrackers to scare away the Nian monster, built bonfires to light the night as though it were day, and put up as much red as possible.

The word *nian* eventually came to mean "year" and thus the customs for passing the end of the year came into being.

Sun Yat-sen

Sun Yat-sen is to China what George Washington is to the United States: he is considered the founding father of the nation. Sun was the leading revolutionary who helped to overthrow the Qing dynasty and found the new Republic of China in 1912.

Sun was born in 1866 outside Canton (now known as Guangzhou) and later lived in Honolulu and Hong Kong, where he studied to be a physician from 1884 to 1886. While overseas, he founded the Nationalist Party (known in Chinese as the Guomindang in pinyin, or by its original English spelling, Kuomintang).

He developed the political philosophy known as the Three People's Principles (Nationalism, Socialism, and Democracy), which became the official ideology of the Nationalist Party and which was later incorporated into the Republic of China's constitution in 1946.

Sun died of cancer in Beijing on March 12, 1925, and was succeeded by Chiang Kai-shek as head of the Nationalist Party. In his last testament, he urged Chiang to continue to work to find solutions to China's political and social problems. He also urged the Nationalists to cooperate with the newly formed Chinese Communist Party.

Sun is an unusual political figure in China because he is celebrated by both mainland China and Taiwan as a political hero. His portrait is displayed next to Chairman Mao's on China's National Day on October 1 at Tiananmen Square. In Taiwan, Sun's portrait is ubiquitous, appearing in school and government offices. Sun was married to one of the famous Soong sisters (Soong Ch'ing-ling), who later became China's vice chairman, an honorary position, when Mao established the People's Republic in 1949. Soong May-ling (also spelled "Meiling") was married to Mao's rival, Chiang Kai-shek, and both Chiang and Soong May-ling fled to Taiwan after Mao's victory in the Chinese Civil War in 1949.

A huge marble tomb was built for Sun Yat-sen on Purple Mountain (Zijin Shan) just outside Nanjing, which was the capital of Republican China from 1928 to 1937 and then again from 1945 to 1949. The tomb, with its stunning blue-tiled roofs and myriad levels of stairs, mirrors some of the architectural elements of the Forbidden City, the former abode of China's emperors in Beijing. Sun Yat-sen's tomb (known as Zhong Shan Ling in Chinese) is one of Nanjing's biggest tourist attractions.

In an interesting bit of political trivia, during Chairman Mao's lifetime, Mao insisted that all Chinese forsake traditional and Western fashions and wear instead simple pantsuits in blue, green, or gray. These outfits became known as Mao suits or Mao jackets in the West. However, in Chinese they are named after Sun Yat-sen, not Mao, for it was Sun who first made famous this style of jacket, with its rounded collar. Thus, in China, the jackets are actually called *Zhong Shan zhuang* (literally, "Yat-sen style"), after the Mandarin pronunciation of Sun Yat-sen's personal name. (Sun used his local Cantonese dialect's pronunciation when he came up with the English spelling of his name.)

Tailors and Clothing

Under Mao, all Chinese were forced to wear uniforms composed of baggy pants and the so-called Mao jacket, both of which came in only three colors of polyester: gray, olive green, or navy blue. (In Chinese, the infamous "Mao jacket" was actually known as a "Sun Yat-sen–style jacket" because it was Dr. Sun who first made this high-collared style famous in the 1910s and '20s.) The idea behind this was to promote egalitarianism and to manufacture enough cheap clothing so that all citizens could afford them.

Today Chinese urbanites are among the most fashionable citizens in the world, a fact not lost on design houses from New York to Paris to Milan. Fashion insiders have already anointed China as an unironic market of glamour gourmands, where the likes of Donatella Versace's sexy, skintight looks can still be appreciated now that changing consumer trends in America and Europe are embracing more somber palettes and looser silhouettes.

For visitors to China who are used to buying cheap Chinese-made clothing in their home countries, it may come as a shock that Western designer clothing is actually more expensive in China than in the United States and Europe. This is because of high tariffs. However, the tariffs do not deter the Chinese nouveaux riches from indulging in buying high fashion. Thus, China is not a good place to buy Western designers if you are looking for bargains. However, if you are Asian and find it difficult to get your size in America or Europe,

China might just be the place to buy, as the sizing and styles are somewhat different from what is made for the Western market.

Another vast change is the resurgence of hand-tailored clothing. Under Mao, many people had to sew their own clothes to save money, but the exquisite embroidery, tailoring, and expertise in silk weaving that marked the traditional Chinese clothing of the Republican era (1911–49) were banned as bourgeois and counterrevolutionary. Today the art of the tailor and traditional-style clothing has returned.

Realizing that many visitors to China also like traditional Chinese clothes as well as the fit of hand-tailored Western-style clothing, tailors in most major cities are fully equipped to provide service in English. For example, on Beijing's most famous shopping street, Wang Fu Jing Avenue, there are numerous tailor shops. If a sign has English on the door or windows saying "Silks" or "Custom Made," it's a good bet that the business is equipped to help non-Chinese speakers. However, the clerks' English may be rudimentary and the process for ordering clothing is not always self-evident.

In shops that sell bolts of fabric, the organization is as follows: Tailors will be located in the corner while the silk will be displayed in front. (Many Chinese prefer to do their own sewing or use their own tailors and so only want to buy the fabric.) Signs in English will appear relatively high up on the walls. Look for the corner labeled "Tailors." Even though some tailors' English may not be excellent, they will generally have a book of designs from which you can choose— shirts, blouses, traditional dresses (known as *qipao* in Mandarin and pronounced "chee-pow"), the works. First, choose the style you want. Then the tailor should have a little dressing room—often just a tiny space behind a curtain—where you can measure yourself in privacy and provide all the data the tailor needs. Finally, you will need to pick out the fabrics and colors you want. The tailor will write down how much you need of each kind of fabric and you can go to the various fabric tables, pick the fabric, and show the form to the salesclerk (usually a woman). If you are in one of the larger, government-run shops, you will be given a receipt and told to pay at a separate cashier booth in the corner. The cashier will give you a stamped receipt, which you give to the salesclerk, who at last gives you your fabric. (It may seem a little cumbersome, but remember China has a lot of people who need to be employed.) Bring the fabric to the tailor and the tailor will give you a receipt and tell you what time to pick up your finished garment.

In smaller tailor shops, you may not have bolts of cloth to choose from but rather a swatch book. There may also be sample garments on hangers. You can ask for different designs to be combined, choose the colors, the trims, the embroidery—and you should try to get hand embroidery rather than machine although this will add to the time it takes to make your garment. Although Hong Kong is famous for the twenty-four-hour hand-tailored men's suit, if you order something more complicated than a stock pattern, expect your garment to take anywhere from a few days to a week to be completed, so plan accordingly. Don't wait to the very end of your trip to go to a tailor.

In Shanghai in the former French concession, you will find many small tailor shops in a row. Don't be shy about checking them all out and comparing prices. If you mention that So-and-so's shop next door is offering you a lower price, most tailors will meet that price or offer you a better deal. But remember, the most exquisite clothing made from quality silk and decorated with unique hand embroidery will not come cheap. In Hong Kong, the most exquisite *qipao*s can start at $1,200. In cities like Beijing and Shanghai, extremely fancy clothes can also run anywhere from several hundred dollars to well over a thousand dollars per item. In smaller Chinese cities, such as Tianjin, which has a long history of producing good tailors but not a lot of famous tourist sites, it's possible to get a solid-colored *qipao* without embroidery for as little as $40.

If you are able to make Chinese friends, ask them for recommendations for tailor shops. They will know where to find the least expensive tailors, the best quality, and the least touristy.

Of course, it is still possible to find funky, folkloric clothes at bargain prices. Many Chinese department stores offer ready-made traditional-style jackets and pants from $8 to $40. (Ask if there are any sales. Clerks are not allowed to give discounts but many department stores have ongoing sales on various types of merchandise.) However, nothing will match the fit of a hand-tailored garment.

Taiwan

Taiwan is more than a geographic island of 23 million people located some one hundred miles off the southern coast of China or the economic powerhouse dubbed a "Little Dragon" because of its success in adapting its market to high technology and other scientific ventures. Taiwan is also a potential hotbed for conflict—even war—between China and the United States.

China has always maintained that Taiwan is a Chinese province that must be reunited with the mainland, while the government of Taiwan prefers to maintain the status quo of de facto independence without declaring itself an independent state. When President Jimmy Carter decided to recognize the Communist government on mainland China as the "true" government of China in 1979, Congress quickly passed the Taiwan Relations Act, which states that the United States will defend Taiwan militarily if necessary should China ever try to use force to reunite Taiwan with the mainland.

The political history of Taiwan is complicated. During the Qing dynasty, the government named Taiwan China's twenty-second province in 1885. However, after China lost a war initiated by Japan in 1895, Taiwan was ceded to Japan as a colony. In 1945, after Japan's defeat in World War II, Taiwan was returned to China and again made a province. At that time that Nationalist government led by Chiang Kai-shek was in power. By 1949, however, the Chinese Civil War had reversed the political scene on the mainland, and Mao Zedong took over the reins of power, making China a Communist state. Chiang fled with his government, troops, and some 2 million refugees from the mainland to the island of Taiwan, which he then named the Republic of China and declared as the seat of the true government of China. However, by this time, the U.S. government had grown weary of the corruption under Chiang and did not offer any aid to his government in Taiwan to fight the Communists.

It looked as though Mao and the People's Liberation Army were poised to take over Taiwan in 1950 when suddenly the Korean War broke out. Fearing an unchecked spread of Communism throughout Asia, President Harry S. Truman reversed course, declaring Taiwan off-limits to the mainland Chinese government and sending the U.S. Seventh Fleet to patrol the Taiwan Strait, the narrow channel of water between the island and the mainland, to protect Taiwan from invasion.

Since that time, the United States provided $4.2 billion in military aid to train Chiang Kai-shek's troops and $1.7 billion in economic aid. These assistance programs, plus a 1954 Mutual Defense Treaty, helped build up Taiwan from an impoverished, underdeveloped island into a strong, prosperous, and modern state. Chiang, however, ruled Taiwan with an iron fist. He declared martial law, forbade divided families from any contact with relatives back on the mainland—forbidding them from even sending mail to China—and used his secret spy force to keep the population under control. These policies, in addition to corruption under his reign, did not engender much love for his Nationalist government among average Taiwanese citizens.

Currently, China is publicly seeking a "peaceful solution" to the Taiwan situation, while insisting still that Taiwan is a "renegade province" and refusing to fully renounce the use of force to reunite Taiwan with the mainland. Meanwhile, after Chiang Kai-shek's death in 1975, Taiwan underwent major political reforms, eventually ended martial law in 1987, and became a full-fledged multiparty democracy in the 1990s. The closest that China and Taiwan have come to war since 1950 was in 1995–96, when China held "missile tests" in the strait between the mainland and the island after then president Lee Teng-hui was invited to Cornell University. China was worried that the United States was treating Lee as a head of state, something the

One China Policy between the United States and China forbids. China launched a missile before Taiwan's first direct election, which was won handily by President Lee, who had previously come to power via government appointment.

There are two major political parties in Taiwan: the KMT (Nationalists) and DPP (Democratic Progressive Party). There is one key difference between the two parties: while the KMT would permit a reunification with China when China becomes a democracy, the DPP would prefer a small and independent Taiwan, not tied with China now or in the future. According to opinion polls, most Taiwanese prefer the status quo, an independent but not legally, permanently independent Taiwan—perhaps because a formal declaration of independence would precipitate a war with China.

The government from 2000 to 2008 was headed by a member of the DPP, President Chen Shui-bian, who before his election often stated his belief that Taiwan should be an independent state. Under pressure by the U.S. government not to provoke an all-out war with China, President Chen toned down his rhetoric. However, the mainland government accused him of practicing what they called "creeping independence" [pinyin: *pufu er xingde duli*]. However, China and Taiwan weathered those years without resorting to force.

While the current state of affairs may seem grim, relations between Taiwan and China have been improving on many fronts. More than a million Taiwanese maintain permanent homes in China; Shanghai alone boasts some 500,000 Taiwanese with their own shops, schools, banks, and apartment complexes. As a result, parts of Shanghai are now called "Little Taipei," after Taiwan's capital, or "Taiwan Town" in a nod to the Chinatowns that have cropped up in other countries around the world. Political relations have also improved considerably since the KMT regained power when Ma Yingjeou was elected as Taiwan's president. He permitted Chinese to visit Taiwan freely and promised that Taiwan would not declare independence from the mainland. Furthermore, China and Taiwan signed a new trade pact in 2010 that cut tariffs on exports from Taiwan to China and vice versa, increasing the economic interdependence between the two. China is now Taiwan's largest single trading partner. Exports to China accounted for 30 percent of Taiwan's total exports since 2007, and the Chinese-Taiwanese cross-strait trade crossed the $100 billion mark that year and continues to grow.

One point of contention between Taiwan and China continues to be media related. While the people of Taiwan have freedom of the press and religion, China blocks many Taiwanese news websites, magazines, and television programs from being viewed on the mainland. Furthermore, all maps in China continue to show Taiwan as a Chinese province, which many Taiwanese find galling.

On the positive side, most Chinese have no hard feelings personally toward the people of Taiwan. Taiwanese speak the same (or very similar) dialect as Chinese from Fujian Province, although many Taiwanese can speak Mandarin as well. Their businesses continue to thrive in China, and more and more Taiwanese businesspeople are relocating to China to take advantage of China's educated but much cheaper labor force. Many Taiwanese students and tourists come to China to study and travel each year, and, conversely, mainland tourists have been flocking to Taiwan since travel restrictions were lifted in 2010.

Technology

Tired of being known as the world's factory, the Chinese government has announced that it aims to make China a leader in technology within the next twenty years. China's funding for research and development is already one of the highest in the world, and China intends to develop the best IT, social media, green technology—from wind to solar to batteries for electric cars—and space satellite technology.

While China still lags behind Silicon Valley in IT, China leads the world in terms of Internet users, bloggers, and gamers. As of 2013, China had more than 513 million Internet users with more than half using microblogging services. However, 60 percent of China's population is still offline, meaning there is tremendous potential for growth. Although the government heavily censors Internet content, it is also spending big money to implement a next generation of the Internet, known as IPv6, that will have far more capacity than the rest of the world's current IPv4 system.

China has already surpassed U.S. technology in seven areas:

- high-voltage transmission
- high-speed rail
- advanced coal technologies
- nuclear power plants
- alternative energy vehicles

- renewable energy (including wind and solar photovoltaic systems)
- supercomputing

China's technological rise has caused some worries. The U.S. government has accused China of cyberattacks on commercial as well as governmental and military targets, including the *New York Times*, *Wall Street Journal*, Google, Yahoo, Lockheed Martin, Los Alamos National Laboratory, and the federal departments of Homeland Security, State, Energy, and Commerce. China has shot back with accusations that the United States is hacking into Chinese sites and conducting its own version of cyberspying, which is undoubtedly true.

The biggest obstacle to China's technological growth is most likely internal, including corruption in the Chinese Communist Party itself, the cost of an aging society, and the cost of cleaning up its pollution-ravaged environment. Despite the central government's focus on science and technology, China has yet to have a single scientist win a Nobel Prize in a scientific field while working in China. (Several Chinese-born physicists have won Nobels for research conducted outside China as citizens of other countries.) Whether China can continue to make major technological advances without reforms and restructuring of its totalitarian political system is a question that is yet to be answered.

Territorial Disputes

There are two major areas of territorial disputes involving China and its neighbors: the East China Sea and the South China Sea Islands. Most of the disputes have occurred because multiple nations have laid claim to the islands, fishing rights, and mining rights to the resources in these seas. As China has begun to assert itself regionally, there have been clashes between China and Japan, Vietnam, South Korea, and the Philippines.

East China Sea

One of the most hotly contested areas in the East China Sea is a group of five uninhabited islets and three barren rocks, known collectively as the Diaoyu Islands to China and Taiwan (the Japanese refer to this area as the Senkaku Islands). Geographically, they are actually closer to Okinawa and Taiwan than to either mainland China or any other major Japanese island. Okinawa itself was once an independent kingdom that historically had been more influenced by Chinese than Japanese culture. However, China ceded these areas, including the island of Taiwan, to Japan in the nineteenth century after the Sino-Japanese War in 1895.

As allies during World War II, President Franklin D. Roosevelt, Prime Minister Winston Churchill, and Generalissimo Chiang Kai-shek agreed that Japan must return all Chinese territories ceded to Japan (except for Okinawa, which was to be administered by the United States). After World War II, however, China itself fell into civil war, and Chiang Kai-shek fled to Taiwan, where he reestablished his government as the Republic of China on Taiwan, while Communist Party leader Mao Zedong established the People's Republic of China on the Chinese mainland. Because the mainland became a Communist country and an enemy of the United States, the question of which government controlled these islands became more ambiguous. In the intervening years, private individuals actually purchased some of the islands in dispute.

The most recent and most heated confrontation between China and Japan over these islands occurred in 2012. In September of that year, the Japanese government "nationalized" three of the Diaoyu (Senkaku) Islands by buying them from their private owner without considering them "disputed territories" with either China or Taiwan. China immediately challenged the purchase, Japan's claim to sovereignty over the islands, and Japan's control of them. Both China and Japan scrambled jet fighters in response to "incursions" into the territory. Tensions between the two countries continue; in 2013, Japanese newspapers reported that the government was considering firing "warning shots" at any Chinese fighter jets spotted over the islands. In response, a Chinese general warned that such an act would be considered the start of "actual combat." Although the United States claims neutrality in this dispute, it is obligated by treaty to defend Japan should China attack Japan in a military conflict, now or in the future.

South China Sea

The South China Sea extends past China to the Philippines, Cambodia, Thailand, Malaysia, Singapore, Sarawak, Brunei, North Borneo, and Indonesia. It is important because it is rich in gas, oil, and other resources; because of this, its hundreds of islands are claimed by mainland China, Taiwan, the Philippines, Malaysia, Brunei, and Vietnam. In 1997, China signed a joint declaration with the Association of Southeast Asian Nations (ASEAN) renouncing the use of force to settle disputes in the region. However, the Philippines signed a separate agreement with the United States in 1999 that provides for a resumption of joint military operations with American warships patrolling the South China Sea. China views this agreement as a sign of American aggression. As new sources of energy become ever more important to the growing economies of the nations of Asia, the South China Sea's contested islands and resources are, unfortunately, likely to become a source of future tensions.

Three Gorges Dam

The Three Gorges Dam in central Hubei Province is the world's largest dam at 607 feet tall and spanning 1.5 miles across the Yangtze (pinyin: Yangzi) River. It became fully operational in 2012, with thirty-two generators that could create 22,300 megawatts of electricity per year. (In comparison, America's national monument, the Hoover Dam, which was built in the 1930s, has an installed capacity of 2,080 megawatts a year.) Chinese government officials say the project is the largest since Emperor Qin ordered the Great Wall built in the second century BCE.

The Three Gorges Dam was a controversial project from its inception in 1993, when then premier Li Peng urged the government to green-light his pet project. His rationale was that China needed electricity for its growing cities and industries in order to become a developed country. Furthermore, the dam was expected to reduce annual floods along the Yangtze River (also known in Chinese as the Chang Jiang, or Long River, as it is the third longest river in the world). These floods have killed an estimated 1 million Chinese in the last hundred years alone.

However, the Three Gorges Dam also displaced some 1.5 million Chinese farmers, as water levels rose, drowning their ancestral villages forever. Some farmers were able to move to land within the various provinces affected by the dam; however, tens of thousands were forced to move to Tibet. Foreigners and Tibetan exiles openly criticized this policy as an effort to "dilute" the native population of Tibet with ethnic Han Chinese. Han Chinese farmers were not exactly thrilled at the move, either, as their new homes in Tibetan cities required them to adjust to an arid, high-altitude, and foreign culture, while giving up the humid, rice paddy–growing agricultural life that was most familiar to them and their families for generations. Furthermore, according to traditional folk religious beliefs, Han Chinese farmers were not supposed to leave the bones of their ancestors unattended nor move them to strange locales. In some instances, the farmers left their homes under duress, only after rising floodwaters threatened their lives. Clan temples, burial sites, ancestors' bones, all had to be abandoned.

Many archaeologists, art historians, and other intellectuals criticized the dam project because the government did not give them adequate time to excavate soon-to-be-flooded areas for their ancient treasures nor first move the priceless archaeological temples and tombs that were found in the 395-square-mile region that is now beneath the lake created by the dam. Among those thirteen hundred known historical sites to be inundated was the four-thousand-year-old homeland of the Ba people, one of the most ancient of the people who settled along the Yangtze.

Environmentalists also decried the rapid and unprecedented change to the natural environment. The dam lies on two faults and could precipitate earthquakes, analysts warn. The diversion of water from the Yangtze has already resulted in massive droughts for the central provinces of Hunan and Hubei, which is costing the government more money as it must divert water to the drought-stricken areas.

The Three Gorges Dam has cost more than $24 billion to build over thirteen years and utilized more than twenty-five thousand construction workers per year, making it the biggest consumer of dirt, stone, concrete, and steel in the history of the world. Officials now admit the dam has been causing water pollution and landslides, and they may begin a new relocation program for 2 million people living in the dam's reservoir region. However, supporters of the dam point out that it is the world's largest man-made producer of electricity from a renewable energy source. The dam could be a model for future Chinese hydropower projects, which would help to alleviate China's current reliance on coal-burning power plants. Whether the benefits outweigh the financial, human, and environmental costs cannot be known at present. Only future generations will be able to weigh what has been lost and gained with the power that the dam brings to China.

Tiananmen Square Pro-Democracy Movement

The Tiananmen Square Pro-Democracy Movement refers to a seven-week period from April 15 to June 4, 1989, when an estimated 1 million students, workers, and other urbanites from all over China joined together at Tiananmen Square in Beijing for the largest demonstrations seen in China since the Cultural Revolution. The movement ended when then prime minister Li Peng, with the approval of paramount leader Deng Xiaoping, ordered the People's Liberation Army to remove all the demonstrators by force. While the students on the square itself were led away before the bullets began to fly, hundreds if not thousands of other civilians died. No official tally has ever been released.

In China the movement's bloody end is called Six Four (*liu si* in Mandarin) in reference to the date of the military crackdown; in the West, it is more commonly called the Tiananmen Square Massacre.

The background to the movement is complex. Throughout the 1980s there had been student protests on a much smaller scale throughout most of China's major cities, on everything from corruption to the slow pace of economic and political reforms to the two-tiered money system that allowed foreigners access to better stores, hotels, and even dormitories while Chinese were treated, in their words, like "second-class citizens in our own country."

When former party general secretary Hu Yaobang died on April 15, 1989, students in Beijing began to set up a makeshift memorial to Hu, at first merely bringing flowers and wreaths to surround a photograph of the reform-minded leader. In 1986, Hu had famously refused to jail a small band of pro-democracy students who had been identified after leading a number of protests. Soon, thousands of students marched to the square to add petitions, memorials, big-character posters complaining about mistreatment or about corruption within the Chinese government, and demanding more openness, including democracy. The movement struck a nerve within China and students from all over the country began flocking to the square. Some students demanded a dialogue with a known "hardliner" who opposed change within the party, Premier Li Peng. A core group of students began a hunger strike, while nearly a million students and other young people camped out on the square in makeshift tents, dancing to rock 'n' roll music, parading around a statue dubbed the Goddess of Democracy that was patterned after the Statue of Liberty, and insisting upon meetings with government officials to read their petition calling for reforms. Students on loudspeakers proclaimed the sins of various corrupt government cadres from around the nation. Workers soon joined in the protest, and journalists from around the world descended upon the square, broadcasting live interviews with the young Chinese activists.

The Chinese central government seemed to be paralyzed and unsure how to react, leading to rumors of internal dissent. Hu Yaobang's successor, Party General Secretary Zhao Ziyang, was rumored to be sympathetic to the student demands and actually visited student encampments in the square, talking with student leaders. However, others urged the ailing Deng Xiaoping to take a firm stance and reassert control. Rumors began to circulate in the government that the CIA or the Nationalist government in Taiwan was going to use the protests as a cover to smuggle in arms and try to overthrow the government. The square was becoming filthy, sanitation was lacking, the government looked as though it had indeed lost control, and finally the hardliners won.

When martial law was declared in Beijing and the People's Liberation Army was first called to the Square on May 20, there was initially no bloodshed. Instead the students faced off against the soldiers, competing against them in sing-alongs as the two groups stood in lines and tried to outsing each other. Other student groups tried to convince the young soldiers to join their side, passing out flyers and posters to describe their movement. Realizing that the Mandarin-speaking troops were already "corrupted" by the students, the central government ordered an isolated division of the PLA from Guangdong Province, where Cantonese is the main dialect, to be brought to the square. The soldiers had not been told of the student protest and apparently were quite shocked to see Beijing inundated with filthy, shouting young people. They were ordered to clear Beijing of the demonstrators on the night of June 3 and in the early morning hours of June 4, the troops and armored tanks moved in. The soldiers were told to fire upon the protesters and, unable to understand a word the protesters shouted at them in Mandarin, they did. Amnesty International estimated that hundreds of civilians were killed outright and as many as ten thousand were injured or arrested. No information has been forthcoming as to how many of the injured eventually died from their wounds.

A horrified world watched as tanks rolled over bicycles and bloody bodies were picked up by students and carried on makeshift stretchers to hospitals.

Some of the protesters turned violent. A few climbed onto the tanks and dropped Molotov cocktails inside. Some managed to find other weapons. These were the images that were shown around China: that of the burned and charred bodies of soldiers, some dead from bullet wounds.

For a year after June 4, the government declared martial law nationwide and began a campaign to paint the pro-democracy movement as a "counterrevolutionary movement." So as not to vilify an entire generation of students, the government claimed that the "young and naive" students had been led astray by "a few bad elements" and "foreign conspirators." Even middle school and elementary school students were obliged to attend a traveling show of photographs taken from the aftermath of June 4—which showed the dead soldiers, with placards describing the tally of injuries that the soldiers received, but did not show the bloodied bodies of the demonstrators, the makeshift morgues in Beijing's hospitals, nor the dead who had been peacefully sleeping in their homes when high-powered bullets pierced the walls and killed Beijing residents in their own beds.

Pictures of student activists were displayed on television and wanted posters placed around the nation as though they were hardened criminals. One activist, Wang Dan, was apprehended while he tried to flee to Hong Kong. He was sentenced to ten years in prison. Others, like Chai Ling and Wu'er Kaixi, escaped and were offered prestigious scholarships to study at Princeton and Harvard. General Party Secretary Zhao Ziyang was stripped of his title and placed under house arrest, where he remains into the present.

Today, a new generation of young people have never heard of the Pro-Democracy Movement or the June 4 Crackdown. Those who have tend to express apathy or at least feign ignorance. In the new post-1989 China, most students will say they are more worried about finding a good job and making a lot of money than they are about politics. While Chinese will express their personal feelings about June 4 to foreign visitors whom they have gotten to know well, by and large they will not express these feelings publicly with strangers. And most Chinese parents who remember that era have taught their children to avoid political protests as they do not want their children to be harmed and they do not believe such protests will lead to political change anyway. Some Chinese express open disgust that the West still views China through the lens of the Tiananmen Massacre, which they feel is ancient history.

(In fact, it is the poorest of the poor rather than the elite who are the most likely to be politically active in China today. Of the more than two hundred daily protests that occur in China, most occur in the countryside in impoverished villages where farmers' land has been seized without compensation, their water has been polluted by factories, or they simply have no way to pay for medical bills, school tuition, and the basic necessities of life.)

Occasionally mothers of slain students from the Tiananmen Movement will petition the government for redress and even a few government officials have hinted that it might be time to stop vilifying the movement and offer an apology. However, at present there is no indication that the central government in Beijing intends to reopen June 4's cold case.

Tibet

Three important things to remember about Tibet when you're in China:

1. The Chinese government truly believes it's helping the Tibetan people with its massive public works programs to build highways, modern hospitals, schools, high-rises, hotels, and most recently the $4.2 billion Beijing-Tibet rail line.
2. The Chinese government is as likely to grant Tibet independence as the United States is likely to give back its land to the Native Americans.
3. The Tibetan people, despite the increased quality in life associated with the modern hospitals, schools, highways, and high-rises, really would rather be an independent state under the spiritual leadership of the fourteenth Dalai Lama, currently living in exile in India.

Tibet, once an isolated land of plateaus set amid massive mountains in the Himalayas, is now accessible to millions of foreign tourists as well as Han Chinese thanks to the new rail line, which has been called an "engineering miracle." At its highest point, the tracks are 16,628 feet above sea level, making it the highest railway in the world. And the entire 2,500-mile trek through some of the world's most spectacular and previously inaccessible scenery takes only two days.

Many Tibetans and Westerners worry that this train will accelerate a process of Sinicization of Tibet that began in 1951, when the People's Liberation Army marched into Tibet, reasserting Chinese control after Tibet had declared independence from China in 1911. In 1959, Tibetans briefly revolted but failed to regain independence. As a result, 100,000 Tibetans along with the Dalai Lama soon fled to India to establish a government in exile. In 1980, the Dalai Lama gave up his previous call for independence and instead now asks that the Chinese government permit him to establish an "autonomous" government for Tibet inside China. The Chinese government has thus far refused to negotiate with him and maintains that Tibet must remain a part of China.

Tibet, once considered by Westerners to be the "Shangri-la" of legend, consists of 471,000 square miles with a low population of slightly more than 3 million people. Ethnic Tibetans have expressed concern that the $4.2 billion high-speed railroad that opened in 2006 will bring ever more Han to their land, making Tibetans a minority. However, as of the 2010 census, ethnic Tibetans still made up some 90 percent of the population. Some Tibetans claim the actual percentage is less if the population of Han Chinese migrant workers were counted. Han have been pouring into the region as workers, business owners, investors, teachers, and soldiers to take advantage of government-funded development projects, including farms, restaurants, hotels, schools, mining, construction, and tourism initiatives. In 2008, anti-Han riots erupted in the capital of Lhasa in which ethnic Tibetans burned Han-owned businesses, resulting in nineteen deaths. Since 2009, more than one hundred Tibetans have self-immolated in protest of Chinese government rule. Meantime, the Chinese government continues to pour in development funds. Though the Tibetan economy has been growing faster than the rest of China, critics contend the money benefits Han migrants more than Tibetans.

Although there has been a growing interest in Tibetan Buddhism among Han Chinese, including many bestselling novels set in Tibet that describe its people's lifestyle and religious beliefs, most Chinese do not understand the West's fascination with the Dalai Lama nor do they understand why Americans, for example, put bumper stickers on their cars saying "Free Tibet" or unfurl banners in

China saying the new railway is going to destroy Tibetan culture (as three women from the United States, Canada, and Great Britain did in 2006 when the railway opened for business). The Chinese truly believe that Tibet is part of their country and serves as an essential buffer zone on its southwest border from potential foreign invasions.

Eventually, a cross-cultural dialogue on Tibet may be possible. At this point, it's a discussion you can hold with friends in China but not necessarily one that will be particularly fruitful.

Urumqi

U rumqi is one of the oldest cities in China and has the unique distinction of being the city farthest from any major source of water in the world. The capital of Xinjiang province, Urumqi is more than two thousand years old. Its name is not even Chinese but comes from an ancient form of Mongolian that was used by the Junggar tribe. It means "beautiful pastureland," a compliment indeed from the nomadic Mongols.

In fact, Urumqi is an oasis of green in Xinjiang, which is known for its extreme terrain—from barren deserts to steep mountain peaks.

Although Urumqi is considered a small city by Chinese standards, with a population of less than 3 million residents, it is extremely diverse. Ethnic Han Chinese are a minority among the forty different ethnic groups living together in the city including Uighurs (Caucasian Muslims), Hui (ethnically Chinese Muslims), Kazakhs, Mongolians, Kirgiz, and Xibe.

Urumqi's diversity is rooted in its long history; the city was a main juncture on the northern route of the Silk Road upon which traders from all over the world came to China. During the Tang dynasty (618–907 CE), trade along the Silk Road was at its apex and Urumqi was a bustling cultural center. Today that diversity is also reflected in the local cuisine, which features kebobs; pilaf; dumplings; mutton (instead of the Han Chinese preference for pork); spicy dishes featuring tomatoes, peppers, and eggplant; poppy seed–covered flatbread known as *nang*; and fruits including apricots, raisins, grapes, and various sweet melons.

The most spectacular tourist attractions are the snowcapped Tianshan ("Heavenly Mountain") Range and Tianchi ("Heavenly Lake") thirty miles southeast of Urumqi.

In recent years Urumqi has been the site of ethnic tensions, including the most violent ethnic clash recorded in China in decades. On July 5, 2009, 197 people were killed and more than 1,000 were injured during the course of Uighur demonstrations against Han Chinese residents, who account for some 75 percent of the population. Two days later, Han Chinese demonstrators retaliated and attacked Uighur neighborhoods. The Chinese government clamped down, tightening security in the city while blaming outside agitators who support Uighur independence from Chinese control. Unfortunately, economic insecurity and increased competition, feelings of ethnic discrimination, and clashes in religious beliefs continue to make this historically diverse city a potential powder keg for ethnic strife in the twenty-first century.

Visiting a Home

Generally, Chinese do not casually invite people over to their homes the same way that Americans do. While it is common in the United States for colleagues to visit each other's homes for dinner, backyard barbecues, and the like, it is not uncommon for Chinese never to visit their colleagues' homes at all. There are many cultural and material reasons for this, including the stricter sense of hierarchy in workplace environments; a feeling of shame or loss of face if one's apartment is not as nice as that of one's coworkers; the fact that unless someone is very rich, their apartment might be quite cramped and they may even have extended family members living with them. However, among young people, it is quite common to visit each other's homes for a meal together or to watch a DVD, although they may actually prefer meeting in an Internet café, trendy restaurant, or other public space that offers a greater variety of activities—as well as freedom from their parents' watchful eyes. (Many Chinese live with their parents well into their twenties or later if they cannot get a good job with a high enough salary to pay for the increasingly expensive apartments in China's urban areas.) Also, many young workers in factories, for example, live in communal dormitories maintained by their employers and do not have their own apartments.

However, if you are invited by Chinese friends to visit their home, there are a few simple rules of etiquette that should help smooth over other cultural differences.

- Remove your shoes by the doorway before entering the living quarters.
- Bring a small gift. Fruit, sweets, flowers, a bottle of wine, and so on are all acceptable. Your hosts most likely will not open the gift in front of you, so if it's something that you want them to eat with dinner, for example, be sure to tell them that they should open it now.
- Don't expect to be shown the entire apartment or house, the way many Americans give tours to guests. However, if your friends have just acquired a very nice apartment or house, or if they are very familiar with Western customs, they may give you a home tour.
- Even if you have not come over for a meal, you will be offered food and something to drink. It is polite to accept these things, but you don't have to actually eat or drink everything you are given. You can just taste a few things if you aren't hungry or don't particularly like the snack you've been offered.
- Be sure to compliment your hosts' living quarters. They will refuse the compliment, saying "Oh, no, this is really not very good." That's simple politeness and the expected Chinese response. Whatever you do, don't agree with them and offer advice on where to find a nicer item if they say something isn't very good, such as a sofa or a set of furniture or a painting. Traditional Chinese manners require the owner to say his or her home, apartment, furnishings, or what have you is somehow inferior (although the nouveaux riches who are building mansions and amassing huge art collections are unlikely to follow these old points of etiquette).
- If you want to reciprocate and invite your Chinese friends to your apartment or college dormitory, remember to offer them a beverage and food as soon as they arrive. Many Chinese are not accustomed to asking for even a drink of water in someone else's home, even if they are very thirsty. They'll keep waiting in agony for you to offer it first.
- If you are a single female and are invited by a single male to his apartment or dorm, this can be seen as sexually forward if you accept. If you don't know the man very well, bring a friend along with you so that no one gets the wrong idea. There are a lot of

stereotypes in China about the sexually free and wild American woman. Best not to put yourself in a potentially awkward or even dangerous situation.

- If you are a single male and want to invite a single Chinese female to your apartment or dormitory, you might want to invite her friends to come along, too, so that rumors don't spread about her behavior. No point in causing someone to lose face if your intentions are just to be friendly. You also don't want to gain the reputation of being a cad.

Xi Jinping

Xi Jinping is China's supreme leader—and, undoubtedly one of the most powerful leaders in the world. He became general secretary of the Chinese Communist Party as well as chairman of the Central Military Commission in November 2012, and president of China in 2013.

Xi [pronounced "shee"] was born in 1953 in Beijing and is considered a "Red Princeling." Xi's father, Xi Zhongxun, supported Deng Xiaoping's reform and Open Door Policy and was appointed a vice premier of the government. At one point, Xi's father was jailed under Mao for openly supporting progressive policies; however, he was later rehabilitated and restored to a position of power. When he was sixteen, Xi Jinping was sent to the countryside in the remote northwestern province of Shaanxi "to learn from the peasants." His official biography records that he was "elected" a "model educated youth" and a village party chief. At age twenty-two, Xi was allowed to return to Beijing, where he enrolled in the prestigious Tsinghua University and studied chemical engineering. He later studied law at the Institute of Humanities and Social Sciences and received an LL.D. degree.

After graduation, Xi became a deputy county party chief in Hebei Province in northern China. He then held a number of posts with increasing responsibility throughout China, including party chief of Ningde Prefecture in Fujian Province (a politically more important post because Fujian is opposite Taiwan). He eventually became governor of the province and later governor of Zhejiang. After proving himself adept in these roles, Xi rose to important party posts in the central government, all the way to the most important decision-making body in the country, the Politburo of the Central Committee of the Chinese Communist Party. By 2008, Xi was named China's vice president, and then vice chairman of the powerful Central Military Commission in 2010. After behind-the-scenes negotiations among factions at the Eighteenth Party Congress in 2012, Xi was selected as party general secretary and chairman of the Military Commission, and unofficially selected to become president. In March 2013 at the National People's Congress in Beijing, the selection was made official when Xi was named president after a symbolic vote of the Congress's delegates.

China's president and general secretary of the party usually keep the positions for two terms for a total of ten years. Among the seven members of the most powerful Standing Committee, Xi and his premier Li Keqiang are the only two members who are expected to stay in power for ten years. The other five members are older and should retire at age sixty-five, according to party rules.

Xi has made two major pledges since becoming president. He said he wants the nation to achieve the "Chinese dream," a phrase that if he did not coin, he has at the very least used so prominently that it has become associated with his presidency. By "Chinese dream," he means national renewal that will make China one of the world's great powers at every level. The second pledge is to combat corruption, which at this point is one of the major factors that could prevent the Chinese dream from being achieved. Along those lines, officials immediately clamped down on banquets and gift-giving after Xi came to office, which resulted in a noticeable decline in luxury sales for European and American brands.

Xi's leadership style is markedly different from that of his predecessors. He has assumed a more down-to-earth style of communicating with the Chinese people, using plain expressions rather than the flowery expressions or jargon typically used by government officials. In the media, Xi is portrayed as a friendly leader, frequently photographed smiling with Chinese citizens or alongside his glamorous wife, the famous folksinger and television personality Peng Liyuan, when traveling abroad. Peng Liyuan often accompanies Xi on state visits, perhaps signaling China's intention to use soft power in the way other nations have been doing for decades. Whereas his immediate predecessor, Hu Jintao, was so formal in appearance and talk that he was commonly mocked (at least in the foreign press) as "robotic," it is clear that Xi is a modern leader who understands the value of both hard and soft power.

Xi'an

Xi'an, the capital of the northwestern province of Shaanxi, is
most famous for the Qin dynasty terra-cotta warriors discovered just outside the city limits. This spectacular archaeological find was uncovered accidentally by farmers digging a well in
1974. To their surprise, an entire army of life-size soldiers was eventually revealed once archaeologists and art historians came to the
scene. The terra-cotta warriors were commissioned by the first emperor of China, Qin Shi Huang Di, who had them constructed to
guard his tomb before he died in 210 BCE. Each of the six thousand
warriors and horses uncovered so far is unique, with different facial
features, weapons, and poses. Today it is still possible to visit the
original dig site and see the soldiers emerging from the ground. There
are two other vaults, containing more warriors and a chariot. A museum nearby houses other archaeological finds. The dig site has not
yet been fully excavated and some scholars believe that Qin Shi
Huang Di, in fact, had a replica of his entire capital built underground for him to enjoy in the afterlife and the warriors are merely
the outermost portion—placed there to guard the city, naturally.

Xi'an, the city, has a long and important history. It served as China's capital twelve times, and its origins have been traced to the Neo-
lithic Age (around 5000–2000 BCE). The city reached its apex in the
Sui and Tang dynasties, when it was known as Changan, the City of
Eternal Peace, and was the center of culture for not only China but

central Asia and all the traders on the famed Silk Road. Diverse, filled with peoples from around the world, wealthy, culturally rich, and renowned for its music and dance, Xi'an/Changan was truly the center of the civilized world. Today, Xi'an's many mosques and large Muslim population attest to its former role as a Silk Road trading center.

Xi'an also played an important role during the Sino-Japanese War, when the local warlord, Zhang Xueliang, kidnapped Generalissimo Chiang Kai-shek in December 1936 and refused to release him until Chiang agreed to concentrate on fighting the Japanese instead of fighting the Chinese Communists and to work with the Communists as a so-called United Front. This event became known as the Xi'an Incident. (After Zhang released the Generalissimo, the warlord agreed to become Chiang's prisoner as a sign of his own sincerity, that he had acted not for personal gain but for the benefit of China as a nation. Even after Chiang Kai-shek fled to Taiwan, he brought Zhang with him and in fact kept Zhang in prison until Chiang's death. Zhang was released by Chiang's son in 1988; he then went into exile in Hawaii, where he later died.)

Xi'an is pronounced "shee on."

Xinjiang Uighur Autonomous Region

The Xinjiang Uighur Autonomous Region is the only other region in China besides Tibet where ethnic Han Chinese are a minority and where the majority of spoken languages are not just different dialects of Chinese but completely different languages. (In Xinjiang's case, they come from Turkic and Persian linguistic groups.) Using the Mandarin pinyin system, the name of the province, Xinjiang, is pronounced "Shin-jong" (hard "j"). Uighur is actually the English name for the majority people, who are Caucasian Muslims with origins in central Asia and Mongolia. It is pronounced "wee-gur." In Mandarin Chinese, the Muslim population are simply called Xinjiang ren, which means "people from Xinjiang." It is called an autonomous region because the people are given somewhat more autonomy in political and cultural affairs than in China's Han-dominant provinces.

A vast province of 615,000 square miles (China's largest in land mass and more than twice the size of Texas), Xinjiang contains both desert plains and steep mountains and borders eight other nations—Russia, Pakistan, Kyrgyzstan, Kazakhstan, Tajikistan, Afghanistan, India, and Mongolia—as well as Tibet. Furthermore, it is the homeland of Uighurs, Kazakhs, and Kirgiz (also spelled "Kirghiz"), as well as Russian, Han Chinese, and other ethnic minorities.

While the Chinese historically viewed Xinjiang with suspicion, referring to its nomadic people as "barbarians," Xinjiang actually holds a very important place in Chinese cultural history. It is the birthplace of the famous Tang dynasty poet Li Po (now spelled "Li Bai" or "Li Bo"), whose father, many scholars now believe, may have been a trader along China's famous Silk Road who married a Han Chinese woman. Xinjiang was also the source of much of Tang China's golden age of arts, music, and dance, as wealth spread by the Silk Road traders also brought an influx of cultural and artistic influences that combined with Chinese traditions to create new and exciting art forms.

Tang China's control of Xinjiang ended in the ninth century CE when the Uighurs invaded from Mongolia. Xinjiang was subsequently ruled for nearly four hundred years by a succession of tribal kingdoms led at various times by Uighurs, Kharakharids, and Kharakhitay minority peoples. While Buddhism was once the prevalent religion, and Xinjiang figures prominently in the Chinese classic Buddhist novel *Journey to the West*, Islam took root in western Xinjiang during the eleventh and twelfth centuries. By the fourteenth century, Islam had spread to eastern Xinjiang as well. However, in 1219, the Mongols took over Xinjiang (and eventually the rest of China during the Yuan dynasty).

Xinjiang did not become part of China again until 1755. After a series of revolts, the Qing dynasty finally succeeded in incorporating Xinjiang as a province in 1884 by moving Han Chinese settlers into the area to dilute the strength of the Muslim tribes. Still, the turmoil did not end.

By the 1930s and '40s, the local population had become closely allied with Kazakhstan and Kyrgyzstan, republics that were part of the Soviet Union. Twice during this time, in 1933 and 1944, Xinjiang was declared to be the Republic of East Turkestan. Only after Mao's victory in 1949 did the Uighurs dissolve their republic and join the Communists as part of the People's Republic of China. Those Uighurs with remaining separatist feelings were brutally suppressed by the People's Liberation Army (PLA) in 1951.

Since that time, the Chinese government, in an effort to win over the people, had the PLA corps reclaim desert land for agricultural use and opened and operated businesses to help improve the economy. Many highways and railway links were built. The government also encouraged Han Chinese migration into the province. By the 1990s, the Uighurs, who had once comprised 90 percent of Xinjiang's population, now constituted less than 50 percent. (These policies of Han migration, economic expansion, and the building of railways and highways to bring in trade are also being used by the Chinese government to diminish separatist movements in Tibet.)

During the early 1990s, Uighur separatists occasionally blew up bombs in China to draw attention to their cause for autonomy, even blowing up a bus in a suicide mission in Shanghai. For a while, the U.S. government expressed sympathy with the Uighurs, but after the terrorist attacks of September 11, 2001, the United States sided with China against the Muslim separatists and China was able to crack down severely on all separatist groups.

In July 2009, China suffered its worst incident of ethnic violence in many years when a riot broke out that pitted Uighur demonstrators against Han Chinese. The dispute resulted in 197 deaths, mainly Han. Uighur neighborhoods then suffered retaliatory attacks from angry Han demonstrators. As a result, the Chinese government increased security in the province, and in 2013, courts sentenced twenty people to prison for "militant separatism." Clearly, the tensions in Xinjiang are not going away anytime soon.

> *Before my bed, the bright moon's beams*
> *are like the earth's dew.*
> *Lifting my head, I stared at the burning moon.*
> *Bowing, I longed for home.*
> — Li Po (aka Li Bai or Li Bo), Tang dynasty poet and
> Xinjiang native (701–62 CE); trans. by May-lee Chai

Yuan

The yuan is China's basic unit of currency.

In Mandarin, it is called *ren min bi*, which literally means "the people's script [money]" and is commonly abbreviated RMB.

Below are what some of the denominations look like. In the case of units worth less than a Chinese dollar (or yuan), both coin and paper versions exist for fifty cents (called *wu jiao* or *wu mao*) and ten cents (called *yi jiao* or *yi mao*). Only coins exist for one cent and five cents.

Please check with your bank or online for the most up-to-date currency exchange rates.

A Chinese 10 yuan note

A Chinese 5 yuan note, 1 yuan note, and 10 cent note

Zhong Guo

Zhong Guo is the name China calls itself in Mandarin. The pronunciation sounds similar to "johng gwoh," with a hard "j." The literal meaning is the "Middle Kingdom" or "Middle Country." This meaning reveals China's oldest conception of itself as the center of the civilized world.

The character for "middle" is a rectangle with a vertical line drawn through it. The rectangle can be seen to represent the world and the line shows China's central place in it.

Of course, the ancient Chinese didn't believe that the world was actually a rectangle. However, this character was created before Chinese used paintbrushes and ink to write but instead wrote using metal tools to carve into bone, tortoise shells, or stone. Thus, circular designs were avoided as it was easier to carve straight lines with hard edges.

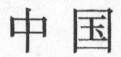

Why is China called China?

The name China originated with Persian traders in the third century BCE. They had discovered that an emperor had unified this land of many kingdoms and now called himself by the reign title Qin (pronounced "chin"). *Na* derives from an ancient Persian word for nation. Thus, as the Persians traveled the world, selling and trading Chinese silks, spices, and goods to other peoples, they described these items as coming from the Nation of Qin, aka Chin-Na. The name has stood ever since. (Of course, the current English spelling is not ancient Persian but the English equivalent of the sounds.)

Notes

The authors have used personal experience, personal interviews, and their own research for most of the information in this book. For additional statistics and information they would like to direct the readers to the following sources, which they found most helpful:

Introduction

For more on China's economic growth:
Wang Zhuoqing, "China's Billionaires on Rise," *People's Daily Online*, Mar. 1, 2013, http://english.peopledaily.com .cn/90778/8148555.html.

Market for art:
Jason Chow, "From Arms Dealer to Art Dealer," *Wall Street Journal*, Dec. 7, 2012, p. D10.

Income inequality:
Sim Chi Yin, "In China, a Vast Chasm Between the Rich and Poor," *New York Times Opinionator Blog*, Feb. 9, 2013, http ://opinionator.blogs.nytimes.com/2013/02/09/in-china-a-vast -chasm-between-the-rich-and-the-rest/.

On air pollution:
Edward Wong, "On a Scale of 0 to 500, Beijing's Air Quality Tops 'Crazy Bad' at 755," *New York Times*, Jan. 12, 2013.

Architecture

25,000 workers statistic and hutong *destruction:*
Jim Yardley, "Olympics Peril Historic Beijing Neighborhood," *New York Times,* July 12, 2006, p. 1A.

BBC quote on 2005 construction:
BBC World News broadcast, December 10, 2005.

Quotes: "land of dreams," 2004 concrete and steel statistics, descriptions of Bird's Nest and the Egg:
Arthur Lubow, "The China Syndrome," *New York Times Magazine,* May 21, 2006.

Shanghai Grand Theater:
Christian Datz and Christof Kullman, *Shanghai: Architecture and Design* (New York: teNeues, 2005), p. 62 (the authors call it the Shanghai Opera House).

Shanghai Grand Theater and Shanghai Heritage Museum information and critique of "big roof" designs:
Peter G. Rowe and Seng Kuan, *Architectural Encounters with Essence and Form in Modern China* (Cambridge, MA: MIT Press, 2002), pp. 168, 187–89.

On the fate of the Bird's Nest:
Jordan Weissmann, "Empty Nest: Beijing's Olympic Stadium Is a Vacant 'Museum Piece,'" *The Atlantic.com,* July 31, 2012, http:www.theatlantic.com/business/archive/2012/07/empty-nest-beijings-olympic-stadium-is-a-vacant-museum-piece/260522/.

On the trend to build imitations of famous landmarks:
Bianca Bosker, "In Chinese Buildings, a Copycat Craze," *Wall Street Journal,* Feb. 9, 2013, C2.

Art

Ch'u Chai, *The Changing Society of China* (New York: Mentor, 1962).

Jason Chow, "Form Arms Dealer to Art Dealer," *Wall Street Journal,* Dec. 7, 2012, D10.

Kelly Crow, "An Art Star's Creative Crisis," *Wall Street Journal,* July 13, 2012. http://online.wsj.com/article/SB100014240527023 04898704577482560576471408.html.

Lynn Douglass, "Rare Chinese Bowl Bought for $3 Sells for Over $2 Million at Auction," Forbes.com, Mar 20, 2013 http://www.forbes.com/sites/lynndouglass/2013/03/20/rare-chinese-bowl-bought-for-3-sells-for-over-2-million-at-auction/

Rita Reif, "'Sunflowers' Buyer: Japanese Insurer," *New York Times*, Apr. 9, 1987.

Beijing

Lara Farrar, "Beijing's Water Cube Now Has Slides, Rides, a Wave Pool and Spa," CNN.com, Aug. 11, 2010, http://travel.cnn.com/explorations/play/beijings-watercube-water-park-now-open-040746.

Jordan Weissmann, "Empty Nest: Beijing's Olympic Stadium Is a Vacant 'Museum Piece,'" TheAtlantic.com, July 31, 2012, http://www.theatlantic.com/business/archive/2012/07/empty-nest-beijings-olympic-stadium-is-a-vacant-museum-piece/260522/

Bo Xilai Scandal

Jeremy Paige, "Briton Killed in China Had Spy Links," *Wall Street Journal*, Nov. 6, 2012, A1.

———. "Chinese Court Sentences Ex-Police Chief to 15 Years," *Wall Street Journal*, Sept. 24, 2012.

———. "Top China Leader Faces Trial," *Wall Street Journal*, Sept. 29–30, 2013, A1.

Edward Wong, "Flamboyant Crime Fighter Now May Face Chinese Justice over Role in Scandal," *New York Times*, Aug. 18, 2012.

———. "Ousted from Party in China, Bo Xilai Faces Prosecution," *New York Times*, Sept. 28, 2012.

Canton

Keith Bradsher, "A Chinese City Moves to Limit New Cars," *New York Times*, Sept. 4, 2012.

Cars

Keith Bradsher, "A Chinese City Moves to Limit New Cars," *New York Times*, Sept. 4, 2012.

Tania Branigan, "China and Cars: A Love Story," *Guardian*, Dec. 14, 2012, http://www.guardian.co.uk/world/2012/dec/14/china-worlds-biggest-new-car-market.

"China to Be Global Premium Car Leader," www.china.org.cn, http://www.china.org.cn/business/2013-03/05/content_28130059.htm.

Bogdan Popa, "The Longest Traffic Jam in History—12 Days, 62-Mile-Long," www.autoevolution.com, http://www.autoevolution.com/news/the-longest-traffic-jam-in-history-12-days-62-mile-long-47237.html.

Edward Wong, "On a Scale of 0 to 500, Beijing's Air Quality Tops 'Crazy Bad' at 755," *New York Times*, Jan. 12, 2013, http://www.nytimes.com/2013/01/13/science/earth/beijing-air-pollution-off-the-charts.html.

Chinese Communist Party

Eric X. Li, "The Life of the Party," *Foreign Affairs*, Jan./Feb. 2013.
Richard McGregor, *The Party*. New York: HarperCollins, 2010.

Confucianism

Anti–Lin Biao campaign:
Jun Jing, *The Temple of Memories: History, Power and Morality in a Chinese Village* (Stanford: Stanford University Press, 1996), pp. 2, 53, 86.
Confucius quote:
Ch'u Chai with Winberg Chai, *The Changing Society of China* (New York: New American Library, 1969), p. 147.
Hu Jintao and Confucianism:
Dr. Cheng Li, "Hu's Opportunity? Our Opportunity Seeking Common Interests at a Time of Mutual Suspicion," speech given before the National Committee on United States-China Relations, Apr. 17, 2006, http://www.ncuscr.org/Cheng_Li_April2006.htm.

Chongqing

Peng Yining, "City Park Dancers Get Their Groove on Chongqing Style," *China Daily USA*, Feb.18, 2013, p. 6.

Corruption

An Baijie, "'House Sister' Associate Accused of Having 12 Houses," *China Daily USA*, Feb. 5, 2013, p. 5.

Jeremy Paige, "Crash Puts New Focus on China Leaders," *Wall Street Journal*, Oct. 22, 2012.

Edward Wong, "Chinese Officials Fired over Sex Scandal," *New York Times*, Jan. 25, 2013.

Cultural Revolution

For more about the 1981 Chinese Communist Party condemnation of the Cultural Revolution policies and young people today knowing nothing about this period see:

Shai Oster, "Why Ping-Pong Star Had to Spend a Week in a Cucumber Patch," *Wall Street Journal,* Aug. 17, 2006, p. 1A.

Dalai Lama

For biographical information:

The Dalai Lama, *A Flash of Lightning in the Dark of Night: A Guide to the Bodhisattva's Way of Life* (Boston: Shambhala Dragon Editions, 1994), trans. by the Padmakara Translation Group, p. vii.

When the Qing took over political control of Tibet:

Jonathan Spence, *The Search for Modern China* (New York: Norton, 1990), p. 68.

Daoism

Quotations from the Dao De Jing:

Translations by Ch'u Chai, from *The Story of Chinese Philosophy* by Ch'u Chai and Winberg Chai (New York: Washington Square Press, 1961), pp. 73, 95.

Dialects

Background on history of Mandarin and on dialects:

Elisabeth Koske, *The Politics of Language in Chinese Education 1895–1919* (Leiden, The Netherlands: Brill, 2007).

UCLA Language Material Project Language Profile: Mandarin
http://www.lmp.ucla.edu/Profile.aspx?LangID=78&menu=004

Subdialects of Mandarin:
From http://en.wikibooks.org/wiki/Written_Chinese.

Number of dialects:
The website www.glossika.com/en/dict/index.php puts the number
at 2,548.
The site www.chinese-culture.net/html/learn_chinese.html says
there are more than a thousand.

The five main dialects of Cantonese:
Prof. Peter Kwan, City College of San Francisco, and Prof. Howard
Choy, formerly of Stanford University, 1999.

Examples of Cantonese:
Professors Kwan and Choy and George Lew.

Dissidents

Internet use:
Ai Weiwei, "A Dissident's Tips for Survival," Dec. 29–30, 2012,
Wall Street Journal, p. C2.
Geoffrey A. Fowler and Juying Qin, "In China, Griping About
Mom and Dad Gets Official OK," *Wall Street Journal*, July 12,
2006, p. 1A.
"Hundreds of Thousands Call for Liu Xiaobo's Release," Am-
nesty International, Feb. 28, 2013, www.amnesty.org/en/news
/china-s-new-leader-urged-free-liu-xiaobo-2013-02-28.
"Liu Xiaobo, China," Freedom Now Campaign, http://www
.freedom-now.org/campaign/liu-xiaobo/.
Paul Mah, "China's Internet Users Pass 500M," Apr. 3, 2012, www
.TechRepublic.com, http://www.techrepublic.com/blog/asian-techn
ology/number-of-chinas-internet-users-passes-500m/122.
Xiao Qiang and Perry Link, "In China's Cyberspace, Dissent
Speaks Code," *Wall Street Journal*, Jan. 5–6, 2013, p.C3.

Arrest and Trial of Chen Guangcheng:
"Update," *Time*, July 3, 2006, p. 16.
Joseph Kahn, "Scuffles in China as Trial of Peasants' Rights
Advocate Is Postponed," *New York Times*, July 21, 2006, p. A11.

Chen's prison sentence:
Joseph Kahn, "China Peasants' Advocate Faces More Than 4 Years in Prison," *New York Times*, Aug. 25, 2006, p. A3.
Andrew Browne, "China Court Sentences Activist to More Than 4 Years in Prison," *Wall Street Journal*, Aug. 25, 2006, p. A6.
Joe McDonald, "Chinese Activist's Sentence Draws Fire," Associated Press report as printed in *The Denver Post*, Aug. 25, 2006, p. 23A.

Chen's appeal:
After he served ten months in detention and then more than two months of his actual prison sentence, an appeals court in Shandong ordered a retrial of Chen's case. While his Beijing-based lawyers lauded this as a rare admission that the first trial had been flawed, the second trial ended in the same sentence for Chen. See, Joseph Kahn, "Rights Advocate Wins a Retrial, a Rarity in the Chinese Courts," *New York Times*, Nov. 1, 2006, p. A14.

Chen's Exile:
Andrew Jacobs, "For China, a Dissident in Exile Is One Less Headache at Home," *New York Times*, May 5, 2012.

Embassy bombing and protests:
"On This Day: 1999: Chinese anger at embassy bombing," http://news.bbc.co.uk/onthisday/hi/dates/stories/may/9/newsid_2519000/2519271.stm.

Invasion of Manchuria:
Jonathan Spence, *In Search of Modern China* (New York: Norton, 1990), p. 391.

Dynasties

The Golden Age of Chinese Archaeology (New Haven: Yale University Press, 1999); for the ax blades see p. 176, information on Fu Hao, p. 125.

Economy

Eric Li, "China's Centralized Meritocracy Fosters Government Entrepreneurship," *Foreign Affairs*, Jan./Feb. 2013.
Minxin Pei, "China's Income Gap Solution: Too Little, Too Late?," CNN.com, Feb.15, 2013, management.fortune.cnn.com/2013/02/15/chinas-income-gap-solution-too-little-too-late/.

Education

Information on unemployed college graduates:

Keith Bradsher, "In China, Betting It All on a Child in College," *New York Times*, Feb. 16, 2013.

Michelle FlorCruz, "Unemployment Report: China's College Graduates Struggle to Find Jobs," *International Business Times*, Dec. 12, 2012, http://www.ibtimes.com/unemployment-report -chinas-college-graduates-struggle-find-jobs-933326.

Paul Mooney, "Unable to Find Work, 20,000 College Graduates Refuse to Move Out of Dormitories in China," *Chronicle of Higher Education*, July 21, 2006, p. A33.

"China: Chaos in the Classrooms," *The Economist*, Aug. 12, 2006 pp. 32–33.

Study abroad trends:

Alexis Lai, "Chinese Flock to Elite U.S. Schools," CNN.com, Nov. 26, 2012, http://www.cnn.com/2012/11/25/world/asia/china-ivy -league-admission.

"Students Studying Abroad Increase 23%," ChinaDaily.com.cn, Aug. 21, 2012, http://www.chinadaily.com.cn/china/2012-08/21 /content_15693813.htm.

Ethnic Minorities

For more information on the Moso matrilineal society, see:

Yang Erche Namu and Christine Mathieu, *Leaving Mother Lake: A Girlhood at the Edge of the World* (Boston: Little, Brown, 2004).

Family

Divorce rates:

"China Simplifies Procedures for Marriage, Divorce," from *People's Daily Online*, Aug. 19, 2003, http://english.people.com.cn /2000308/19/eng20030819_122589.shtml.

"China's Divorce Rate Increases in 2011," ChinaDaily.com.cn, June 21, 2012, www.chinadaily.com.cn/china/2012-06/21/content _15517559.htm.

Michelle Florcruz, "China's Divorce Rate Rises for a Seventh Consecutive Year," *International Business Times*, Feb. 27, 2013,

http://www.ibtimes.com/chinas-divorce-rate-rises-seventh
-consecutive-year-1105053.

Divorce website:
Chen Hong, "Breaking Up Is Hard, Picking Up Pieces Harder,"
China Daily, Sept. 1, 2006, p. 1.

Marriage counselors:
"Shanghai: Marriage Counselors," *China Daily*, Aug. 28, 2006, p. 2.

WHO statistics:
Christopher Allen, "Traditions Weigh on China's Women," BBC
News broadcast, June 19, 2006, http://news.bbc.co.uk/1/hi
/programmes/5086754.stm.

Farmers

*For information on services cities must pay for as well as expansion
efforts:*
Andrew Browne, "Growing Pains: Booming Municipalities Defy
China's Efforts to Cool Economy," *Wall Street Journal*, Sept. 15,
2006, p. 1.

Efforts by Xi'an to provide services to farmers:
Ma Lie, "Xi'an District Grants Farmers Equal Treatment," *China
Daily*, Sept. 1, 2006, p. 3.

Number of peasants and description of protests:
Edward Cody, "For Chinese, Peasant Revolt Is Rare Victory,"
WashingtonPost.com, June 13, 2005, http://www.washington
post.com/wp-dyn/content/article/2005/06/12
/AR2005061201531.html.

Peasants' burdens:
"Authors of Ground-Breaking Book on China's Peasants Nominated for Award," *Radio Free Asia*, Sept. 29, 2004, http://www.rfa
.org/english/news/social/2004/09/29/china_peasants_book/.
Chen Guidi and Wu Chuntao, *Will the Boat Sink the Water?
The Life of China's Peasants* (New York: Public Affairs Books,
2006).

Chinese peasant income:
Xia Yunfan, "The Great Chinese Land Grab Is On," *Asia Times
Online*, July 17, 2004, http://www.atimes.com/atimes/China
/FG17Ad03.html.

On Hukou modifications in Xi'an:
Ma Lie, "Xi'an District Grants Farmers Equal Treatment," *China Daily*, Sept. 1, 2006, p. 3.

Rural population:
"China's Urban Population Exceeds Countryside for First Time," www.Bloomberg.com, Jan. 17, 2012, http://www.bloomberg.com /news/2012-01-17/china-urban-population-exceeds-rural.html

Fashion

On Alexander Wang and the Chinese market:
Eric Wilson, "An American in Paris, Again," *New York Times*, Dec. 7, 2012.

On the taste for luxury goods:
Laurie Burkkitt, "In China Race, Adidas Is Hot on Nike's Heels," *Wall Street Journal*, Mar. 8, 2013, p. B6.

Michael J. Silverstein, "Don't Underestimate China's Luxury Market," *Harvard Business Review*, HBR Blog Network, Dec. 12, 2012, http://blogs.hbr.org/cs/2012/12/chinas_luxury_market_and .html.

Lingling Wei, "China Flaunts Austerity," *Wall Street Journal*, Mar. 16–17, 2013, p. A9.

On the cross-dressing grandfather model:
Laurie Burkkitt and Josh Chin, "A Retailer Discovers China's New 'It' Girl: Grandpa," *Wall Street Journal*, Jan. 9, 2013, p. A1.

Festivals

Carol Stepanchuk and Charles Wong, *Mooncakes and Hungry Ghosts: Festivals of China* (San Francisco: China Books and Periodicals, 1991).

For a moving story about Ghost Festival *(gui jie)*, see Lan Samantha Chang's short story collection *Hunger* (New York: Penguin, 2000).

W. G. Astor, "Chinese Valentines [sic] Day," Colorado Springs Chinese Cultural Institute, http://www.cscci.org/tradition.htm.

Feng Shui

Peng Yining and He Na, "Wealthy See Their Fate Linked to Feng-shui," *China Daily*, Jan. 10, 2013, http://www.chinadaily.com.cn /cndy/2013-01/10/content_16100637.htm.

Forbidden City

For a complete guide, see:
Gilles Béguin and Dominique Morel, *The Forbidden City: Center of Imperial China*, trans. Ruth Taylor (New York: Harry N. Abrams, 1997).

Gay and Lesbian Culture

As Normal as Possible: Negotiating Sexuality and Gender in Mainland China and Hong Kong, edited by Yau Ching (Hong Kong: Hong Kong University Press, 2010).
Zi Heng Lim, "For Gay Chinese, Getting Married Means Getting Creative," TheAtlantic.com, Apr. 2013, http://www.theatlantic .com/china/archive/2013/04/for-gay-chinese-getting-married -means-getting-creative/274895/.
"What's Up with LGBT Rights in China?" Nov. 15, 2012, http ://chinalawandpolicy.com/2012/11/15/whats-up-with-lgbt-rights -in-china/.

Government

Party statistics:
Eric X Li, "The Life of the Party," *Foreign Affairs*, Jan./Feb. 2013.
Richard McGregor, *The Party*. New York: HarperCollins, 2010.
On the Central Committee's power:
Robert Lawrence Kuhn, "The Seven Who Will Run China," *China Daily USA*, Nov. 19, 2012, p. 12.
Edward Wong, "Ending Congress, China Presents New Leadership Headed by Xi Jinping," *New York Times*, Nov. 15, 2012, p. A16.

Great Leap Forward

For more on various estimates of deaths:

Frank Dikötter, *Mao's Great Famine: The History of China's Most Devastating Catastrophe, 1958-1962* (New York: Walker, 2010).

Hong Kong

For film history:

Mette Hjort, *Stanley Kwan's Center Stage* (Hong Kong: Hong Kong University Press, 2006).

Geography:

"Background Note: Hong Kong," Bureau of East Asian Affairs, January 2006, www.state.gov/r/pa/ei/bgn/2747.htm.

Human Rights

Amnesty Report 2012: China, http://www.amnesty.org/en/region/china/report-2012.

Austin Ramzy, "After Deadly Riots, Ethnic Tensions Heat Up in Urumqi," *Time*, July 7, 2009, http://www.time.com/time/world/article/0,8599,1908969,00.html.

World Report 2012: China, Human Rights Watch, http://www.hrw.org/world-report-2012-china.

Jiang Zemin

Clifford Coonan, "Jiang Zemin's Appearance Ends Rumours of His Death," *Independent*, Oct. 10, 2011, http://www.independent.co.uk/news/world/asia/jiang-zemins-appearance-ends-rumours-of-his-death-2368134.html

Edward Wong, "Ending Congress, China Presents New Leadership Headed by Xi Jinping," *New York Times*, Nov. 15, 2012.

Kunming

"'Flying Tigers' Veterans Visit Memorial in Kunming," *People's Daily Online*, Aug. 23, 2005, http://english.people.com.cn/200508/23/eng20050823_204174.html.

"The U.S. Flying Tigers," www. yunnantourism.com/kunming/flying_tigers.html.

"Yunnan Province to Build Three International Transport Corridors," *People's Daily Online*, Aug. 18, 2005, http://english.people .cn/200508/18/eng20050818_203310.html.

Li Keqiang

"China's Next Premier, Li Keqiang, Has Mixed Record," *South China Morning Post*, Nov. 6, 2012.
Andrew Jacobs, "In China, New Premier Says He Seeks a Just Society," *New York Times*, Mar. 18, 2013.
———. "Liberal Background, But Limited Leeway, for a New Premier," *New York Times*, Nov. 16, 2013.
Profile: Li Keqiang, BBC News, http://www.bbc.co.uk/news /world-asia-china-19870221.

Long March

Edgar Snow, *Red Star Over China* (New York: Grove Press, 1968), p. 194.
Jonathan Spence, *In Search of Modern China* (New York: Norton, 1990), pp. 405–9.
Removal from new textbooks:
Joseph Kahn, "Where's Mao? Chinese Revise History Textbooks," *New York Times*, Sept. 1, 2006, p. 1A.

Macau

"Macau to Overtake Las Vegas by 2007," Agence France-Press, Aug. 3, 2006, Yahoo! News site.
Keri Geiger, "In Macau, It's Time to Bet," *Wall Street Journal*, June 30, 2006, p. C13.
"Macau: The Seven-Year Itch," *The Economist*, July 29, 2006, p. 40.
Crime:
Alexandra Berzona and Kate O'Keeffe, "Sands China Deal Scrutinized," *Wall Street Journal*, Aug. 10, 2012.
Alexandra Berzon, Kate O'Keeffe, and James V. Grimaldi, "Vegas Bet on Chinese VIPs Raises Red Flags with Feds," *Wall Street Journal*, Sept. 20, 2012.
Kate O'Keeffe, "China Tightens Reins on Macau," *Wall Street Journal*, Dec. 4, 2012.

Martial Arts

Putin visit and Shaolin Temple origins:
"Trade, Martial Arts Dominate Second Day of Putin's China Visit," Xinhua News Agency, as reported on www.gov.cn/misc/2006-03/220content_233993.htm.
"Putin Visits Shaolin Temple," from *China Daily* as reported by *People's Daily Online,* http://english.peopledaily.com.cn/200603/23/print20060323_252837.htm.

For number of styles, foreign contestants, and disciples, see:
Zhao Rui, "At Shaolin, the World Takes on Wushu," *China Daily,* Oct. 17, 2006.

For historical background and competition rules, see:
Liang Shouyu, "An Introduction to Chinese Martial Arts," trans. Bill Chen and Mike Sigman, www.nardis.com/~twchan/liang.html.

Additional background on Japanese forms:
"Origins of Kodokan Judo," http://www.judoinfo.com/jhist3.htm.

Medicine (Traditional)

Information on acupuncture:
Personal interview with Qing-Mei Chen, L.Ac., M.S., Center of Harmony: Acupuncture and Herbal Medicine, San Francisco, California, www.chcherb.com.

Information on Dr. Ing Hay:
Shehong Chen, *Being Chinese, Becoming Chinese American* (Chicago: University of Illinois Press, 2002), p. 158.

Migrant Workers

Bob Davis and Tom Orlik, "China Seeks to Give Migrants Perks of City Life," *Wall Street Journal,* Mar. 6, 2013, p. A12.
Kristie Lu Stout, "China's Great Migration from 'Hukou Hell,'" CNN.com, Feb. 8, 2013. http://www.cnn.com/2013/02/07/world/asia/china-lu-stout-great-migration.
Xinhua, "China's Busiest Travel Season Breaks Records," *China Daily USA,* Mar. 7, 2013, p. 2.

Novelists

On "Bureaucracy Lit":
Louisa Lim, "Masters of Subservience," *New York Times*, Feb. 1, 2013.

On the publishing industry:
Clarissa Sebag-Montefiore, "The Bookworms of China," *New York Times*, Sept. 4, 2012, latitude.blogs.nytimes.com/2012/09/04 /the-promise-of-chinas-publishing-industry/.

On Mo Yan:
Carolyn Kellogg, "What a Bummer: Nobel Laureate Mo Yan Defends Censorship," LATimes.com, Dec. 6, 2012, latimes.com/features /books/jacketcopy/la-et-jc-bummer-nobel-prizewinner-mo-yan -defends-censorship-20121206,0,3452308.story.

On Yiyun Li:'
Clare Wigfall, "A Conversation with Yiyun Li," *Asymptote Journal*, http://asymptotejournal.com/article.php?cat=Interview&id= 14&curr_index=0.

One Child Policy

Mao's indifference to family planning:
Austin Head-Jones, "The Economics of Chinese Birth Planning," from http://economics.about.com/cs/moffattentries/a/birth_plan.htm.

War of nuclear attrition:
Jonathan Spence, *In Search of Modern China* (New York: Norton, 1990), p. 576.
Mao Zedong, "The Chinese People Cannot Be Cowed by the Atom Bomb," Jan. 28, 1955, from *Selected Works of Mao Tsetung*, Vol. 5 (Beijing: Foreign Language Press, 1977).

Population statistics:
The figure 116.86 males to 100 females born in 2000 is from "China's Missing Girls," *Shanghai Star*, Oct. 24, 2002, http ://app1.chinadaily.com.cn/star/2002/1024/fo5-1.html.
Eric Baculinao, "China Grapples with Legacy of Its 'Missing Girls,'" NBC News, Sept. 14, 2004, http://www.msnbc.msn.com/id/5953508.
Rob Brooks, "China's Biggest Problem? Too Many Men," CNN .com, Mar. 4, 2013, http://www.cnn.com/2012/11/14/opinion /china-challenges-one-child-brooks.

Kathleen E. McLaughlin, "China's Staggering Male-Female Ratio Worsens," *Alaska Dispatch*, Jan. 5, 2013, http://www.alaskadis patch.com/article/chinas-staggering-male-female-ratio-worsens.
Societal Attitudes:
Leslie T. Chang, "Why the One-Child Policy Has Become Irrelevant," TheAtlantic.com, Mar. 2013, http://www.theatlantic.com /china/archive/2013/03/why-the-one-child-policy-has-become -irrelevant/274178/.
He Fenglun and Zhou Yan, "What Shall I Call You, Auntie?" *China Daily USA*, Feb. 15–17, 2013.
"Let Them Choose," www.ChinaEconomicReview.com, Jan. 28, 2013, http://www.chinaeconomicreview.com/let-them-choose.

Peng Liyuan

Lily Kuo, "China's Hip New First Lady," TheAtlantic.com, Mar. 2013, http://theatlantic.com/china/archive/2013/03/chinas-hip -new-first-lady/274005/.
Jeremy Page, "Meet China's Folk Star First Lady-in-Waiting," *Wall Street Journal*, http://blogs.wsj.com/chinarealtime/2012/02/13 /peng-liyuan-meet-chinas-folk-song-singing-first-lady-in-waiting/.
Jane Perlez and Bree Feng, "China's First Lady Strikes Glamorous Note," *New York Times*, Mar. 24, 2013.

People's Liberation Army (PLA)

Statistics on soldiers:
"Chinese Defence Today," www.sinodefence.com/army/default.asp.
On plans for growth:
"China's Military Rise: The Dragon's New Teeth," *Economist*, Apr. 7, 2012.

Qingdao

On women's aversion to tanning:
Dan Levin, "Beach Essentials in China: Flip-Flops, a Towel and a Ski Mask," *New York Times*, Aug. 4, 2012.

Religion

On the Taiping Rebellion:
Jonathan Spence, *The Search for Modern China* (New York: Norton, 1990), pp. 170–78.

Statistics for new Christian converts:
Simon Elegant, "The War for China's Soul," *Time*, Aug. 28, 2006.

Incidents of government crackdowns:
Howard W. French, "China Adds Restrictions in Effort to Shake the Faith of Independent Congregations," *New York Times*, Aug. 18, 2006, p. A7.

Filmmaker jailed:
Geoffrey A. Fowler, "An Arrest in China Spotlights Limits to Artistic Freedom," *Wall Street Journal,* July 3, 2006, p. 1A.

Respect for Elders

On influence of Jiang Zemin:
Edward Wong, "Long Retired, Ex-Leader of China Asserts Sway over Top Posts," *New York Times*, Nov. 7, 2012.

Shanghai

"Meet Shanghai's Old Jazz Band" *TimeOut Shanghai*, Oct. 2010, http://www.timeoutshanghai.com/features/Music-Music_features/2567/Meet-Shanghais-Old-Jazz-Band.html www.timeoutshanghai.com/features/Music-Music_features/2567/Meet-Shanghais-Old-Jazz-Band.html/.
Shi Yingying, "The Brilliant Bund" and "A Shanghai Jewel Dazzles On," *China Daily USA*, Dec. 2-8, 2011.

Shenzhen Special Economic Zone

For more on the other Special Economic Zones in 1979 and 1986:
Jonathan Spence, *In Search of Modern China* (New York: Norton, 1990), p. 805.

For more descriptions of wealth, wigeon blankets, and gold bottles, see:
"Ready for Warfare in the Aisles," *The Economist*, Aug. 5, 2006, p. 59.

Shopping

For more on American big-box stores in China:
Laurie Burkitt, "Home Depot Learns Chinese Prefer 'Do-It-for-Me,'" *Wall Street Journal*, Sept. 14, 2012, http://online.wsj .com/article/SB1000087239639044443350457765107291115 4602.html.

For more on Chanel's strategy in China:
James T. Areddy, "How Chanel Sells Itself in China," *Wall Street Journal*, Feb. 4, 2011, http://blogs.wsj.com/scene/2011/02/04 /how-chanel-sells-itself-in-china/.
Xu Junqian, "Chanel Builds a New Channel in China," *China Daily European Weekly*, Feb. 11, 2011, http://europe.chinadaily .com.cn/epaper/2011-02/11/content_11984506.htm.

Sino-Japanese War

Tally of casualties in Battle of Shanghai:
May-lee Chai and Winberg Chai, *The Girl from Purple Mountain* (New York: St. Martin's Press, 2001), pp. 145, 166.

Panay vessel bombing:
Iris Chang, *The Rape of Nanking* (New York: Penguin Books, 1997).

Sorties and bombings over Chongqing:
Chai and Chai, *The Girl from Purple Mountain*, p. 202.

Spring Festival

Travel numbers:
Sylvia Hui, "Mass Travel for Chinese New Year," January 28, 2004, http://www.int.iol.co.za/index.php?set_id=1&click_id=3&art _id=qw1138443484453B255#.
"The Chinese New Year Travel Crush," Jan. 29, 2003, http ://www.cbsnews.com/stories/2003/01/29/world/main538505.shtml.

Customs:
Carol Stepanchuk and Charles Wong, *Mooncakes and Hungry Ghosts: Festivals of China* (San Francisco: China Books and Periodicals, 1991).

Tailors and Clothing

Information about Versace and the China market:
Ariel Levy, "Summer for the Sun Queen," *New York Magazine*, Aug. 28, 2006, p. 54.

Taiwan

Fiona Foster, "Chinese Tourists Go It Alone in Taiwan," BBC News, Oct. 6, 2011, http://www.bbc.co.uk/news/world-radio-and-tv-15173456.
"Historic Taiwan-China Trade Deal Takes Effect," BBC News, Sept. 12, 2010, http://www.bbc.co.uk/news/world-asia-pacific-11275274.
Michael Roberge and Youkyung Lee, "China-Taiwan Relations," *Council on Foreign Relations*, Aug. 11, 2009, http://www.cfr.org/china/china-taiwan-relations/p9223.

Technology

John Fingas, "China's Tianhe-2 Supercomputer Could Hit 100 Petaflops in 2015, May Have a Race on Its Hands," *Engadget*, Nov. 1, 2012, http://www.engadget.com/2012/11/01/china-tianhe-2-supercomputer-could-hit-100-petaflops-in-2015/.
Leslie Horn, "Number of Chinese Internet Users Climbs to 513 Million," www.pcmag.com, Jan. 17, 2012, http://www.pcmag.com/article2/0,2817,2398956,00.asp.
Leo Mirani, "China's Internet Is Better Than Yours," QZ.com, http://qz.com/68972/chinas-internet-is-better-than-yours/.

Territorial Disputes

On the risk of combat over the Diaoyu (Senkaku) Islands:
"The Senkaku/Diaoyu Islands: Dangerous Shoals," *Economist*, Jan. 19, 2013.

Three Gorges Dam

Statistics on the dam:
"Visions of China-Asian Superpower," CNN In-Depth Specials, http://www.cnn.com/SPECIALS/1999/china.50/asian.superpower.

Edward Cody, "Dam Big: The Great Second Wall of China," *Washington Post* (as reprinted in *Denver Post,* May 18, 2006).

Brian Handwerk, "China's Three Gorges Dam, by the Numbers," *National Geographic,* June 9, 2006, http://news.nationalgeographic.com/news/pf/48061222.html.

Graham Hutchins, *Modern China: A Guide to a Century of China* (Cambridge, MA: Harvard University Press, 2003), pp. 419–21.

Hoover Dam statistics:

From http://www.usbr/gov/lc/hooverdam/History/storymain.html.

Deaths from flooding in the past:

Jonathan Spence, *The Search for Modern China* (New York: Norton, 1990), pp. 695–96.

Environmental impact:

"Three Gorges Dam Has Caused Urgent Problems, Says China," Associated Press, May 19, 2011, http://www.guardian.co.uk/environment/2011/may/19/china-three-gorges-dam.

Jim Yardley, "Chinese Dam Projects Criticized for Their Human Costs," *New York Times,* Nov. 19, 2007.

Tiananmen Square Pro-Democracy Movement

Estimated number of deaths:

From Amnesty International, http://web.amnesty.org/web/ar2001.nsf/webascountries/CHINA?Opendocument.

See also Jonathan Spence, *In Search of Modern China* (New York: Norton, 1990), p. 743. Spence writes that hundreds died immediately on June 4, 1989, and thousands more were injured.

Tibet

Tim Johnson, "Tibetans See 'Han Invasion' as Spurring Violence," McClatchy Newspapers, http://www.mcclatchydc.com/2008/03/28/31913/tibetans-see-han-invasion-as-spurring.html.

"Tibet's Population Tops 3 Million; 90% Are Tibetans," Xinhua, http:/news.xinhuanet.com/english2010/china/2011-05/04/c_13858686.htm.

Edward Wong, "China's Money and Migrants Pour into Tibet," *New York Times,* July 24, 2010.

Urumqi

Chris Buckley, "China Convicts and Sentences 20 Accused of Militant Separatism in Restive Region," *New York Times*, Mar. 27, 2013. Austin Ramzy, "After Deadly Riots, Ethnic Tensions Heat Up in Urumqi," *Time*, July 7, 2009, http://www.time.com/time/world /article/0,8599,1908969,00.html.

Xi Jinping

Biographical details:
"Profile: Xi Jinping: Man of the People, Statesman of Vision," Xinhua, *China Daily USA*, Dec. 25, 2012, http://www.chinadaily .com.cn/china/2012-12/24/content_16046049.htm.

Cave Dwelling:
"Xi Jinping: Cave Dweller or Princeling," Damian Grammaticas, BBC News, Feb. 14, 2012, http://www.bbc.co.uk/news/world -asia-17022763.
Edward Wong, "Tracing the Myth of a Chinese Leader to Its Roots," *New York Times*, Feb. 16, 2011, http://www.nytimes.com/2011/02/17/ world/asia/17village.html?pagewanted=1&ref=xijinping.

Education:
"Xi Jinping: One of China's Top Future Leaders to Watch," Brookings Institution, http://www.brookings.edu/about/centers /china/top-future-leaders/xi_jinping.

Luxury spending decline:
Andrew Jacobs, "Elite in China Face Austerity Under Xi's Rule," *New York Times*, Mar. 27, 2013.

Xinjiang Uighur Autonomous Region

Ethnic riots and separatist charges:
Chris Buckley, "China Convicts and Sentences 20 Accused of Militant Separatism in Restive Region," *New York Times*, Mar. 27, 2013.

Zhong Guo

Thanks to Prof. Howard Choy of Wittenberg University for the explanation of the origins of the name China.

Index

Note: Page numbers in **bold** indicate
the primary discussion of subjects.